Contemporary Poland

Changing Eastern Europe

Editors:
David M. Smith
Queen Mary & Westfield College
University of London
R. Antony French
University College London

Contemporary Poland
Space and society

Grzegorz Węcławowicz
Institute of Geography and Spatial Organization,
Polish Academy of Sciences

First published in 1996 by UCL Press.

UCL Press Limited
University College London
Gower Street
London WC1E 6BT

The name of University College London (UCL) is a registered
trade mark used by UCL Press with the consent of the owner.

ISBNs:1-85728-046-6 HB
1-85728-047-4 PB

British Library Cataloguing in Publication Data
A catalogue record for this book is available from the British Library.

Typeset in Times New Roman.
Printed and bound by
Biddles Ltd, Guildford and King's Lynn, England.

CONTENTS

To the memory of my grandparents Genowefa and Leon Szymczak

PREFACE

This book has been written for my English-speaking friends, principally scholars and students of the geographical and social sciences. The rapid transformation taking place in Poland demands explanation and interpretation beyond mere description and it prompts the question as to why certain things are happening in particular places. The 79 maps and charts in the book show not only how Poland's space is differentiated but also provide a basis for the conceptual integration of space with society.

The list of those who deserve acknowledgement is very long. I would like to acknowledge personally David M. Smith of Queen Mary and Westfield College, University of London, for encouragement and constant assistance in writing this book. Also, I deeply appreciate the following English speakers for revising, criticising and discussing preliminary versions of selected chapters: Keith Grime, Mike Ingham, Vic Duke, Sharon Moran, Roger Bivand and Don Dunlevey.

My Polish perspective has been moderated thanks to the opportunity to pursue research at the Austrian Academy of Sciences in Vienna, to lecture at Université de Paris X (Nanterre), and to a grant from the Brussels government that allowed me to undertake research at the Université Libre de Bruxelle. Also, I would like to acknowledge a research project founded by the European Union programme, Co-operation in Science and Technology with Central and Eastern Europe, which provided a platform for stimulating discussion.

I owe a great deal to my colleagues at the Institute of Geography and Spatial Organization, Polish Academy of Sciences. Particular thanks are due to Piotr Korcelli for tolerating my involvement in writing a book outside normal research activities. I am greatly indebted to Bożena Gałczyńska, Marcin Rościszewski and Ewa Kulabko for reading parts of the manuscript and making useful comments, and for the support of other colleagues. Thanks are also due to Ewa Kulabko, Andrzej Jarosz and Danuta Bodzak for technical support.

Finally, I owe an immense debt to my family. To my wife Alina for her discourse, presence and inspiration; to my younger children, Ania and Krzysztof, for tolerating their father sitting so long in front of a PC; and to my elder son Piotr, whose participation in entrepreneurial activity and student life became for me a source of shared reality evaluation.

Grzegorz Węcławowicz

PART I
The specificity of Poland

Introduction

This book is an attempt to describe and interpret contemporary Polish society, with particular reference to its spatial differentiation. It has been written in the context of conflicting attitudes and opinion, confrontation of different views, and very rapid system transformation. A question arises as to whether this sort of analysis could be in any sense objective or unbiased; however, this is what has been attempted. One of the methodological approaches is to provide a description as close as possible to popular experience. This is thought to be as valuable as what may be provided by any other more "sophisticated" analytical instruments.

It must be stressed that there was no theory that could have predicted the events of 1989–90 in eastern Europe. As Ralph Dahrendorf (1990) said, although we have a theory predicting the downfall of capitalism and the inevitable rise of socialism, we have none that could help us understand the transition from socialism to the open society. The most spectacular failing of "theoretical" explanations of world events applied to eastern Europe was the domino theory, which reversed the direction in which the dominoes would actually fall. Many scholars will investigate the roots of the collapse of communism in eastern Europe, which is attributed to different phenomena: economic, social, political, ideological. Some assert that collapse occurred first of all in the institutional and systemic arena (Kamiński 1991).

The unpredictability of events in eastern Europe reflects the unrealistic expectations of some Western and Eastern scholars and politicians that all evolution in this part of Europe could be initiated only from above. In spite of that, society revealed that it could react and become the subject as well as the object of evolution. Why it happened at this particular moment of history, and why society adapted to the imposed system 40 years ago, needs to be explained even if only in outline.

Since 1989 contemporary Poland has been in a particular period of systems transformation. This transformation can be labelled in various ways according to the particular interpretation adopted. Exemplifying just a few of these, the transformation could be described as:

- real socialism to an open society
- totalitarianism to democracy
- socialism to capitalism
- centrally planned economy to market economy
- egalitarian society to inegalitarian society
- Soviet political and economic domination to economic dependency on western Europe.

These descriptions, however, do not contain an explanation of exactly what type of socialism existed in Poland and what version of capitalism is going to come about. So, for the description of contemporary Poland in the period of transition, it is crucial to describe the starting point of the transformation. By describing the nature of socialism as it existed and its role in the social, economic and regional development of Poland, we will be better able to provide a basis for understanding the contemporary situation.

During the twentieth century, Polish society has faced at least three transformations and, during the Second World War, the threat of physical annihilation. On each occasion this was conditioned by strong external causative factors, whereas the internal development has been considered of only secondary significance by many scholars and politicians.

The first transformation, after the First World War, was political independence and unification after 124 years of partition. The successful re-establishment of the Polish state and its consolidation was possible because of the will and the long struggle of Poles, but occurred in the political vacuum caused by the collapse of Tsarist Russia, Germany and the split of the Austria–Hungary Monarchy. Despite this, the reborn Poland had to fight to establish its frontiers, often with only verbal support from Allied Powers; however, without this support it would have been impossible to maintain access to the Baltic sea. The tremendous effort involved in the unification of the territories, which for more than a century were developed under conditions imposed by the states responsible for partitioning, was rewarded when Polish statehood was internationally recognized. The short period of 20 years of authentic independence, democratic or semi-democratic development, particularly after 1926, was characterized by political pluralism, which was crushed by the German and Soviet invasions in 1939. The reaction to the attempt at physical extermination of Poles and the holocaust of the Jewish population was armed resistance, which continued throughout the whole period of German occupation. It is also worth mentioning the substantial military contribution of Polish forces to the final victory of the Allies, from the Battle of Britain to the capitulation of Berlin.

The second transformation occurred after the Second World War. The superpowers at Yalta, and later in Potsdam, allocated Poland together with other central European countries to the Soviet sphere. This was done against the will of the people of Poland, but was settled by a rigged election on 19 January 1947, which gave communist rule an aura of legitimacy. The imposed communist system, together with the consolidation of its power, has had the most dramatic influence on the contemporary state of the country.

The third transformation was the rejection of the communist and totalitarian system by most of Polish society. This act of will seems to have been prior to the regaining of political independence, which accompanied the collapse or substantial weakening of the Soviet Empire.

Above all, these transformations of Polish society have been subjected to more universal processes of modernization characteristic of the whole of Europe, including industrialization and urbanization, or the process of transformation from traditional society to mass or modern society.

The contemporary transformation is taking place in conditions of a complete lack of experience and of any single precedent. No single country has been transformed from socialism to capitalism. No wonder then that there is no clear conceptual or theoretical framework to understand such a transformation. The aim of this book is not to create such a framework; however, several possible explanatory considerations may be suggested.

The general process now taking place in Poland is the transformation of the entire social, economic and political system, which is composed of several less abstract and more narrowly defined arenas. In the political and ideological arena, we can observe the creation, from the very beginning, of the new democratic organizational structure of society, the formation of new social structures, and the struggle for creation of new relationships between state and society. In the economic arena, the reorganization of all economic structures is occurring with varying success, adapting to the great efficiency and competitive requirements of the capitalist world economy. Psychologically, transformation concerns the moral value system and imposed ways of thought, including abandoning the collective claiming attitude in favour of more individualistic attitudes of enterprise and autonomous self-dependence. Bearing all these different aspects of transformation in mind, in this book we attempt to filter them through the space dimension.

The introductory part of the book is concerned mostly with historical and conceptual frameworks. It is not intended here to provide comprehensive historical information; deeper analysis and detailed information can be found in specialized historical writings. This part provides necessarily selective background, without which any attempt at reliable description – and particularly interpretation – of contemporary Poland is impossible. The pivotal issue in historical evolution is the place of Poland in the eastern European context (Ch. 1). The second chapter is an attempt to place communist ideology as a dominant phenomenon of the post Second World War era in eastern Europe in other conceptual contexts. The third chapter provides a description of the key element of political development leading to the decline and collapse of the communist system.

The intention of the second part of the book is to look at the impact of communism, and particularly its declining phase, on the state of selected aspects of social, economic and regional differentiation. The spatial structure formed under communism will remain for a long time and will substantially contribute to the future development of Poland, both as a constraint and as providing a set of opportunities. Chapter 4 considers the impact of spatial policy on the urbanization and industrialization of the country. Describing the main element of regional structure, particular attention has been devoted to industry and agriculture. More detailed analysis is devoted to the key issues of population trends (Ch. 5) and, because Poland has become urbanized, to urban issues (Ch. 6). The state of the environment, which under communism became a basic element of regional differentiations is described in Chapter 7.

In the third part, an attempt is made to describe and interpret the present. The present is understood as development occurring during the past few years, starting in 1989. In the first place (Ch. 8) the transformations in social structure are described and the evolution of public opinion is analyzed. In Chapter 9, the formation of a new political structure is described in the light of electoral geography. The basic elements of the new regional differentiation are described in Chapter 10, where particular attention is devoted to privatization, unemployment, ethnic differentiation, and spatial consequences of transformation. Chapter 11 offers some conclusions about and interpretations of the new geopolitical situation, which is becoming a security challenge for Poland. Finally, the consequences of a drift towards European integration as a modernization challenge are described in Chapter 12.

The aim of the third part is an analysis of the impact of the multidimensional aspects of transformation on the emergence of new regional structures. The general intention is to illuminate questions frequently raised by social geographers: Who gets what and why? Who gains? Who loses? and also the question of Where in space?

Frontispiece The administrative divisions of Poland.

CHAPTER 1

Poland in a European context

The past decade of political transformation in eastern Europe raises the question of regional differentiation at the macro level. The traditional divisions have been called into question, and new ones are beginning to emerge. Do we have in our continent one, two or three Europes? What exactly do we mean by western Europe, eastern Europe and central Europe? Where are the boundaries, where does one end and another begin? The answers to these questions depend on many considerations: subjective opinion and political, economic and, above all, cultural interpretations. The division of Europe into east and west could be traced from the division of the Roman Empire into eastern and western parts in AD 395; however, it did not appear in its full, rigid form until after the Second World War (Krasuski 1991).

The predominant way of political thinking for several decades has been dominated by the Cold War perspective, which to a greater extent also influenced Western mass media, social science studies and diplomatic attitudes.

Historians sharply distinguished the western from the eastern part of the continent. Historians have typically distinguished the densely populated west from the lower density east; Romance and German languages as opposed to Slav languages; Catholic and Protestant church against the Orthodox church; urban development and export of manufactured goods against the decline and stagnation of towns, export of food and raw material; in the western part, peasants turned into smallholders or landless labourers, whereas in the eastern part peasants were turned into serfs. In spite of these over-generalizations, central Europe sustained a sense of identity with the western part and frequently contrasted itself with the east.

In Poland, Western Christianity, in the form of the Catholic Church and its organizational and spiritual structures, was adopted a thousand years ago, along with the Latin alphabet. The cultural and historical connection meant that, throughout the past millennium, Poland shared with varying intensity most aspects of feudalism and medieval Christian universalism. It also participated actively in Renaissance culture, to a smaller extent in the Reformation and Counter-reformation, and again more intensively in the Enlightenment. However, the last period overlapped with a sharp economic and political decline of the country.

The historian's dichotomous way of thinking is congruent with the centre–periphery concept accepted by many economists and geographers. The inclusion of central Europe in the Medieval Ages in international trade resulted in economic revival, but position designated this region as a raw material supplier. In a sense, this role remained relatively stable through the centuries. The only period when central Europe and Poland played an important European role was during the Jagielonian dynasty. The Commonwealth of Poland and Lithuania, as a strong republic and "gentry democracy", was at that time the subject of European political intrigues. The collapse of this dynasty, together with a weakening of its economic position, initiated a long process of depression. Poland slowly lost the opportunity to play an independent role in international politics and economics. At the same time, the surrounding absolute power of the Prussian Kingdom and the Russian and Austrian empires grew in significance. The final result was that, for 124 years from the end of the eighteenth century, Poland ceased to exist as an independent state.

Between 1795 and 1919 the development of Poland experienced three different conflicting traditions (Fig. 1.1). Prussian absolutism overlapped with an increasing Germanization tendency and with the economic integration of connected territories to the rest of Prussia. In the Austrian monarchy, Poles adapted to the relatively liberalized parliamentary monarchy, and in the Russian part, people were the subject of Tsarist autocracy with its Eastern style of executive power. Across Polish territory for more than a century, the political frontiers that had become the boundary of "civilization" between East and West had been raised. During the absolute domination of central Europe by Prussia, Austria and Russia, there was no need for any concept of distinctiveness.

In Europe, the west was constituted as the areas of France, Netherlands and Great Britain, central Europe was attributed to Germany, and Russia became part of eastern Europe. The other division was between Southern Europe and Northern Europe, separated by the Danube River. By the end of the nineteenth century, the concept of Mittel Europa had been launched. This geopolitical concept was a sort of ideological instrument for legitimizing German domination in this part of the continent, with two attempts at implementation by initiating the First and Second World Wars.

The 40 years of existence of the Iron Curtain and the ideological confrontation between NATO and Warsaw Pact countries added a new line dividing Europe after the Second World War. All central European Countries had no choice. The Iron Curtain severed cultural and economic contacts. This separation contributed substantially to the gradual growth of a new differentiation between two parts of the continent. The notion of "Europe" became limited to the territory beyond Soviet domination. The result of that attitude has been the growing and deepening distinctiveness of easterners. So the decision of the Yalta and Potsdam conferences drew the most dramatic division in the past century of European history.

The notion of eastern Europe was used mostly in political terms in order to distinguish communist countries from democratic countries. All notions concerning the middle, eastern, central, or Mittel, were used in western Europe in order to denote regional differentiation, and in Poland and other central European countries they were adopted mostly to distinguish themselves from eastern Europe understood as Russia.

Poland, however, preserved within eastern Europe (understood as the Soviet Empire) a specific character through the whole communist period and was the most

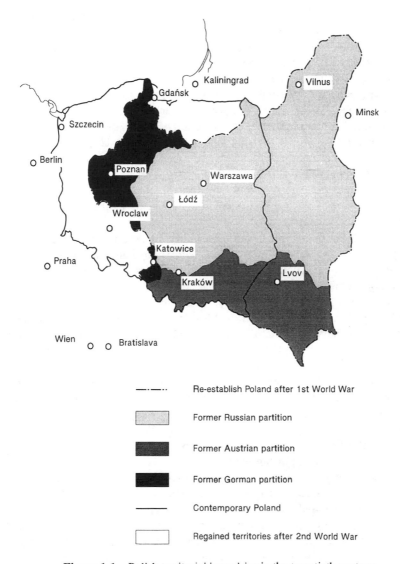

Figure 1.1   Polish territorial boundries in the twentieth century.

difficult satellite. The repeated political upheavals in 1956, 1968, 1970, 1976, and 1980–81 challenged the position of the Polish Communist Party, although only the 1956 and 1980–81 disturbances were really significant. Almost all these upheavals of society brought some political and economic concessions from the authorities (Kamiński 1991). The major ideology in Polish communism, ostensibly, was the declared different version of its "own road towards socialism". In other socialist countries for two decades (between 1968 and 1988) not a single confrontation with the communist system occurred.

This Polish specificity has been based on several factors. First the Church, which was the only national-scale institution in the Soviet Block remaining independent of the state; Catholicism became the basis for preservation of a national spirit and moral value system. Secondly, the existence of a private sector in the economy, and particularly the domination of private ownership in agriculture, allowed some economic freedom for citizens. Thirdly, the Poles did not allow themselves to become separate from western European cultural and scientific development. Except for the short Stalinist period of the 1950s, Polish culture was not developed in "the realist socialist cage". Fourthly, Sovietization was never accepted, and was constantly challenged by the Christian moral value system and the Polish national spirit. Fifthly, the communists never had complete control of all areas of public life. These factors help to explain why Poland was the first country in this part of Europe that rejected communism, as the conditions conducive to such actions emerged.

In spite of all the favourable developments in central and eastern Europe, it is a long step to replacing these popular notions with a more general notion of Europe as a whole. The key conditions of integration are of course political stability in the region and economic prosperity of particular countries.

Two contradictory processes are now occurring in western as compared to eastern Europe. In western Europe, the emergence of the Common Market has led to a form of unification. In eastern Europe, the collapse of the communist system has resulted in dramatic regional disintegration. In western Europe, economic development has led to integration and the partial elimination of borders, in spite of some problems with the Maastricht Treaty. In eastern Europe new political boundaries have emerged. The most dramatic examples are in Yugoslavia, the painful division of Czechoslovakia, and the disintegration of the Soviet Union. In comparison with other countries in central Europe, Poland seems to be the most stable in this respect. In spite of substantial support for democratic development in post-communist countries from western Europe, the west does not seem to be fully convinced that the economic development and prosperity of the eastern part is also in its own interest. Eastern European economies, after centuries of backward development and several decades of communist economics, need radical and long-term capital and political support, not just short-term trade agreements. Through the past ten centuries, central Europe (understood as contemporary Poland, the Czech Republic, Slovakia and Hungary) contributed substantially to the formation of Western civilization. This region is not merely a raw material supplier, a reserve of cheap labour or a protective zone from eastern invaders. It brings its own cultural diversity, has huge economic potential, and acts as a bridge to Asia.

The spontaneous and idealistic concept of the "return to Europe" was met at the beginning with optimistic (however rhetorical) notions from western Europe of the "unity of the continent" or "a new European architecture". This indicates that the European Community was not prepared for the suddenly emerged "eastern challenge".

Figure 1.2 The countries bordering Poland before 1990.

The contemporary unification of Europe creates what I call the "modernization challenge" for Poland, whereas the collapsed Soviet Union created a "security challenge". Both types of "challenges" could have a major influence on the future of Poland. Suddenly the number of countries bordering Poland increased from three (Soviet Union, Czechoslovakia, German Democratic Republic in 1989; see Fig. 1.2) to seven! (Russia, Lithuania, Byelorussia, Ukraine, Slovak, Czech, Germany in 1991; see Fig. 1.3).

Having a common border with European Union and NATO countries could ease integration with Europe. During the early years of transformation, a very popular feeling was that, for the first time for several centuries, Poland had a chance to be freed from the threat of two large neighbours. The traditional "German question" is solved by the absorption into the EEC or the Europeanization of Germany. At the same time, "the Russian question" seems to be solved by the split of the Soviet Union into much smaller countries released from imperialistic Russian domination. However, political developments in Russia indicate the possible rebirth of the old-style policy of domination.

Re-unification with western Europe is now blocked by a new curtain – the wealth curtain. There is a threat of division of Europe into two worlds: of misery and wealth.

11

Figure 1.3   The countries bordering Poland after 1990.

The significance of the international context is still crucial. All the countries of this part of Europe have been too weak in economic and political terms to complete democratization without integration into more international and regional structures. Greater political domination, or economic subordination to any superpower, will inevitably lead to instability in this region. The path to democracy without economic assistance is impossible and could only lead, in the most favourable circumstances, to the creation of a "semi-democratic system". The only solution in the international context will be rapid integration with the European Union and NATO.

The widely accepted notion of the "return to Europe" was treated, not only in Poland but in all central European countries, as an immediate guarantee of full success in the struggle for a solution to the security and modernization challenges. It has very quickly become evident that neither side is ready. In the European Union, on the one side, the process of integration is in a very fragile period and cannot be risked by premature enlargement. In spite of that, the substantial issue is the lack of will for enlargement of the European Union. The central European countries, on the other side, have for centuries been without a voluntary tradition of peaceful co-operation (except in Jagielonian's times of the fifteenth and sixteenth centuries), and have been trying to reach their goals in isolation. The formation and the development of a different regional co-operation organization seems to be a necessary transitional step towards full membership of the European Union. It has been done with varying success, for instance as Polish participation in the Council of Europe, Visegrad Four, the Council of Baltic States, and an attempt at the formation of many Euro-regions along Polish borders. Additionally, the economic transformation must take much longer than was expected at the beginning. European membership was one of the mythical "single factor solutions" for all economic and political problems.

Integration with the European Union and NATO, as the latest political developments show, will take much longer and could even be stopped. The existence of a security vacuum in central Europe could become the basic constraint on political and economic transformation. One can argue that there is no external power threatening central Europe right now, but the future is uncertain. The "Alliance for Peace" of 1994, in a situation of an evident attempt to re-establish the nationalist power of Russia in the region, seems to have very limited significance. The widely shared feeling in Poland is that, once more, Poland's citizens could be pushed into external (i.e. Eastern) political domination).

CHAPTER 2

Ideology and social
and economic structure

There is no universal and widely accepted explanation for the post-war evolution of Poland. Many interpretations attempt to explain just one part of a very complex reality. I do not attribute explanatory power to one single phenomenon, or treat all phenomena as equally significant. For the purposes of this book, the strategy adopted has been to assign a different level of significance and generality to different processes. The following hierarchy of levels is adopted:
- political
- ideological
- economic
- living conditions.

This hierarchy of explanation emphasized the fact that, since the Second World War, the most important phenomenon was the struggle for political power. Since power was monopolized by the communists, ideology was quite freely modified by the ruling group, as the history of the Polish People's Republic indicates.

The ruling group had a monopoly on judgement concerning which ideology principles are correct or are "revisionist". Ideology was also a tool for the mobilization of social action and individual behaviour, and was frequently used for the elimination of potential political opposition. The best guarantees of the maintenance of power on the part of ruling groups was first of all to extend their bases of support, both material and social. The main strategy for achieving this was nationalization of the economy, in order to control it and force industrialization.

Industrialization created the material basis for military power in the conditions of Cold War, increased the number of supporting working class, and was also supposed to create the material means for implementation of egalitarian social policy. So both ideology and economy have been freely used to safeguard the principal political objective: to maintain power.

The subordination of the economy to political and ideological objectives limited the scope for conducting a rational economy in other respects. The imposed war-time, Russian style, economy remained for all the communist period the predominant background. It has substantial influence on maintaining a relatively low standard of living, and caused the appearance of the succeeding crisis. Interdependences of economic and political processes are characteristic of all systems, but in the case of socialist countries the political processes had absolute priority.

15

Ideological and political considerations have their own hierarchy. At the highest level was subordination to the Soviet Union in most important issues from 1944 to 1989. At the national level, the absolute domination of the Communist Party and the ruling group was evident, and this pattern was reproduced at the regional level. On the national and regional scales, the economy became the instrument of struggle for power and political influence.

The subordination of the economy to political priorities, or fusion of these two domains (as Kamiński 1991 put it) has its roots not only in imposed ideology. The ground had been prepared during the inter-war period, when the state sector dominated the national economy. However, the economy remained to a high degree independent of political confrontation. The post-war take-over of German and Jewish property in both the old and regained territories substantially eased nationalization of industry and subordination of the entire national economy to ideological and political aims (Bolesta-Kukułka 1992). The institutionalization of this subordination according to Bolesta-Kukułka (ibid.) had been achieved by the introduction of the following attributes:

- the centralization of the most important economic decisions at the central government and central committee party levels
- the utilization of the economy as a tool to fulfil the ideological aim of social justice by redistribution according to criteria imposed by political and ideological priorities of national production and accompanying investment and price policies
- the integration of economic management with the state administration
- the formation, parallel to administration and management, of a political structure of party organization down to lowest organizational level
- the use of political affiliation as the main criterion for recruitment of managers (the nomenclature)
- the elimination of formal legal structures, and
- the subordination of international economic exchange and co-operation to the interests of the Soviet economy.

To these attributes of the "politicization" of economic processes should be added the struggle for power between different actors. These actors were more than just the ruling group and society. The ruling strata has been increasingly differentiated internally, for example on a regional basis. The regional party rulers and administration had their own political interests, conflicting frequently with other regional rulers or with interests of the central authority. In this articulation of their own interests, these groups treated the economy as a tool in the struggle.

The logic of maintenance of power of the new post-communist elite is similar to the old communist logic, albeit implemented in a more democratic way. The principal objective of the communists was to create social support by the development of the working class and gradual liquidation of the economic basis of other social classes that could challenge communist hegemony. The propaganda slogans were an egalitarian society and industrialization. To assure the continuation of transformation and maintenance of power, the new political elite looks to the development of a middle class as a base for their social and political support. The propaganda slogans are efficiency and an open society. So the communist maxim "to everyone according to their need" has been evolving towards "to everyone according to their work" and, "to everyone according to impartial principles of social justice". However, the impartial principles have each time been determined by the ruling group, according to participation in supporting the existing power structure. The most popular slogan of contemporary transformation is "to everyone according to their efficiency in the market".

It seems that the post-1989 transformation has not changed the basic relationship between politics and economics. It is the result of the fact that political democracy has come first, before a market economy has been formed (Gołębiowski 1993). The democratic opposition before 1989 also used the economy as a tool for political purposes – to eliminate communism. The strategy was based on the widely shared illusion that implementation of democracy would automatically bring free market prosperity similar to that of western Europe. The widespread misperception of the economic costs and benefits of the transformation was evident. Now its increasing costs create a situation in which the idea of transformation could be rejected or diluted in a democratic way, or recognized and adopted.

Through time, as support for the economic transformation dropped, the only possibility that remained was its implementation by political means, or its continuation with partial concessions. It seems that this last strategy was used by all Solidarity governments up to the dissolution of parliament in 1993. So the trajectory of the economic transformation was partly determined by voters during the parliamentary election in September 1993, although in a very fragmented and differentiated political arena. The winners – the left-wing alliance of Peasant Party (PSL) and former communists under the Social Democrat label (SLD) – maintain the direction of transformation in the economic system. However, it has used the economy extensively to improve its political influence.

The economy and standard of living remain all the time the most important instruments in the struggle for power. Economic benefits are still based to a large extent on political influence in the old and new power structures (Bolesta-Kukułka 1992). The new dimension of these phenomena was the enfranchisement of the communist nomenclatura before 1989, a process that continued afterwards with the enfranchisement of a new political elite. The wealth of the communist nomenclatura has been a classic example of the transition of the former power elite into an economic elite, with the maintenance of its indirect political influence and its higher standard of living.

The contemporary transformation, which has taken place in conditions of the collapse of old ideas and the creation of new ones, is still in the formative stage. First of all, new rules of political and social life are only partly established. The only pattern frequently exposed as an aim is the example of well developed Western countries with a well established liberal and democratic order. The idea of market transformation, widely accepted in the beginning, is losing much of its appeal. The liberals are confronted with ideas emanating from the Church, and bad

17

economic conditions are stimulating favourable sentiments towards the old order.

The political transformations are at a very early stage, because there is a lack of well established rules of public conduct and no widely approved mechanism for the articulation of interests of local social groups and for conflict resolution. The emerging political system in Poland will probably be a compromise between the principles of liberal democracy and former attitudes, along with the resolution of the conflict between aspiring power groups. There is particularly strong opposition to the establishment of a new political and economic system as an intellectual construct, to be imposed on society. The best example is the resistance of interest groups, both employees and managerial elite, to the privatization processes, which resulted in substantial delays and in its "adaptation". So the theoretical aim of privatization – efficiency – may be sacrificed to the political aim of "social equity".

The democratically and market-oriented political elite has no economic resources, and the support from Western democracies, however visible, falls short of the radical and decisive action needed to provide the time necessary for the establishment of a market economy and democracy and the demonstration that it will guarantee increasing standards of living. So far the number of those losing their standard of living exceeds the number of those who gain.

The move towards the separation of the economy from politics since the collapse of communism has been only partly successful. The private sector has grown substantially in significance. However, the state sector still dominates politically, with a huge concentration of a frustrated industrial working class. Additionally, the substantial unemployment and impoverishment of society, particularly the rural population, keeps economic issues at the core of the agenda of every political party. The persistence of the politicization of the transformation provides the opportunity to treat the economy as an object of political intrigue. The popular belief still persists that improvement of living conditions can be reached only by political protest. It is inherited from the previous behaviour of workers in using strikes as a political weapon to guarantee their interests, instead of using newly introduced democratic means of negotiation with the government. For most Poles, the state remains responsible for their standard of living, and is evaluated according to that criterion.

The continuation of the fusion of politics and the economy in the perception even of the pro-democratic elite could be exemplified by the reports prepared by the resigning governments of Bielecki, Olszewski, and Suchocka. These reports indicated how political prerequisites strongly shape the way the state of the economy is presented, and how the different evaluation of the same fact and interpretation of the same processes could be presented.

Two options are still under consideration as possible future scenarios: neoliberalism and social democracy. The neoliberal option, which has been pushed forwards during the first four years (up to 1993), would lead to the separation of the economic, political and social systems. Social democracy, implemented since the parliamentary election of 1993, stresses strong ties between these systems, because of the requirement of social justice and the existence of a welfare state (Morawski 1994).

CHAPTER 3

Towards transformation – the decline and rejection of the communist system

The post Second World War history of Poland could be described in terms of several phases, differentiated by many criteria. However, the last phase is the most important, and only selected features of others have had a direct influence on the maintenance and ultimate rejection of the communist system. In the political arena, all these phases could be defined in terms a struggle around power.

The first years of communist Poland (1945–9) were dominated by a struggle for power between different social groups and parties, but with decisive external intervention in favour of communism. The next three decades (1950–81) were characterized by the struggle of society with the totalitarian system and particularly with its communist rulers, for mostly economic concessions. However, this struggle was only a moderate challenge to the ruling role of the party. Inside the communist elite, a struggle for power between interest groups also emerged, defined regionally and by sectors of economy. The years 1981–9 were characterized again by struggle for power, in all arenas, completed by rejection of communism. The introduction of martial law in 1981 changed the situation, with opposition beginning to struggle for participation in real power, which finally succeeded during the Round Table negotiation in 1989.

The contemporary phase began with the elimination of the communists from power. The disappearance of the common enemy brought polarization in the former opposition, and a gradual increase in the struggle for power between different social strata and newly created elites. The last (1993) electoral success of the post-communist parties does not reverse the transformation. It could be treated as a "normal" democratic game in the articulation of the interests of the different social categories. The leading post-communist parties, in spite of their origins and communist roots, cannot be fully identified with old, pre-1989 ruling parties.

3.1 The phases of post Second World War evolution

For the purposes of this book, the following substantially different phases must be borne in mind.

19

The first (1944–9) was the early phase of people's democracy, characterized by the forced introduction of the communist system from above and abroad. The Communist Party (the Polish United Workers' Party: PZPR), subordinated two formerly independent allied parties: the United Peasants' Party (ZSL) and the Democratic Party (SD), and ruled the country in a totalitarian manner. The second (1950–5) was the Stalinist phase characterized by a classic totalitarian attitude of authority, although this was moderate as compared with other communist countries. The third (1956–70) began with the "Polish October" and the formulation of the concept of "own road towards socialism", and ended with stagnation and political crisis. This phase became crucial in preserving Poland's distinctiveness in the Soviet empire. The collectivization of agriculture had been halted and reversed, political liberalization and greater freedom had been re-established, and strong cultural and scientific ties with non-communist countries had been formed. The fourth phase (1970–79) was dominated by the modernization programme through large-scale economic growth, technological upgrading and consumerism (which collapsed after 1976). This programme, financed partly by foreign credit, resulted in a mounting of debt. The inflow of modern technology was not adjusted to the centrally planned style of economy, and substantial delays and waste of investment resources resulted in reducing the possibility of repayment. The political aim of this programme was to maintain power, to give the population better living conditions, to improve the political system, and to corrupt society into remaining docile. The economic decline caused frustration and growth of open opposition. However, the price rise of 1976 and crushed strikes resulted for the first time under communist rule, in the unification of workers' and intellectuals' opposition. The most visible was the foundation of the "Committee for the Defence of Workers" (KOR), which was transformed later into the "Committee for Social Self-Defence (KSS–KOR). The fifth phase (1980–81), the Solidarity era, was characterized by open challenge to communist domination. The sixth (1981–9) began with the introduction of martial law, involved attempts at economic reform, and ended with the so-called round-table negotiation and the peaceful rejection of the communist system. The last phase began in 1989, and is characterized by the peaceful struggle for a democratic system based on a free market economy.

3.2 The roots of decline

The shape of post Second World War Poland's political and economic system was decided by the Yalta treaty. The development of the democratic and free-market system of inter-war independent Poland had been halted and had no chance to flourish. In spite of that, some scholars maintain that the direction of development of Polish society led to an authoritarian solution. The most radical opinion indicates that socialism in Poland was determined because this was the direction of the increasing role of the state sector in the economy, along with the absence of a middle class as a result of their war-time extermination. So, sooner or later, the democratic system would collapse in favour of authoritarian bureaucracy.

The first post-war economic programmes of most important political parties were to a great extent similar. The question, however, was who would introduce this programme, so it was mostly a struggle for power rather than for a model of national economy (Bolesta-Kukulka 1992).

The election of 1947 legitimated communist power and provided the basis for the formation of segments of society supporting the change. The idea of industrialization and elimination of unemployment gained substantial social support in post-war conditions. Agricultural reform also provided political support for the communists. However, the economy remain mixed and 65–70% of Poland's GNP came from the private sector (Gołebiowski 1993). The communists, however, reinforced their absolute power and introduced their own order.

The nationalization of the economy created supporting social strata, in particular working class, and led to the political subordination of the economy. Parallel to that, independent economic activities were eliminated. Up to 1956 only the private agricultural sector resisted, however, the forced industrialization policy accompanied by impoverishment of the rural population substantially constrained economic improvement of this sector.

The gradual replacement of the whole administration and management by Communist Party members, and centralization of all economic, social and political activity, gave the communists basic control of the country. The party officials formed the ruling apparatus, which became alienated from society at large, and for which maintenance of central control and power became the main objectives. Very quickly the official dictatorship of the proletariat has been replaced in reality by dictatorship of the communist apparatus (Lange 1966). The economic base for any social protest had been eliminated. The only resource exchangeable for survival at minimum level by society was obedience (Bolesta-Kukulka 1992). The mechanism of obedience created different interest groups, which obtained guaranteed jobs and enjoyed a better standard of living in exchange for supporting the system.

The absolute domination of the party and ideology over the economy, together with the formation of the ruling social strata, created the basic mechanism for the ultimate self-destruction of the communist system. The roots of collapse of state socialism could be traced from the institutionalization of this phenomenon (Kamiński 1991). The ruling social strata opposed any rationalization of the existed system because this reduced its privileged position.

The collapse of the six-year plan (1950–55), divisions in the elite of the Communist Party in the Soviet Union and in Poland, and strong worker protests, caused a substantial withdrawal from the orthodox totalitarian attitude. The economic and political concessions to society did not change the power structure; however, for the first time the mass protest of workers from large factories created the possibility of challenging communist power. This possibility came to be appreciated by both the working class and the ruling strata. Since the "Polish October" (1956), the working class became increasingly aware of its power and came to form an interest group struggling for improvement of living conditions. The rebirth of worker self-government in 1956, although gradually eliminated by the Communist Party from any influence on the economic management of enterprises, did contribute to the formation of working-class consciousness. At the beginning of the 1960s, the communists re-established absolute control over the economy.

The 1956 changes created favourable conditions for the formation of interest groups in the ruling strata, defined regionally and by branches of the economy (particularly industrial branches). The new leader of the party, Wladyslaw Gomulka, while struggling to establish his power over the Communist Party in confrontation with the central bureaucratic apparatus, sought to find support from regional leaders and mid-level bureaucrats. The regional apparatus gained additional influence in bargaining for shares of national income and the form of new investment (the distribution of scarce resources), thus increasing its political influence.

The decentralization of economic administration, together with a strategy of investment in heavy industry, provided substantial pressure for the formation of economically and politically strong regional power and of regional–industrial sector interest groups (Bolesta-Kukulka 1992).

In the 1960s, forced industrialization was maintained and the share of national income devoted to investment increased in relation to consumption, so the gap between expectation and reality remained. The decline of living standards, and increasing polarization between those in power and the rest of society, became more visible in spite of the declared egalitarian principles.

The disillusionment of society, particularly the growing gap between indicators of economic development and everyday living conditions, increased dissatisfaction and political tension. People became aware that investment progress was proceeding at their own expense, and comparison with standards of living in western European countries became more frustrating. A revolt of the intellectuals in 1968 was easily put down; however, it created the intellectual infrastructure for the formation of political opposition.

The workers' explosive protests in December 1970 against price increases was used by the strongest regional party group to take power. Gomulka was replaced by Edward Gierek, leader of the largest industrial voivodship in Poland (Katowice). The new ruling elite was, in the first place, trying to gain support from the industrial working class of the large enterprises and farmers. The intellectuals remained passive.

The economic concessions in the form of withdrawal of price increases, abolition of compulsory supply to the state in agriculture, and particularly promises of improvement in the future, calmed down the political tension. The parallel carefully prepared propaganda and social engineering around the image of the new rulers once more persuaded society to suppress its aspirations and wait for substantial improvement in their living conditions.

Based on large-scale economic growth and stimulated consumerism, the early 1970s brought remarkable progress as compared with the constraints of the 1960s.

The rapidly increased consumption and rising standard of living had been accomplished primarily by borrowing, but also by the release of resources the productivity of which was repressed in previous stagnation periods

Modernization strategy and further development, particularly of the heavy industry, was undertaken in conditions of strong regional polarization of interests. This was facilitated by "official" diffusion of many economic decisions to regional party groups and branch ministries; however, "unofficially" they already had an important influence on the economy by lobbying for their interests in the Central Committee. The strongest regional power groups and industrial lobbies managed to absorb all state resources in their branches or regions, in spite of other planning priorities and other sources of economic efficiencies. As one of the former party leaders confessed, between 1971 and 1975 the Political Bureau undertook economic decisions, concerning the development of different branches and regions, which exceeded the most optimistic hopes for building the national economy by four times (Bolesta-Kukułka 1992). And the largest investment of the 1970s, the huge steel complex of Huta Katowice and new sea port in Gdańsk, had been undertaken and located independently from the officially approved national plans.

The economic sector, with weak political lobbies, had simply been ignored, in spite of its evident economic irrationality. For example, agriculture had been excluded from the investment boom in circumstances when purchase of food by credits accounted for 20% of all credits in the 1970s (ibid. 1992). Subordination of the economy to the interests of the regional power elite reached its apogee. The workers' protest in June 1976 against price increases was put down. But the evident inefficiency of the entire system and the deterioration of the economic situation since 1976 caused a gradual consolidation of opposition and the formation of alliance between intellectuals and the working class. The repression only consolidated opposition; however, it was relatively moderate, and sometimes withdrawn because of external pressure. The KOR gained support from public opinion in Western countries while the Polish government was attempting to maintain a good image in order to secure additional loans. The level of fear of confrontation with authority had been diminished.

The development of an opposition movement had been associated with the development of underground publication and press, which resulted in a substantial limitation of the communist monopoly of information.

The election of Karol Wojtyla, the Archbishop of Cracow, to the papacy on 16 October 1978, and particularly his visit to Poland in June 1979, substantially improved the general mood and brought some relief to wide social groups from the moral captivity of communism. These events became the starting point for the rejection of communism on moral grounds.

The state of the economy and its management in the second half of 1970s became so disorganized that the hard winter of 1978/9 disrupted the functioning of all public services and the productive economy for several days. In the ruling strata, different groups were struggling between themselves for power, and nomenclature members accumulated wealth illegally. This time the authorities had very

23

limited resources with which to placate society, because there were no new sources of borrowing.

The price increase introduced by the communist government on 1 July 1980 caused the first widespread reaction of society, which resulted in the final stage in the creation of the first independent trade union in the Soviet sphere. A social agreement was signed on 31 September 1980 in Gdańsk. By December the union had 3.5 million members, which grew the following year to 10 million. In spite of massive support for Solidarity, the government tried to impose some constraints on its activity. The Communist Party was in internal crisis and in September Edward Gierek was replaced by Stanisław Kania as leader of the Party.

The concessions of the Polish communists caused increasing pressure from the Soviet Union, to the extent that in December 1980 General Jaruzelski was informed by Moscow that within a week the Soviet, Czechoslovakian and East German armies were going to intervene in Poland. Direct diplomatic intervention by President Carter and the Pope, along with Jaruzelski's plans to mobilize the Polish army, stopped the Soviets from intervening. However, the Soviet army was concentrated on the Polish border for a month.

The Polish communists remained under increasing pressure from the Soviet Union and other communist parties to withdraw their concessions. The major military exercises begun in March 1981 had been a direct threat and pressure. The already huge military presence of the Soviet army on Polish territory had been further increased. However, the greatest general strike in the history of Poland, on 27 March, was also supported by local branches of the Communist Party.

The crisis in the Communist Party had been made more visible by resignations from membership and by the formation of an alternative structure (struktury poziome) at the regional levels. The deteriorating economic situation caused the extension of rationing for provision of basic food.

The consolidation of the trade union organization Solidarity had been accompanied by the first sign of internal differences. The programme of the Solidarity meeting on 26 September 1981, and agreed document, mention that Solidarity is a pluralist organization aimed at representing and protecting the dignity, rights and interests of employees. The economic reforms should be based on both the planned and market systems, stressing the self-government of employees. In the final resolution, no single word "socialism" was used, and this became an object of strong attack from the party and the government side.

The continuous deterioration of the economic situation, and social and political confrontation between the Solidarity movement and the authorities, radicalized opinion and action on both sides. The wave of barely controlled strikes was accompanied by many deliberate provocations and preparations for martial law. Because the collapse of the economy would be associated with the collapse of authority, the Solidarity leaders were not fully interested in supporting it.

During the Party congress on 16–18 October 1981. General Wojciech Jaruzelski replaced Stanisław Kania as a party leader. This concentrated in one pair of hands power over the party, the government and the army.

The martial law declared on 13 December 1981 was final proof that communists can rule only by direct use of force. From the legal point of view it was a coup d'état. It was suspended in December 1982 and officially lifted in July 1983. However, the new set of laws created the situation of a "legislative cage" for any free and anti-communist social or political action. Officially, Poland was ruled by the Communist Party, but in practice by the generals organized in a declared Military Committee for Salvation of the Nation (Wojskowa Rada Ocalenia Narodowego) and a secret Committee of Country Defence (Komitet Obrony Kraju). The Communist Party remained in crisis and apathy. The ideological argumentation had been limited to the minimum requirement of the communist leaders of the Soviet block (Roszkowski 1994). The evident aims of the rulers was to intimidate and, having lowered the resistance of society, they began to lift the harsh marshal law regulations. The most popular reaction in society was different forms of escapism and frustration, described as internal emigration, and increasing involvement in the black economy. The government strategy of co-option of the opposition and society as a whole was unsuccessful. However, the steps towards normalization of the law had not changed the apathy and increasing resistance of society.

The economic reform programme the "3-S" (i.e. self-direction, self-financing and self-management), introduced in 1982, together with austerity measures at the beginning, brought very limited economic recovery. Under martial law, the economy ceased to be the object of political intrigue for power because it was now determined by military force (Bolesta-Kukułka 1992). The introduction of the army apparatus to the economy imposed additional bureaucratic authority, parallel to the government administration and the Communist Party apparatus. This fusion of the different spheres of apparatus brought only a radical increase in administration; however, the nomenclature system started to be diluted. However, the industrial and regional lobbies preserved their monopolistic positions, as producers, and contributed substantially to the collapse of the first stage of reforms.

The rejection in a national referendum of the second stage of economic reform in 1987 could be interpreted as a rejection of the socialist economy as a whole. The collapse of economic reforms, pressure from the International Monetary Fund, and favourable external factors such as liberalization in the Soviet Union, pressed the government for radical liberalization of the economy in Poland. The liberalization of 1987–9, however, come too late, particularly in that the rate of inflation had now risen to hyperinflation. Parallel to that, the majority of the ruling group lost its will to defend socialist principles by force, or realized the very limited possibility of success. So the ruling group had only one solution: bargaining with the opposition to maximize its own security in the expected transfer of power.

The rejection of communism on economic grounds had been determined by the introduction of martial law and the collapse of attempts to run the economy since 1981. Equally important, however, was the moral rejection initiated by the first visit of the Pope to Poland. The final turning point, however was the assassination of priest Jerzy Popiełuszko on 19 October 1984 by members of the state security force. This murder, probably organized as a provocation by an orthodox faction of the communist ruling group, failed in its aim. It brought about a moral consolidation of democratic opposition and society. The communists finally lost any moral support from the majority of Polish society.

3.3 The rejection

On 18 December 1988 the "Citizens' Committee" had been formed by Lech Wałesa, aimed at negotiating with the government. The meeting of 20 December of the Communist Party resulted in the decision to undertake negotiation with the opposition, in spite of strong orthodox opposition within the party. The Round Table negotiations, begun on 6 February 1989, concluded on the 5 April 1989 by re-legalization of Solidarity, free access to mass media, and preparation of a semi-free parliamentary election.

The basic political agreement concerned the partly free parliamentary election organized for 4 June 1989. The absolute victory of the Solidarity candidates was the final proof of the rejection of the communist system. Since that electoral verdict, an irreversible process of transformation began in a peaceful way.

The Polish society during this election questioned immediately the Round Table agreement that communists could form a majority of the government. The idea of the division of power between opposition and communists was launched in July 1989 by A. Michnik, under the slogan "your president, our prime minister". The initial threat of Soviet intervention had been calmed down, but in Solidarity several groups of leaders warned about sharing executive power and responsibility for events without full freedom of execution of power. As a result, General Jaruzelski was elected to the presidency, by one vote. The voting in parliament showed division in the Solidarity camp and in the communist coalition for the first time. Not all members of the communist coalition supported Jaruzelski. It was the final collapse of that coalition that led to splits inside the Communist Party.

Additionally, the economic situation had been worsening in 1989. The high rate of inflation, and uncontrolled budget spending by the last communist government of Mieczysław Rakowski, caused a dramatic increase of shortages in the shops. The policy of freezing prices meant that factories were trying to limit the delivery of their products to the market, waiting for new price increases. The economic chaos of empty shops and falls in production, together with speculation, created additional pressure for radical political changes.

The final result, after several unsuccessful attempts, was the formation of the first non-communist government, by Tadeusz Mazowiecki. In spite of N. Ceausesku's attempt to organize Warsaw Pact intervention in Poland, the Soviet Union refused to intervene in the internal affairs of Poland. This also indicated the end of the Brezniew doctrine, and that the Soviet Union was ready to accept the political consequences of Poland's transformation.

The Mazowiecki government had been approved by 402 votes from 415 deputies. This was the situation before the Prague Autumn and East Germany's revolutionary transformation. In September 1989 Mazowiecki declared the policy of the "thick line" (gruba kreska), which indicated partial release of communists from responsibility for 45 years of totalitarian government and allowed many former officials to adopt the new political system. The aim of this policy was to reduce the resistance of old communists to the democratic transformation, and the avoidance of common responsibility and acts of revenge. However, the "thick line" policy caused much social frustration, particularly in the conditions of massive impoverishment of society on one side, and wealth accumulated by former communist officials by privatization of different sectors of the national economy on the other. In spite of this policy, the police structure and the security service had been reorganized. The changes and replacement of the old communist administration had been substantial in all ministries and particularly in the Ministry of Internal Affairs and the Army. By the end of 1989, the 29 December Polish diet (Sejm) legally ended the existence of the Poland Peoples Republic as a communist state. The name was changed to the Commonwealth of Poland (Rzeczpospolita Polska), and a democratic state of law was declared. The Communist Party, which existed under the name of the Polish United Workers Party, was itself dissolved in January 1990.

The period from 1990 to the parliamentary election of 1993, when the post-communist parties came to power, changed the country in a way that meant that there was no threat of a return of communism either as an ideology or as a system of authoritarian government. This situation continued through 1994, when post-communist government dominated by the left-wing continued in principle the transformation process, but with some modification and delays.

The parliamentary election of September 1993, and success of post-communists, ended the period of absolute domination of post-Solidarity parties. The market economy and parliamentary democracy has been established in a non-reversible way. The return of the post-communist elite to the political arena, regaining some political power, serves rather to maintain its privileged economic position, which it never completely lost.

The interest of the post-communist elite is to continue the market and democratic transformation. The main post-Communist Party, the Democratic Left Alliance (SLD), has evolved into a Social Democracy party in the Western sense. Also, the Polish Peasant Party (PSL) seems to have evolved in a Christian Democracy direction, or has become a party representing only the narrow class interests of the peasantry. There is also no threat of military power or external interventions in favour of communism.

There is no longer any coherent social group that will really support the former political system or ideology. However, there are many groups of losers, frustrated peoples and those not satisfied with the direct consequences of the transformation. There remains an open question about the speed, the manner, and the cost of future transformation. The direction of transformation – towards the market economy and more mature democracy, has been finally determined.

PART II
Regional differentiation and post-communist transformation

CHAPTER 4
Regional and spatial structure

The reduction of regional disparities inherited from the nineteenth century has been the aim of each Polish government throughout the twentieth century. The unification of Poland in 1918, after the First World War, raised immediately the question of elimination of disparities inherited from 125 years of partition between three powers. The post Second World War shift of Polish territory westwards again raised the problem of strong regional disparities (see Fig.1.1). So the idea of spatial justice gained wide acceptance. However, the implementation of spatial policy was shaped by ideological priorities. Additionally, in spite of many successes in the reduction of regional inequalities, some new forces arose causing an increase in disparities. In particular, the idea of the equal spatial allocation of productive forces, in order to achieve regional equalization of standards of living, itself proved to be ineffective. The key element was the issue of planning. Under a command economy, planning is a part of ideologically determined social engineering.

Substantial spatial disparities exist in Poland. On the broad scale the most evident are those between the western and eastern parts of the country and between urban and rural areas. For example, the difference in the level of urbanization between eastern and western voivodships is estimated at 1 to 10. A relatively new dimension of differentiation in standards of living is between polluted and "green" areas. The geography of contemporary Poland has been an arena of radical changes, the most important stimulated by spatial planning policy. After 45 years of communist rule, new patterns of regional differentiation have emerged; however, the macro-structural pattern remained relatively stable.

Two important processes were most evident in this period: spatial policy, and industrialization connected with urbanization. So the actual state of Poland's regional disparities is only partly the result of the inherited spatial structure of the pre-war situation; to a very great extent it is also a result of communist spatial planning. Now, the elimination of the strong mechanism of wealth and income redistribution will inevitably increase disparities in the future.

31

4.1 The impact of spatial policy on urbanization and industrialization

The study for the national physical plan undertaken just after the Second World War was never finished and approved. The vision was deconcentrating industry from Upper Silesia towards a strong industrial axis connecting the coal basin with the Baltic Sea, as well as new industrial centres to activate underdeveloped regions (Malisz 1986).

The reorganization of the planning apparatus in 1949 subordinated physical planning to economic planning. The first target of this sort of planning was to guarantee the interests of branches of national economy rather than territorial units. Despite all this, the vision of Polish space originating from the post-war years has to some extent influenced the emerging spatial pattern.

The second planning objective emerged in the years 1971–4. The new socio-economic policy adopted in 1971 aimed officially at raising living standards and satisfying the consumption needs of the population. Achieving this seemed possible at that time because of the favourable international situation and easy access to Western credits and technology.

Three prospective concepts in the spatial arrangement of the country had a direct impact on the national physical plan prepared by the Planning Commission in the years 1971–4 for the 1990 time horizon. The first concept emphasized the growth of urban agglomerations. The second concept is known as the node-band system. The third concept emphasized the urban–regional approach (ibid.).

The target model of the country's spatial structure has been referred to as a moderate, policentric concentration. It has assumed shifting part of the national industrial potential to the northern and eastern territories of the country, by allocating part of new industrial investment to economically less developed regions. In reality this concept could not be fulfilled because of the strong impact of the regional political lobbies of already industrialized voivodships, and because of declining economic prospects in general.

The spatial structure of Poland in 1950 was a result of many historical processes. Poland inherited from the period of capitalist economic development areas peripheral to three powers, and in which economic development proceeded in different stages. The best developed was the Prussian part, with for example 6.3% of people employed in industry as compared to 3.4% in the Russian part and 0.6% in the Austrian part. So the spatial structure inherited from economic development and political partition of the nineteenth century has been impossible to integrate. Additionally, the world economic crisis of 1929–33 stopped any progress in this field. The basic elements of the inter-war transformation of spatial structure were the construction of the sea port of Gdynia together with the railway line connecting Upper Silesia and the creation of the Central Industrial Region (COP) in 1936–9 (Dziewoński 1988) (in the contemporary voivodship of Rzeszów, Tarnobrzeg and Tarnów).

In the inter-war period, Poland was predominantly a rural country, with a huge employment in agriculture variously estimated at between 4.5 to 8 million people. The Second World War completely devastated Poland. Additionally, the shift westwards and resettlement of northern and western Territories have changed the regional arrangement of the country. In terms of population, however, the pre-war number was reached in the 1960s.

The scale of war-time devastation provided a unique opportunity for planners for radical transformation of the spatial structure of the country, and for equalization of spatial disparities. This was the aim of all spatial planning in 1945–9. In practice, however, this idea was not realistic. The immediate need and priority of the country was to restart production as soon as possible, so the renovation of the industry petrified the old spatial structure. The stress on industrialization meant that employment in industry in 1950 reached 8.5% as compared with 4.7% in 1938 (Dziewoński 1988).

The first forced industrialization plan, the so-called "six-year plan" designed under totally new socialist principles, aimed to create the productive basis for economic development and a more equal distribution of productive forces in space. More than 1200 new industrial plants were designed, some of which were located in less developed areas. However, the collapse of this plan and beginning of the Cold War caused a drastic reduction, so 470 projects were postponed, mostly those that were intended for non-industrial areas. The next plan, the five-year plan of 1956–60, was characterized mostly by completing the investment initiated under the previous plan and raising the effectiveness of investment in underdeveloped areas (Dziewoński & Malisz 1978)

The first phase of forced industrialization could be attributed to the 1950–70 period, when the fundamental structural changes occurred that shaped later regional development. During the next period, 1971–90, the process of urbanization had priority; however, industrial development, particularly in the 1970s, has been regarded by some scholars as "the second phase of industrialization, with its intensive industrial development, the concomitant scientific–technological revolution, and the rising share of qualified labour in the production processes." (Dziewoński 1988).

The second period of industrialization was characterized by the concentration of investment on the mining and energy sectors. This investment was located outside existing industrial regions. The spatial policy became more of a compromise between economic objectives working in favour of concentration and the political objective of egalitarian development and social justice.

After 20 years of centrally planned spatial policy and imposed industrialization, processes of regional differentiation had changed. In 1950 more than 77% of total industrial output came from the inverted T-shaped areas defined by the contemporary voivodships of Wrocław, Opole, Katowice, Kraków, Częstochowa, Piotrków and Łódź (Fig 4.1), with a small concentration in Warsaw (5.2%) and Poznań (6.3%) voivodships (Dziewoński & Malisz 1978). Substantial disparity also

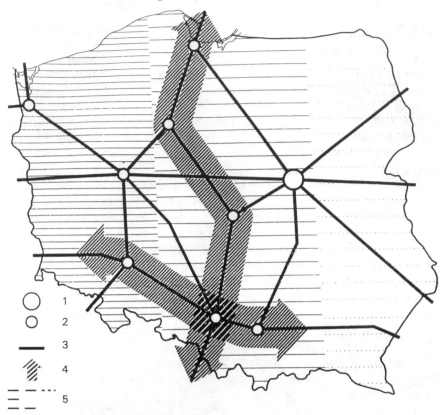

Figure 4.1 The pattern of the spatial structure of Poland, 1950. 1. Capital. 2. Largest urban centre. 3. Principal communication network. 4. Main axes of industrial development. 5. Schematic pattern of the intensity of investment in infrastructure, decreasing toward east. After: Dziewoński & Malisz 1978, p. 26.

existed in the technical infrastructure, reflecting cultural development and the level of inherited disparities. The same was true of the urbanization level and other indicators.

By 1970 the spatial structure showed some evolution, however. The three voivodship of Katowice, Wrocław and Łódź, whose share of industrial output was 60% in 1950, produced only 36.4% of total industrial production in 1970. The old T-shape pattern had weakened. The most industrialized voivodships now form a triangle (Fig. 4.2). However, the strongest industrial development remained within a radius of 300 km from Katowice. Thus, almost the whole country was now under the influence of the industrialization process (ibid.).

The most important spatial outcome of many errors of the centrally planned economy (described by various scholars) was the delay of urbanization in comparison with industrialization. Industrialization, as the most important modernization process of Polish society in the twentieth century, gained considerable popular support at the beginning, in spite of the imposed character of its socialist version.

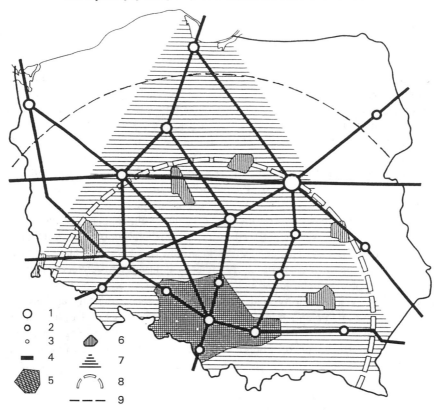

Figure 4.2 The pattern of the spatial structure of Poland, 1970. 1. Capital. 2. Biggest urban centre. 3. Medium size urban centres. 4. Principal communication network. 4. Main axes of industrial development. 5. Southern industrial region. 6. New industrial region. 7. Areas of high industrialization level. 8. Circle of 300 kilometres radius from Katowice. 9. Zone of influence of the new industrial regions. After: Dziewoński & Malisz 1978, p. 32.

But during the past two decades the unfavourable side of this process became very visible. The socialist version of industrialization had produced first of all a tremendous housing shortage, concentrated mostly in urban areas. Even in comparison with other eastern Europe countries, Poland has the most severe housing problem. Another outcome of socialist industrialization was tremendous pollution of the natural environment.

Polish regional structure, however, revealed some positive features. The degree of regional differentiation is smaller than in other countries, and the present spatial structure of the country creates favourable conditions for future development (Malisz 1986).

4.2 The position of industry in the national economy and its spatial structure

Industrialization has became the most stimulating process of modernization in Polish society. It has contributed decisively to the existing pattern of spatial differentiation. The regional level of industrialization (Figs 4.3, 4.4), measured by employment per 1000 inhabitants (Misztal & Kaczorowski 1983), shows the scale of transformation of the country. At the national scale, this indicator has increased from 61 in 1946 to 130 in 1988. The share of industry in GNP increased from 31% in 1949 to 50.2% in 1980; however, it dropped to 44.9% in 1990 and to 38% in 1992. In short, under communism Poland became an industrialized country. The rate of industrialization was one of the highest in Europe.

The structure of industry, however, was shaped by the demands of the Soviet Union and the military sector, and by the division of labour imposed by the Council of Mutual Economic Assistance (CMEA). From the very beginning, industry was to suffer from hypertrophy, particularly of heavy industry. This concerns particularly mining, steel, shipbuilding and chemicals, whereas light industry and the service sector were underinvested. In addition, the technological gap between western Europe and Poland gradually increased. The modernization of industry in the 1970s was concentrated on the traditional sectors of metals, mining and chemicals. The massive import of modern technology was not capable of absorption within the organizational structure of centralized Polish industry. The final result

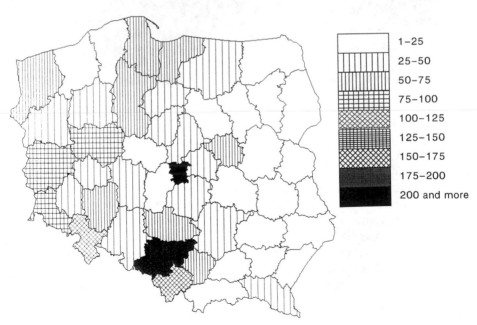

	1–25
	25–50
	50–75
	75–100
	100–125
	125–150
	150–175
	175–200
	200 and more

Figure 4.3 Employment in industry, 1946, per 1000 inhabitants. After: Misztal & Kaczorowski 1983.

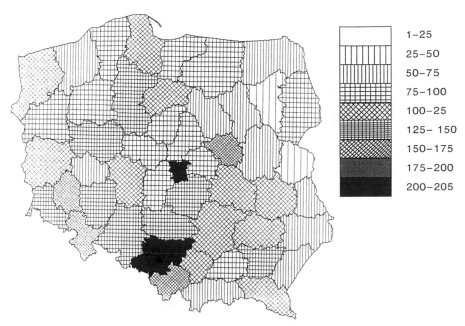

	1–25
	25–50
	50–75
	75–100
	100–25
	125– 150
	150–175
	175–200
	200–205

Figure 4.4 Employment in industry, 1988, per 1000 inhabitants. After: *Rocznik statystyczny przemysłu* 1989. Warsaw: GUS.

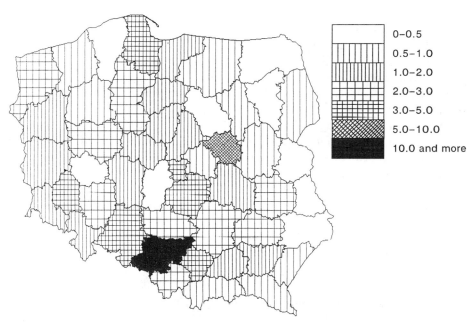

	0–0.5
	0.5–1.0
	1.0–2.0
	2.0–3.0
	3.0–5.0
	5.0–10.0
	10.0 and more

Figure 4.5 Distribution of investment expenditure in industry, 1950–85 (%). After: Lijewski 1993.

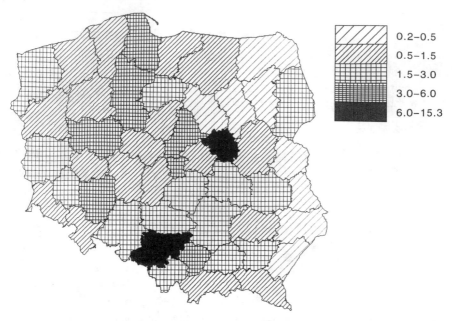

0.2–0.5
0.5–1.5
1.5–3.0
3.0–6.0
6.0–15.3

Figure 4.6 Distribution of Gross Domestic Product in industry, 1992 (%). After: Zienkowski 1994.

was a huge waste of capital and fixed assets. In addition, Polish science to a great extent remained outside the modernization process.

In spite of the ideological objective of balancing regional development, in reality over 40% of investment was allocated to the Upper Silesia, Cracow and Częstochowa industrial regions. The Katowice voivodship absorbed 21.8% of all industrial investment in the period of 1950–85, Warsaw received 6.4%, and 18 voivodships (out of a total of 49) located mostly in eastern and northern parts of the country gained below 1% (Lijewski 1993; Fig. 4.5). As a result, in 1992 the regional structure of industry, in terms of gross domestic product, tended to repeat the old pattern, and is much the same today (Fig. 4.6).

The most capital-consuming branches of heavy industry, coal mining and electric power production have 28% of the fixed assets of the whole of Polish industry. The old mines were substantially enlarged, and the new coal mines have been located around Upper Silesia, particularly in the new Rybnik region. The creation of a new mining region east of Lublin, initiated in 1975, was stopped in 1988.

Coal was and still is of key importance as a resource for electric power and is the most important Polish export product as a hard currency earner. Production grew strongly during whole communist period, and in 1979 reached its highest level of 201 million tonnes. It dropped during the 1980s to 190 million tonnes, to 140 million tonnes in 1991, and 131 million tonnes in 1993. There will be further decline in the near future. Another important source of electric power is the production of brown coal, which reached 73.5 million tonnes in 1988. Since then it started to decline, to 67 million tonnes in 1992.

The absence of oil and the very limited gas resources mean that production of electric power is based on coal and brown coal, providing basic self-sufficiency at the national scale but also causing substantial environmental problems. Power-generating plants are located close to coal mining, and in the largest cities they operate as central heating plants. Some of the largest new plants are close to rivers, generating power for industrial plants.

The metal industry has a greater concentration than even mining and power production. In 1985, 45% in terms of employment and 48% in terms of value was concentrated in Katowice voivodship. Adding Cracow, Legnica, Częstochowa and Kielce voivodships raised this to 87% of Poland's total employment and production. The spatial concentration is associated with size of plants. More than half of employment in the metal industry is in factories with more than 5000 workers (Lijewski 1993). The electro-engineering, technical and machinery industry generated the most new employment during the post-war period. It is the most modern branch of industry developed in the centres existing before the Second World War, and had little impact on the subsequent evolution of the spatial structure of production. It is concentrated in all large cities and pre-war centres of the Central Industrial Region and in Kielce, Bielsko–Biała and Opole voivodships. Poland is the producer of a whole range of machinery and engines.

The chemical industry is located in medium-size towns, and during the post-war period was shifted northwards generally along the Vistula and Odra rivers. The largest post-war investment was determined by the location of domestic natural resources, such as copper in Legnica, and sulphur mining in Tarnobrzeg, which were the bases of industrial development in those voivodships.

The textile industry was discriminated against, in term of investment, during the whole post-war period. It was well developed before the Second World War and was left relatively unscathed by the hostilities. In 1946, 44% of total national employment was concentrated in Łódź, but by 1985 its share had dropped to 16% (Lijewski 1993). In spatial structure this industry had become dispersed.

The food industry is the most evenly distributed in national space. Throughout the whole post-war period its share of industrial investment was around 10%; however, this was not enough to satisfy demand. Additionally, the small size of many factories makes the industry inefficient.

This spatial structure of industry has undergone substantial restructuring since 1990. The whole industrial economy was in crisis throughout the 1980s. The political and economic transformation of the 1990s entailed a great fall in industrial production. This primarily affected the industrial branches dependent on exchange with the former CMEA countries, that is, mechanical and electrical engineering and textiles. Liberalization of international trade and competition from Western products suddenly reduced demand for domestic industrial products.

The state of Polish industry, as evaluated by OECD experts, indicates features created by the centrally planned economy that serve as constraints on the transformation to a market economy (OECD 1992). First is the size distribution of firms. The lack of small and medium-size enterprises limits the possibility of finding a niche in the competitive market. The second feature is the outcome of the egalitarian spatial policy, locating heavy industry in rural regions. In contemporary conditions there is a lack of financial resources to maintain the ineffective and generally low-quality production in such locations. The result is high unemployment and constraints on economic development in these regions. The third feature concerns high and inefficient energy consumption, with the side effect of tremendous environmental pollution. The fourth concerns the poor telecommunications infrastructure.

The substantial overemployment in industry, by international standards, has become a source of increasing unemployment. However, the proportional decrease of employment, for example in 1990, was much smaller than the decrease of industrial production. In spite of that, 1992 was the first year of stabilization, and in 1993 industrial production started to expand again. The re-orientation of international trade, from CMEA to OECD countries, occurred in two years. The sharp recession in state-owned industry was accompanied by rapid development of the private sector, which was however unable to compensate for the national scale of decline in the early 1990s.

The recession in industry concerned mostly the branches dependent directly on co-operation with the former CMEA. In 1992 (compared with 1989) the greatest falls were in the textile industry (52%), in the leather industry (43%), in the non-ferrous metal industry (43%), and in the machine industry (42%) (Central Office of Planning 1993).

According to the Central Office of Planning, the downward trends in industrial production ceased by 1992, and since April 1992 growth resumed. Sales of industrial products for 1992 were 4.2% greater than in 1991. However, it was still lower than in 1989 by 30.4%, and only at the level of 1974. This figure indicates how deep the recession was. In 1993, sales of industrial production grew again, this time by 6.2%.

The regional differentiation of sales of industrial production in 1993, compared with 1991 (in constant prices), indicates the regions where the economic situation improved relatively, and where recession is still present (Fig. 4.7).

This improvement is the result of following advantageous transformation factors. The first is increasing production in the private sector, and particularly increasing productivity (much higher than in the public sector), and the increased number of private industrial entities of small and medium size as a result of changes in ownership of state enterprises through liquidation or capital privatization. The second is the partial restructuring, in terms of quality and quantity of production, to the requirement of a market economy. The competitiveness of domestic products had to increase in relation to foreign goods. The third is the growth of labour productivity.

The problem of inefficiency of energy consumption still remains. However, the constant increase of prices of energy transmission creates the basic condition for

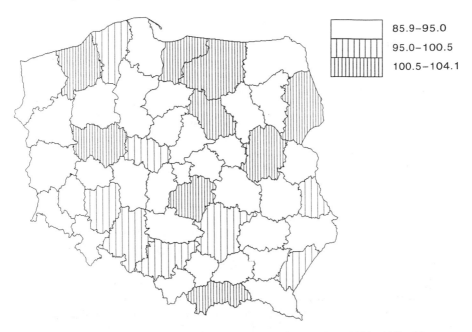

85.9–95.0

95.0–100.5

100.5–104.1

Figure 4.7 Sales of industrial production, 1991–3 (fixed prices 1991: 100). After: Central Office of Planning, 1993.

rationalization. This is one of the most important issues, because the Polish economy uses two to three times more energy than those of highly developed countries. This situation is inherited and is impossible to change in the short term, because the production of energy is based on inefficient solid fuels, the existing industrial structure, which is based on energy-intensive raw material industries, and the low efficiency of energy use by the population living in buildings with inadequate insulation. It has been estimated that the potential effect of the rationalization of energy use in Poland would save 50 million tonnes of theoretical standard fuel per annum (Central Office of Planning 1993).

4.3 The role of agriculture in the national economy and its spatial structure

The existence of private agriculture in the centrally planned economy was treated as a threat to the ideological principles of communism. After the Second World War, it was understood that such agriculture would sooner or later be eliminated. Its continued existence, however, became one of the main characteristics of the "Polish way towards socialism", and distinguished Poland among Soviet block nations. The resistance of Polish peasant landholders to collectivization changed the communist strategy from direct use of force in the early 1950s to

41

gradual transformation in the subsequent period. Techniques for gradual transformation included industrialization, and also creating unfavourable conditions for
private farms in relation to the state and co-operative sector. As a whole sector of
the national economy, agriculture became one of the main sources of capital accumulation for industrialization and a reserve source of cheap labour.

The position of the private sector became strong under conditions of insufficient
production, aggravated since the 1970s by the general shortage of foodstuffs in the
Soviet block. In Poland, private farming survived and the peasant became more
influential in state agricultural policy. The most important successes politically
were: the constitutional recognition by the communist government of the right of
individual peasants to their property; the abandoning of discriminatory treatment
in access to consumer goods and means of production; and the promise to maintain
income parity between urban and rural dwellers.

The rapid increase in farmers' income in the early 1980s resulted in a rapid
expansion of agricultural production. Also, for the first time since 1945, the transfer of land from the state sector to the private sector was possible. Some observers
even claim that, in terms of wellbeing, peasants gained more than workers (Wilkin
1989). At the same time it was possible to observe an inflow of people to agriculture because of martial law restrictions and the recession. As a result, the growing
food shortage was reversed to overproduction in the late 1980s. But since 1989,
hyperinflation has reduced the economic effects of the successes in agricultural
production.

Despite being politically successful in their struggle with the communist
regime, peasants in Poland remained socially and economically backward, and
unprepared for the introduction of market economics after 1989. This social category became one of the first to be negatively affected by the transformation, and
threatens to become the most conservative section of Polish society.

In terms of employment structure, agriculture's share dropped from 53.6% in
1950 to 43.3% in 1960, 34.3% in 1970, 29.87% in 1980 and 25.8% in 1990. The
1990s saw this reduction level out, and in 1991 there was an increase to 26%; however, the proportion fell again to 25.2% in 1993. Employment in private agriculture
has increased from 87.7% of total agricultural employment in 1989 to 95.4% in
1993 (GUS 1994).

4.3.1 THE SPATIAL STRUCTURE

Polish rural areas are inhabited by people who can be characterized as peasants.
This type of society has almost disappeared in western Europe. In communist
Poland, discrimination against rural areas in terms of supply of consumer goods
and modern means of production resulted in farmers consuming more than 60%
of their own production. This has limited the increase of productivity and has
become the most important barrier to the commercialization and modernization of
private agriculture. The contemporary consequence of 40 years of communist

policy is an organizational and technological gap, estimated at 25–30 years, between Polish and Western standards.

Favourable climatic conditions for agriculture facilitate the development of this sector of the economy. However, soil conditions are relatively poor. The majority of soils are of average or poor quality. In the classification of soils the two top classes cover only 3.3% of the country, in the "good" category 22.7%, and rest is covered by average or poor soils. The best quality soils are concentrated in the southeast and in small areas of Żuławy, Kujawy and Pyrzyce.

Most important for the state of Polish agriculture, however, has been the level of economic development of particular regions. In the agricultural sector, more than in any other, the regional differentiations rooted in historical development are very visible. This is true of all economic indicators, organizational structure, productivity and level of modernization.

The ownership and size structure is the outcome of many historical factors, but above all the agrarian reforms introduced by the communists after the Second World War. In 1990 there were three types of ownership in the agricultural sector: individual–private comprising 76% of farmlands; state 18.6%; and co-operative 4% (Szczęsny 1992). During the post-war period the share of the private sector decreased from 89.6% in 1950 to 86.9% in 1970 and 74.5% in 1980 (Stola & Szczęsny 1994). The co-operative sector is the least important; in 1955 it reached only 11.2%, dropping in 1960 to 1.2% of farmland, with a gradual increase thereafter.

Deliberate communist policy, together with the more general process of urbanization and industrialization, has also had a direct influence on the size structure of individual farms. Through the whole post-war period, the average size of the farm shrank to 5.1 ha, but generally the size structure has not changed very much. This size and ownership structure is a considerable barrier to the future modernization of the agricultural sector, and to accommodation to the competitive free market economy at the national and international scale. The domination of private agriculture in eastern and central parts of the country contrasts with the domination of state agriculture in western parts (Fig. 4.8).

At the regional scale, the average farm size is smaller in the south (Katowice, Tarnów, and Krosno voivodships: around 4 ha) than in the north (Great Poland: over 8 ha; and more than 10 ha in Mazurian and Żuławy regions) (Szczęsny 1992).

Throughout the communist period the socialized sector was favoured in terms of technical infrastructure and supply of means of production. All sorts of tractors and more modern machinery were provided for the state sector, which was dominant in the western and northern part of the country. The situation changed only in the early 1970s, and radical improvement occurred only in the 1980s. The scale of progress can be measured by the fact than in 1960 in the private sector 94% of haulage power was animals (horses), whereas in 1988 over 87% of haulage power was mechanical, mostly tractors (Szczęsny 1992). In 1990 it varied markedly: 4.3 tractors per 100 ha in Olsztyn, 5.2 in Cracow, and 11.1 in Opole voivodships. The problem of the 1990s is the increasing share of old and very old tractors,

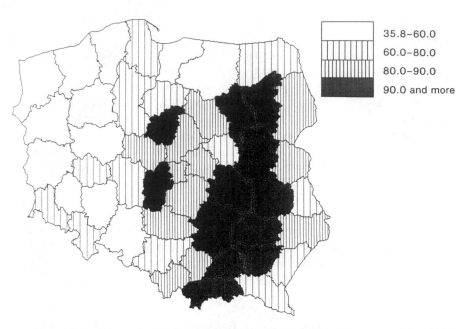

	35.8–60.0
	60.0–80.0
	80.0–90.0
	90.0 and more

Figure 4.8   Private farmland, 1992 (%). After: *Rocznik statystyczny województw* 1993. Warsaw: GUS.

particularly in the northern and western territories where individual farmers have second-hand tractors from the deteriorating state farms and now have no capital for modernization.

There is also great regional differentiation in fertilizer application (Fig. 4.9). The application rate dropped from as high as 193 kg per ha in 1980 to 95 in 1991. The highest application is in the western part of the country, in Leszczyńskie, Pozanańskie and Opolskie, with lower levels in eastern parts. The difficult economic situation of both individual private farms and state farms has resulted in a drop in fertilizer application, particularly in the 1990s. The economic changes have also resulted in a decrease in the use of higher quality seeds and of prevention chemistry.

In spite of considerable progress in piped water supply during the 1980s, only 60% of individual rural households have running water supply. The best conditions are in western parts, where more than 70% of households have piped water, and the worst in eastern voivodships, where only 25–35% of farms have such facilities.

The economically active population in agriculture fell in 1950–88 from 54.5% to 27.1%. In absolute numbers the size of the economically active rural population remained fairly stable, and in the post-war period fell by only 1 million, to 4.8 millions in 1988. At the regional scale, over 30% of the population based its income on agriculture in eastern parts of the country (Fig. 4.10). The rural population at the national scale is characterized by a relatively high proportion of post-productive age (15%); however, in the private farm sector this was higher (18% in 1988).

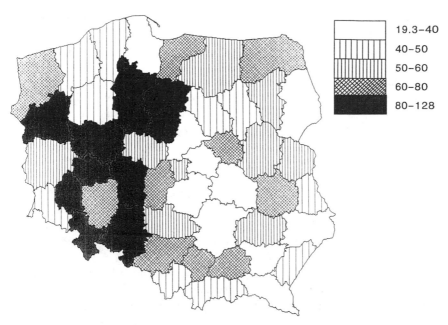

☐	19.3–40
▥	40–50
▦	50–60
▨	60–80
■	80–128

Figure 4.9 Use of artificial fertilizers, 1992 (farmland/ha). After: *Rocznik statystyczny województw* 1993. Warsaw: GUS.

The under-urbanization, together with the shortage of labour force in industry, resulted in a continuous increase in the proportion of peasant-workers, particularly those having both industrial and rural jobs. Numbers have increased strongly around large urban and industrial agglomerations, and in the southeast. Families holding small-size farms are characterized by high shares of peasant workers.

A particular disadvantage for the future development of individual agriculture is education. Private agriculture has the lowest educational level among sectors of the national economy, in spite of substantial progress. This has a direct impact on productivity and on prospects for future improvement. Significant post-war advances in the educational level of the rural population have partly been eroded by migration.

In spite of an increase in the share of farmers with higher than primary school education, and a substantial decrease in the share of farmers with less than complete primary education, the educational level of the rural population is much lower than that of the urban population (Gałczyńska 1993a,b). In 1988, among people working mainly on their own farms, there were only 28.1% with more than primary education, including only 0.5% with university education, 7.6% with secondary education and 20% with vocational education. Farmers with only primary education dominated the statistics at 60.2%.

The areas of Greater Poland, Cuiavia, Krajeńskie and Chełmskie Lake Lands, as well as Lower Vistula, are characterized by larger proportion of people with more than primary education. This especially applies to Greater Poland, where in the communes of Poznań and Leszno voivodships the share of farmers with more than primary education exceeded 40%, and in almost every second commune it even exceeded 50% of people working primarily on their own farms (Gaclczyńska 1993a).

The differentiation in technical infrastructure and education of the rural population amplifies the traditionally strong regional polarization of productivity. Generally, the lowest agricultural productivity is in the eastern and central part and the highest is in Greater Poland, Silesia and Żulawy. The overall picture of regional differentiation shows the distribution of the value of production of agriculture (Fig. 4.11).

At the beginning of 1980s the private sector employed nearly 30% of the total labour force of the national economy, but produced only 15% of the national income. Peasant households account for 40% of the Polish population, and 60% of farmers had additional occupations outside agriculture. The spatial distribution of the importance of agriculture in generating GDP provides an indication of its share in the regional economy (Fig. 4.12).

The transformation of the national economy to a free market system in 1989 introduced, from the very beginning, substantial adaptive problems for Polish agriculture. The share of agriculture in gross national income dropped from 12.8% in 1976 to 6.8% in 1992. The regional differentiation of the share of GDP derived from agriculture indicated highest values in the best agricultural region in the western part and the worst in the eastern part, whereas the lowest values indicate the most

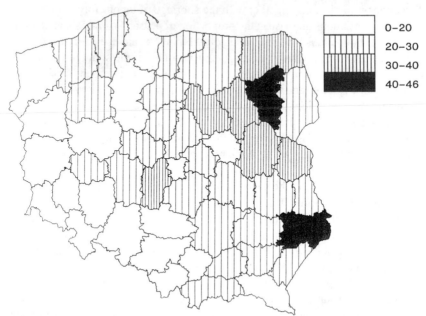

0–20
20–30
30–40
40–46

Figure 4.10 People living off agriculture, 1988 (%). Average for Poland: 17.7%. After: *Rocznik statystyczny województw* 1990. Warsaw: GUS.

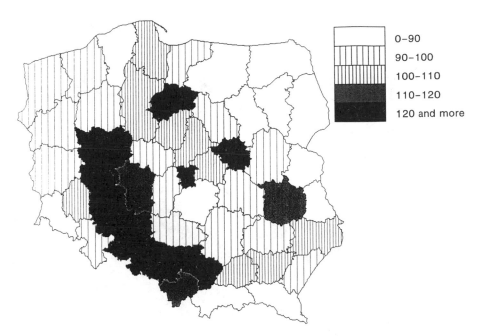

Figure 4.11 Total agriculture production by value, 1985–6 (average for Poland: 100).

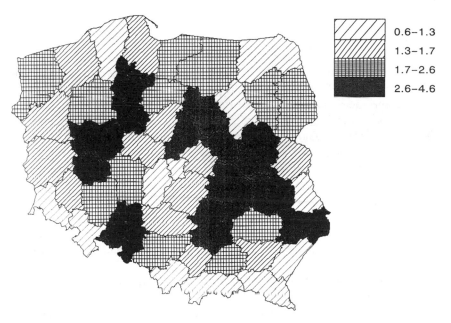

Figure 4.12 The distribution of Gross Domestic Product in agriculture, 1992 (%). After: Zienkowski 1994.

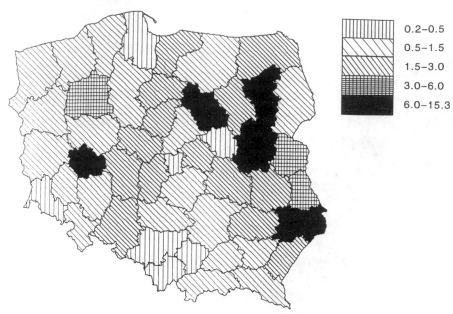

▥	0.2–0.5
▧	0.5–1.5
▨	1.5–3.0
▦	3.0–6.0
■	6.0–15.3

Figure 4.13 Share of agriculture in Gross Domestic Product, 1992 (%). After: Zienkowski 1994.

urbanized and industrialized areas, except for Nowosądeckie voivodship (Fig. 4.13).

4.3.2 THE FREE MARKET CHALLENGE

Most of the agricultural sector and the rural population have become losers during the transformation. This situation creates strong counter-pressures, from one side on modernization and adaptation to the market economy, but from the other grounds for political rejection of the speed and direction of transformation. The peasant parties, particularly those of post-communist origin, received an increasing share of support in each election.

The transformation has brought the following consequences for agriculture:
* the collapse of the existing organizational structure of supply of means of production
* the collapse of the state purchasing system for agricultural products
* the collapse of the former Soviet Union's market and a dramatic drop in exports, which has been accompanied by a fall in purchasing power in the domestic market
* the increasing gap between prices of agriculture on the one hand, and industrial products and services on the other
* low customs barriers introduced competition from very cheap and attractive Western products (subsidized by Western countries while Polish products ceased to be subsidized)

- uncontrolled importation of Western products up to 1991
- high inflation rate and non-affordable credits.

The freeing of prices, cuts of food subsidies and inflation impacted heavily on the agricultural sector. The most important factor was the collapse of the state purchase system, generally transforming the relations between producers and traders and suppliers of means of production.

In the 1990s the problem of decreased demand and profitability developed partly as a result of the opening of Polish markets for Western agricultural products and the simultaneous collapse of the eastern market in the Soviet Union.

The recession in industry substantially limited the double jobs of peasant-workers, and precipitated a return to single jobs in agriculture. As a result, the productivity of agriculture has fallen. However, the drop in production is greater than the drop in employment. The agricultural sector has become a niche for unemployed people of rural origin. The rural sector has become an employment buffer for the peasant workers, losing their additional jobs.

The economic recession and the fall of demand, together with inflow of food products from Western countries and inflation, placed this sector of the economy in a very difficult position, particularly in the period 1989–91. The ratio between the prices of agricultural products and of services purchased for agricultural production worsened from 107.3 in 1989 to 49.5 in 1990 (Central Office of Planning 1993). The decrease in the purchase of production exacerbated the problems of the agricultural sector. For example, the use of mineral fertilizer fell considerably between 1989 and 1992. The sale of tractors fell from 62 400 in 1989 to 12 700 in 1992, creating a recession in this branch of industry.

The economic recession also exacerbated the west/east disparity in the regional structure of Polish agriculture. All the depressed areas of private agriculture are concentrated in the eastern and southern part of the country. The problem for agriculture in the western part is the collapse of the majority of state farms, where they represented a high share of land ownership.

For the western and the northern part of the country the problem of conversion of the state farms into productive units must be solved. The newly established State Treasury Agricultural Property Agency has at its disposal 4.5 million ha for sale or lease.

One possible part of a comprehensive modernization strategy could be the development of ecological agriculture. The actual size of farm in Poland is favourable; unfortunately its implementation on a large scale is impossible because of the low level of education, lack of capital, and traditional agricultural practice.

The contemporary problems of agriculture are aggravated by migration from rural areas. The continuous depopulation of some rural areas, particularly from central and eastern parts, has changed the demographic structure to such a degree that any modernization potential is limited.

Agriculture, in spite of all its difficulties, still comprises a substantial part of the national economy. It has a chance to become an important element of future specialization in the international division of labour. Already, Poland is one of the largest producers and exporters of apples, currants, cabbages, carrots, potatoes and beetroot. The country is also self-sufficient in the production of meat, cereals and milk.

The fundamental issue is, however, adaptation to the European Union standards and future integration. The large and medium-size private farms in Poznańskie, Leszczyńskie voivodship and western Poland, and highly specialized farms in sub-urban zones, are modern and will survive. The problem will be with small farms in eastern and central Poland.

CHAPTER 5

Population

The population of Poland increased from 23.9 million in 1946 to the pre-war size of 35 million in 1977, and to 38.5 million by the end of 1993. This increase was the result of both long-term and short-term trends. The theory of demographic transition is helpful in describing and explaining long-term trends in Polish demographic evolution. This theory, as applied to European countries, describes the process of population development from traditional to industrial and post-industrial society in four phases, from high natural population reproduction and high mortality to low reproduction and low mortality. From the beginning of this century up to 1970, Poland was in the third phase, strongly distorted by the First and Second World Wars. Today Poland is in the middle of the fourth phase, characterized in the long term by a decline in the fertility rate and a slow decrease and ultimately stable mortality. Most western European countries have already passed through or are at the end of this phase. It is estimated that Poland will reach the end of the fourth phase by 2020, when the number of births will equal the number of deaths and the population will be stabilized at 43 million (Korcelli et al. 1992).

The contemporary population structure and evolution trends are also the result of short-term conditions, particularly the consequences of the Second World War and fluctuations caused by changing population policies. In 1945 Poland's territory was shifted westwards (only 67% of the land area is the same as before the Second World War), the total area of the state was reduced by 20%, and the population dropped by 11 million as compared with 1939 (ibid. 1992). These losses were strongly compensated for by waves of baby booms and demographic peaks and troughs through the whole of the post-war period. In addition, the enormous scale of post-war migration increased the regional differentiation of population characteristics. Economic development was also important to short-term trends during the post-war period.

Since 1950, the processes of industrialization connected with urbanization, together with changes in the population policies of the state in each decade, have had a substantial impact on demographic evolution. Predominantly pro-natalist attitudes of government, together with policies to encourage return migration, were characteristic of the immediate post-war period. The 1960s were dominated by an anti-natalist policy, and in the 1970s new pro natalist measures were implemented. The impact of this pro-natalist attitude was being limited by the mounting economic crisis in the late 1970s and early 1980s (Holtzer 1991). During this period of increasing cost of living and devaluation of wages, the impact on fertility of

51

social legislation such as paid maternity leave, family allowances, and the provision of day infant's nurseries and kindergartens, was gradually reduced.

The 1980s revealed a new dimension in population trends. The gradual decline of the fertility rate after its second boom in the beginning of 1970s ended. In 1980 and 1981, the fertility trend was revived as the consequences of a wave of marriages related by some demographers to a "Solidarity fever". The increase in 1982 and 1983 has been attributed to the outburst of religious activity, and return to the ideal of family life in the frustrating economic and social conditions of the post martial law period (Okólski 1989).

The deterioration in health conditions in the 1960s and 1970s was reflected in the gradual decline of life expectancy at birth, the increase in the standardized mortality rate, and the increasing gap between the numbers of females and males more particularly in middle age (ibid.), had an accumulating effect by the early 1980s. Some of these trends, if they became more permanent, could threaten the development of a more prosperous Poland.

The latest report of the Governmental Population Commission (1993) described the demographic situation of Poland in 1991 and in 1992, which has its roots in the 1980s, stressing the following points. First of all, since 1989, a reproduction rate below the level of simple generation replacement rule has been established. This is a consequence of: a decrease, since 1981, in the rate of new family formation by 30.8%; a drop in fertility, with a substantial increase in the number of babies born (by 28.5% since 1984), which in 1992 reached its lowest level in the postwar period; and an increasing death rate and decline of real natural increase. Secondly, worsening health conditions and the subsequent increase of mortality rates have also helped shape the population profiles of the 1990s. Thirdly, the population in some regions suffers from higher mortality rates than in others. Fourth, mortality rates by accidents have increased. Finally, the worsening psychological state of society also contributed to demographic changes.

The new pro-natalist attitudes of government, connected with the strongly politicized issue of abortion, do not seem likely to impact on existing demographic trends in the foreseeable future, because of the persistent economic crisis.

All the demographic processes outlined above have their regional dimensions. The most regionally differentiated processes will be analyzed in the following sections.

5.1 Distribution of population

The two basic processes with the greatest impact on the distribution of population in Poland are: first, the resettlement of the Regained Territories immediately after the Second World War, and during the first decade of 1950s, and secondly, the concentration of the population arising both from a move from rural to urban and from regional shifts. The move from rural to urban itself has a regional character,

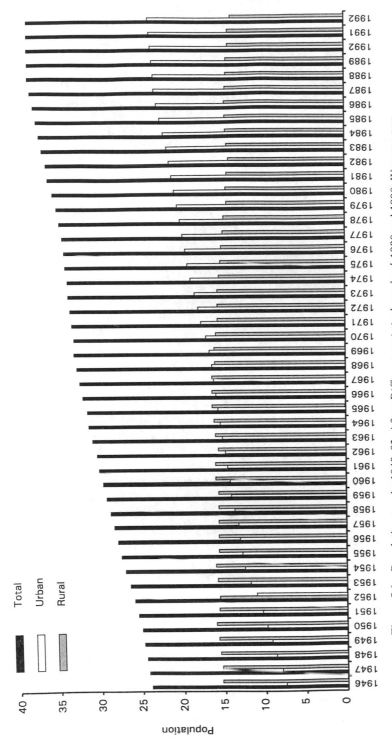

Figure 5.1 Population trends, 1948–92 After: *Different statistical yearbook* 1980 and 1990. Warsaw: GUS.

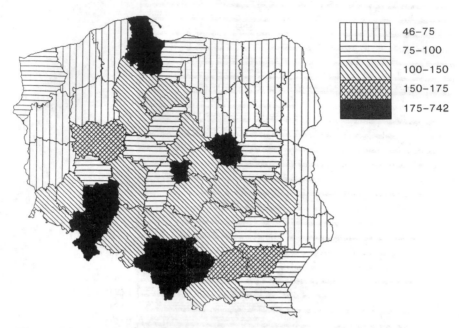

Figure 5.2 Density of population, 1992, per km². After: *Rocznik statystyczny województw* 1993. Warsaw: GUS.

that is, the predominant movement was to the nearest large city. By 1966 the urban population exceeded the rural population (Fig. 5.1). The interregional migration led to a concentration of population in the largest agglomerations: Upper Silesia, Warsaw, and Gdańsk–Gdynia–Sopot. During the period of construction of particular new industrial centres, medium-size cities were temporarily the object of immigration on a national scale.

The regional distribution of population in Poland at the macro scale, measured by density of population, has been relatively stable (Fig. 5.2). The general pattern of population density looks much the same as in the pre-war period (on the same territory), but the densities have increased substantially. During the past few years, however, certain trends have become more visible. This concerns a slowing down in urbanization in the already urbanized western part, as the share of urban population became more stable, and a continuous, relatively strong increase of urban population in eastern areas (see Fig. 6.2).

The largest concentration of population is in the south, particularly in Katowice and neighbouring voivodships (Fig. 5.2). The central part of the country has average population density, with higher concentrations around the Warsaw and Łódź agglomerations. The northeastern and northwestern regions are characterized by the lowest density. The only higher density areas in the northern part are the metropolitan areas of Gdańsk, Gdynia, and Szczecin. Population density is lowest along the eastern border of Poland, resulting from a long-lasting depopulation process, particularly of the rural areas.

5.2 Sex and age structure

The existing age and sex structure is usually treated as an end result of many demographic features, such as level of fertility, mortality and migration. In the age and sex structure in 1991 (Fig. 5.3), we can observe the characteristic deficit and surplus that reflects the demographic history of Poland. The first two deficits are the residue of the First and Second World Wars. The third deficit reflects the demographic depression of the 1960s. The largest booms are the result of the post-war compensation baby-boom in the 1950s, and its echo in the 1970s.

In sex distribution, women outnumber men. In 1946, there were 118.5 females per 100 males; however, in urban areas the differences were much greater (130.7 as compared with 117.4 per 100) than in rural areas. Since 1950 this divergence has become less pronounced and in 1992 it reached 105.3 at the national scale, 108.9 for urban areas and 99.9 for rural areas.

At the regional scale, the divergence in sex structure is strongly marked, particularly between urban and rural areas. The urban areas are differentiated according to their economic functions; for example, the textile towns are more dominated by females, whereas in the heavy industrial towns the sex balance is more even. In rural areas, particularly in northern and eastern territories, a shortage of females has emerged as a result of more women migrating to urban places. This has had serious social and economic consequences, because of the limited number of marriages and the reduced chance of creating new family farms. In statistical terms, in 1988 as many as 135400 people in the 20–25 years old age group had no opportunity to find partners in the same age group. This concerns males in rural and females in urban areas (Korcelli et al. 1992).

The spatial distribution of this phenomenon in 1992, for the larger demographic cohort of 18–39 years old, revealed a sharp regional differentiation. Females outnumber men in all western parts and in the more urbanized areas (Fig. 5.4). For rural areas the regional disparities are more striking (Fig. 5.5). Nowhere in Polish rural areas is there a balance between the sex groups in this cohort, and in Suwałki, Lomża, Ostrolęka and Bialystok voivodships there are fewer than 80 females per 100 of males. The situation is partly reversed in urban areas (Fig. 5.6), where more balance is found in western parts, and an over concentration of females in towns, particularly in eastern voivodships.

In the whole of the post-war period, the regional differentiation of age structure in Poland has been relatively stable. For example, throughout this period we can identify a west/east regional dichotomy arising from post-war resettlement. With respect to the age structure, the two groups revealing the greatest regional differentiation are the elderly (population over 60 years old) and children (population 0–14 years old). Generally, the central and eastern territories are characterized by higher concentrations of elderly people, whereas the population in the west remains relatively young in spite of all the post-war demographic changes.

The slowing down of the rate of population increase in urban places during the past few decades was accompanied by an increase in proportion of the elderly at

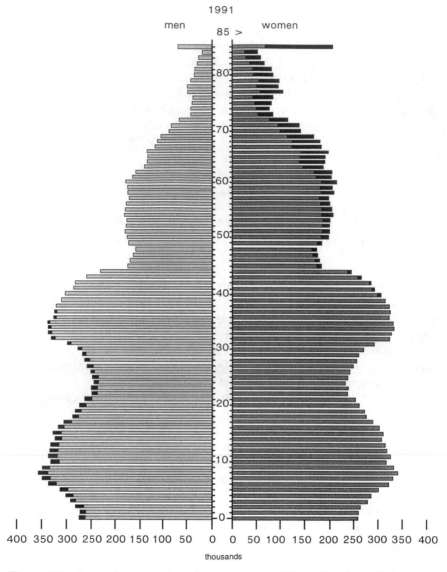

Figure 5.3 Age and sex structure of the population, 1991. After: *Rocznik demograficzny* 1992. Warsaw: GUS, 1993.

all scales: national, rural and urban. In urban areas the elderly population reached 13.08% in 1988, compared with 8.97% in 1960. But for the five largest cities the elderly population increased to 16.88%.

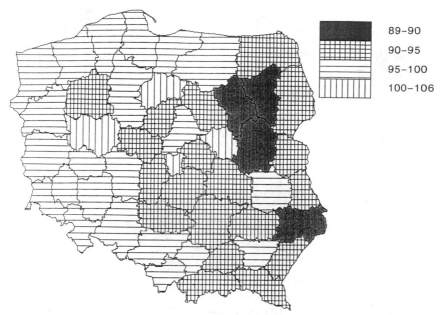

Figure 5.4 Females per 100 males, 1992, for the age group 18–39. After: *Rocznik statystyczny województw* 1993. Warsaw: GUS.

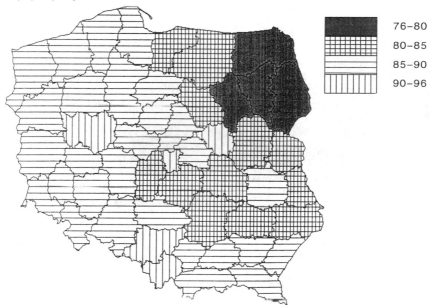

Figure 5.5 Females per 100 males in rural areas, 1992, for the age group 18–39. After: *Rocznik statystyczny województw* 1993. Warsaw: GUS.

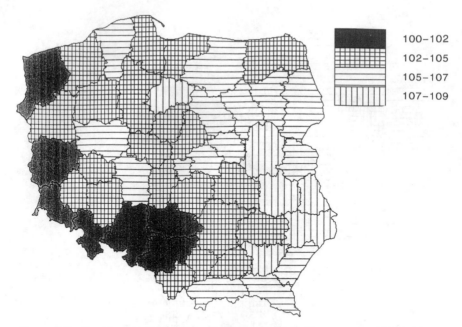

Figure 5.6 Females per 100 males in urban areas, 1992, for the age group 18–39. After: *Rocznik statystyczny województw* 1993. Warsaw: GUS.

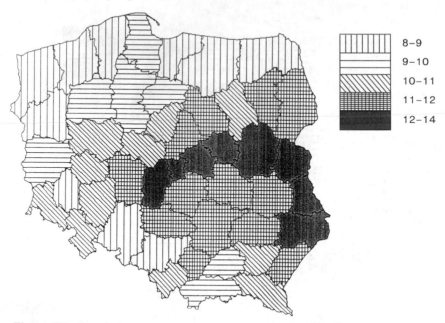

Figure 5.7 Population aged 65 years and over, 1992 (% of total population). After: *Rocznik statystyczny województw* 1993. Warsaw: GUS.

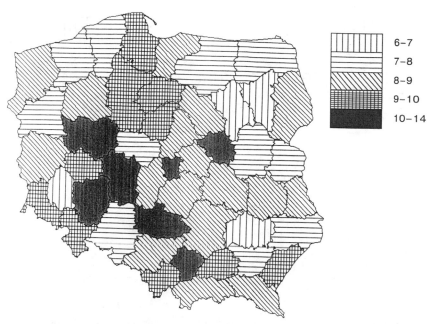

Figure 5.8 Population aged 65 years and over in urban areas, 1992 (% of total population). After: *Rocznik statystyczny województw* 1993. Warsaw: GUS.

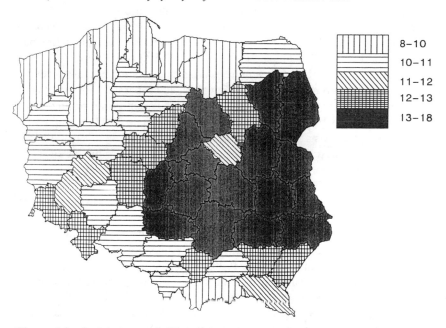

Figure 5.9 Population aged 65 years and over in rural areas, 1992 (% of total population). After: *Rocznik statystyczny województw* 1993. Warsaw: GUS.

Population

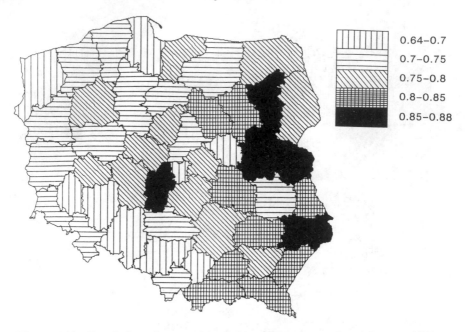

Figure 5.10   Population of non-working age per 100 persons of working age, 1992.
After: *Rocznik statystyczny województw* 1993. Warsaw: GUS.

The increase of the elderly population at the national scale during the past decade has been 118.8, whereas in urban places it was 125.56. There was a particularly high increase in Wroclaw (162.16); however, this city still has a low percentage of elderly (14.66%) compared with Lódź (19.05%) and Warsaw (17.86%).

The regional differentiations are more acute if analysis is undertaken for the narrower elderly group of 65 and older (Fig. 5.7), and separately for urban (Fig. 5.8) and rural areas (Fig. 5.9). The share of this population group has increased from 5.3% in 1950 to 10.7% in 1992. In economic terms, in 1992 the population of productive age consists of 57.7% of the total, whereas in the post-productive age group it is 13.2%. At the regional scale, the population of productive age compared with the population of non-productive age varies considerably (Fig. 5.10). Most of the eastern voivodships are in a very unfavourable position for future economic development in terms of their local labour force.

The general process of the ageing of the population, that is, the gradual increase in the share of elderly in the population, will continue up to the end of this century. Parallel to the predicted decline of the younger population will be an increase of the productive age groups. For the 1990s, the economic problem will be this anticipated increase in population, as compared with the predicted increase in unemployment associated with continuous recession. In 1992 alone, the increase of population of productive age was 118000, and in 1993 the increase was around 139000. In total, the estimates of the Governmental Demographic Commission suggest an absolute increase of that group in 1991–5 by over 400000.

60

5.3 The evolving demographic structure

5.3.1 MARITAL STATUS

The number of marriages reflects the demographic structure of a society and its prevailing customs. A continual decline in the index of marriages (except for the 1970s), from the highest post-war level of 12% to 6.5% in 1988, reached its lowest value at 6.1 in 1991. Regional differentiation overlaps with other demographic variables; the only disparities are in the east between urban areas (with relatively high indexes) and rural areas (with very low indexes), caused by structural demographic deformation in depopulating areas. In western parts, in both urban and rural areas, the level of marriages remains relatively high.

One of the social problems connected with the changing demographic structure is the increase in one-parent families. In 1992 the rate of increase exceeded the rate of family formation by three times. It has been estimated that there are 2 million children in one parent families. These families are usually poor, particularly in the latest period of economic recession and unemployment (Governmental Population Commission 1993).

The divorce rate has been gradually decreasing since 1987. But still, substantial rural/urban differentiation exists, with divorce five times higher in urban areas. Questionnaire studies indicated that in 1991 the most important reason for divorce had become alcoholism (28.6%), and the traditionally most popular reason, that is, deceit and incompatibility of character was placed second. Other surveys, conducted in 1987–9, indicated a correlation with the housing situation: over 16% of respondents indicated lack of dwellings as a reason for divorce. Forty per cent of divorces occurred in a situation where they had not owned their flat; after divorce, 80 per cent were still sharing a flat with each other.

5.3.2 MORTALITY AND LIFE EXPECTANCY

The greatest anomaly in the demographic situation of Poland is the dramatic increase of mortality, caused not only by the natural process of the ageing of society but also by other factors. These anomalies are a consequence of the Second World War (Okólski 1989), and of economic and sociopolitical factors. But the most direct influence on the high rate of mortality and its specific structure has been the deterioration of health conditions and environmental pollution. It is very significant that the most dramatic rise of mortality has occurred in the most polluted areas.

In 1991, for the first time in the post-war period, the number of deaths exceeded 400000. From its lowest post-war level of 7.3 per 1000 inhabitants in 1966, the death rate gradually increased to 10 in 1989 and 11.7 in 1991. The increase occurred mostly among males, particularly in the cohort of 35–49, so the gap between age-specific groups and between men and women continues to increase.

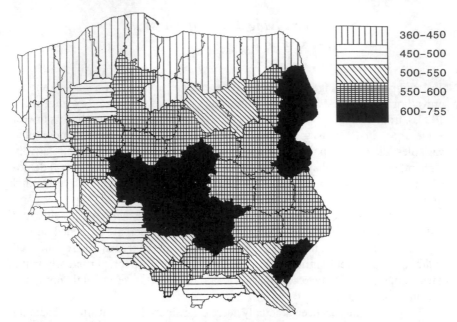

⦀⦀⦀⦀	360–450
≡≡≡	450–500
◪	500–550
▦	550–600
■	600–755

Figure 5.11 Death rate caused by cardiac problems, 1992 (per 100 000 of population). After: *Rocznik statystyczny województw* 1993. Warsaw: GUS.

The international comparison provided by WHO for 1986–7 showed that the standardized over-mortality rate among men placed Poland in a very bad situation, third from the bottom. Only Hungary and Czechoslovakia had higher male over-mortality. The over-mortality of men is caused largely by cardiovascular diseases, to the greatest extent in the cohort of men aged as 30–54.

The main cause of deaths for the population as a whole is cardiovascular disease, which for several years has been increasing and in 1991 accounted for 52.7% of deaths (Fig. 5.11). The risk of deaths from this cause will continue to increase in the future, with the ageing of the population and the unfavourable economic conditions causing stress, hard living, unemployment, and lack of adequate health care, both preventive and overall.

The scale of deaths caused by cancer is also very high, and in addition is usually under-registered. Deaths from cancer increased dramatically between 1963 (when for the first time sufficient information was available for comparison) and 1991; in absolute numbers from 34 500 to 73 959. The main cause of the increase of population numbers and the ageing of the population has been the increase in the number of carcinogenic factors in the environment, and a life-style involving poor diet and high tobacco and alcohol consumption (Zatoński & Tyczyński 1994). At the regional scale (Figs 5.12, 5.13) the dichotomy between the west and east is very significant. According to some estimates nearly 13 million people live in ecologically polluted areas. The mortality rate from lung and laryngeal cancer occurring in smokers is one of the highest in the world.

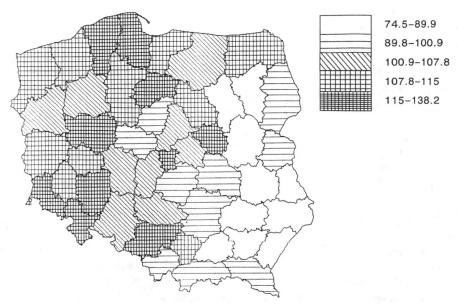

	74.5–89.9
	89.8–100.9
	100.9–107.8
	107.8–115
	115–138.2

Figure 5.12 Standardized mortality rate from cancer for females, 1991 (per 100000 of population). After: Zatoński & Tyczyński 1994.

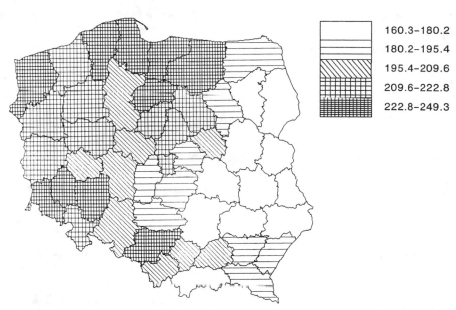

	160.3–180.2
	180.2–195.4
	195.4–209.6
	209.6–222.8
	222.8–249.3

Figure 5.13 Standardized mortality rate from cancer for males, 1991 (per 100000 of population). After: Zatoński & Tyczyński 1994.

A social problem having direct influence on the state of population health is alcoholism. Alcohol consumption has risen by 40% since 1989 to 1993. The average annual consumption had risen from 7 litres of pure spirit per head to 10.5 litres. There are around 1 million adult alcoholics in Poland, and 2–3 million adult Poles are drinkers, although not yet dependent on drink. The only positive change has been that drinking at work, a widespread habit in earlier years, has dropped significantly, probably because of an increase in discipline at work and a fear of redundancy.

An additional factor influencing the increase in mortality rate is connected with a deterioration of the epidemiological situation. There are significant disparities between central and eastern Poland and the surrounding voivodships.

Life expectancy increased up to the end of 1970s, and began to decline in the 1980s. In 1992, life expectation for males at birth was 66.71 years, and for females 75.70 years, as compared with 67.15 and 75.67 respectively in 1988 (Governmental Population Commission 1993). Also, the gap between the sexes has continued to increase, approaching 8.99 years in favour of females in 1992. The small decline of life expectancy since the mid-1960s, and the marked acceleration from the 1970s into the 1980s (particularly for men), has no precedent in the post-war demographic development of Europe except in some other post-communist countries.

5.3.3 INFANT MORTALITY

The infant mortality rate, although decreasing in the past few years, remains at a relatively high level compared with other European countries. The official index of infant mortality in 1991 was 15 per 1000 live births; however, estimated according to the criteria of WHO it was higher at 18.2 per 1000. These different estimates are even more visible regionally (Figs 5.14, 5.15).

5.3.4 ABORTION

Another demographic "problem" that became the object of strong political controversy is the issue of abortion. A strict anti-abortion law was introduced in 1993. After the September 1993 parliamentary election the new law was challenged by the new left-wing parliament; however, a weak legislative proposal was rejected by presidential veto.

According to official statistics, abortion decreased from 1960 to 1991. In absolute numbers it fell from 223 800 in 1960, to 132 600 in 1980 and 30 900 in 1991. The number of induced abortions per 100 live births dropped from 33.4 in 1960 to 5.7 in 1991. However, this statistic is unreliable. Research conducted in the mid-1980s indicated that, compared with the official figure of 200 000 induced abortions, in reality there were 400 000–450 000. Another estimate gives the number of abortions at 620 000–700 000 (Józniak & Paradysz 1993). This could be one

	11–14
	14–15
	15–16
	16–17
	17–22

Figure 5.14 Infant mortality by Polish criterion, 1991 (per 1000 live births). After: *Sytuacja demograficzna Polski.* Raport 1992 Rządowa Komisja Ludnościowa. Warsaw: Maszynopis.

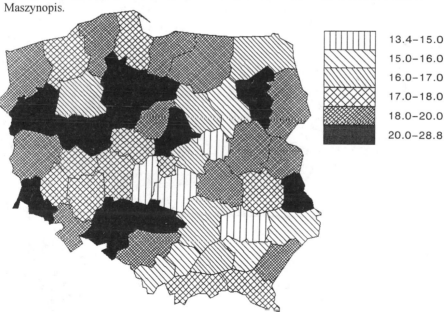

	13.4–15.0
	15.0–16.0
	16.0–17.0
	17.0–18.0
	18.0–20.0
	20.0–28.8

Figure 5.15 Infant mortality by WHO criterion, 1991 (per 1000 live births). After: *Sytuacja demograficzna Polski.* Raport 1992 Rządowa Komisja Ludnościowa. Warsaw: Maszynopis.

explanation for the decrease in the birth rate since the mid-1980s. The other deter-mining factors, such as marriages, the shift in demographic structure and contra-ceptive attitudes and behaviour, have not changed, so their impact is of minor importance.

5.4 Migration

There was a gradual decrease in all types of migration at the end of 1980s and beginning of 1990s. The evident causes have been economic recession, unem-ployment and the permanent acute housing shortage. This concerns in particular net rural–urban migration, which dropped from 143 600 in 1988 to 106 400 in 1991 and to 85 707 in 1992.

The redistribution of the population at the national scale is a matter for future development and adjustment to a market economy. This obviously determines the economic prosperity of particular regions in the longer term. However, the depop-ulation of rural areas of eastern and central Poland, observed thorough the entire post-war period, will be magnified in the future. This will lead to a changing func-tion for those areas, possibly abandoning agricultural production.

The external emigration rate is more stable, and is likely to decline gradually. In the 1980s, emigration from Poland was 26 670 per year; in 1990 it was 18 400,

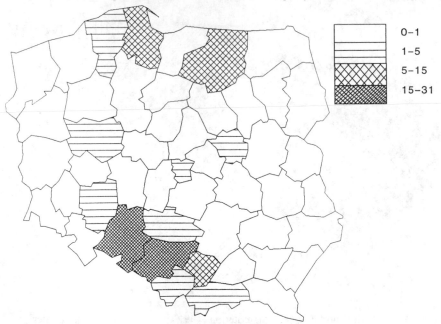

Figure 5.16 Emigration from Poland, 1979–88 (% of total external emigration). After: Central Statistical Office, Warsaw.

21000 in 1991 and 18100 in 1992. The majority of emigrants abroad come from urban places. Its regional specificity is reflected in the fact that 67% of those emigrating abroad came from seven voivodships: Katowickie, Opolskie, Gdańskie, Szczecińskie, Wrocławskie, Krakowskie and Olsztyńskie (Fig. 5.16).

A specific case is Opole voivodship, inhabited by a high proportion of mixed Polish and German descent. The ethnic situation and great differences in the living conditions between Poland and Germany resulted in a relative high propensity to emigrate. Emigration from this voivodship mostly involves population of German descent; between 1959 to 1991 this accounted for around 200000, and has distorted the demographic structure particularly in the rural areas (Kupiszewski 1993). In some communes, between 1975 and 1983, more than a quarter of the population emigrated, mostly in the twenties and early thirties age cohorts.

At the national scale, Germany has become the more important destination, whereas North America is losing its historical importance. In total however, Germany and North America took over 72% of legal emigration from Poland in 1984–8 (ibid.).

The most important reasons for emigration from Poland under communism were both political and economic. However, the new political situation and elimination of border constraints has not created massive waves of emigration, as had been expected by some Western countries. An important factor in emigration remains differentiation in the quality of life; however, this emigration now has rather a consumer character (Kurcz & Podkański 1991). After 1990 many social and economic needs could be satisfied in Poland, and the travel cost, together with fear of a relatively hostile reception, discourage emigration.

The new push factor for emigration is high unemployment in northern and eastern Poland. In addition, the traditional brain drain from Poland to western Europe lost its political constraints; however, this trend is partly limited by the booming expansion of the private sector. The most important factor stimulating emigration from Poland is the future economic prosperity of the country. Even at the most optimistic rate, the economic development of Poland in the 1990s, can hardly absorb the predicted increase in the number of adults seeking employment. Although emigration will increase, high unemployment in western Europe is creating rather unfavourable conditions.

Emigration will probably involve two extreme social categories: the population without education, for work in the shadow economy and illegally employed in menial jobs; and highly skilled professionals employed on a legal basis.

CHAPTER 6

Urban Poland

6.1 Post-war urbanization: from rural to urban society

Understanding the urbanization of Polish society and what happened in Polish towns in the post-war period requires some historical background. The urbanization of Poland has its specific character, which is based on: the historical location on the periphery of the main economic core of western Europe; the persistent Polish cultural distinctiveness and identity through several centuries; the lack of political and economic independence through the whole of the nineteenth century; devastation of the Second World War; and the imposed communist system.

Leaving more detailed consideration for historians, there is a need here to stress the following general facts. Polish culture had, from the sixteenth to the twentieth centuries, a gentry and a rural character. The landed gentry and their influence contributed to the emergence of a distinctive Polish culture compared with other European countries. This was compounded, after the Renaissance period, by the weakening of cultural links with towns of western Europe. The significance of towns, as expressed through legal regulations, had been declining in Poland from the sixteenth century. The landed gentry, being a group representing the cultural and political prosperity of the state, gained absolute domination over towns. In addition, the economic breakdown and military defeats of the seventeenth and eighteenth centuries inflicted civilization agrarization in Poland. Thus, the degree of urbanization of Polish territories was higher in the sixteenth century than in the middle of the nineteenth century (28.8% in 1578 as opposed to 20% in 1842). Such a situation was also partly attributable to loss of independence and the long period of partition of Poland (1795–1918). It was only at the beginning of capitalist industrialization that a new vision of urban life could start taking shape. Regaining independence in 1918 also partly changed the overall situation.

Radical changes, accompanied by the formation of a vision of an urban life style, occurred after the Second World War. More than at any time before regaining independence, reconstruction and development of towns, together with industrialization, became a symbol of social progress and improvement of living standards, accessible for almost everyone who decided to move into town.

The urbanization process was also encouraged by the ruling communists. The territorial shift westwards, that is, the resettlement of the Polish population from mostly rural territories allocated to the Soviet Union, to the territory regained from Germany, was of special importance. In spite of war devastation, this area was urbanized, at least in terms of technical infrastructure and the urban network. The cumulative industrialization process was accompanied by state discrimination against the agricultural sector in favour of the industrial sector. The obvious result was an increase in urban–rural inequalities, which amplified migration to urban areas.

The industrialization and urbanization process did not develop in its classic western European mode, however. Before the Second World War it developed as a part of the peripheralization process of the capitalist world-system. After the Second World War this process was shaped by communist ideological priority. It has sometimes been called "managed urbanization" (Musil 1984), which has been stimulated by "imposed industrialization" (Morawski 1980).

The process of socialist industrialization and accompanying urbanization has changed Polish society from a rural to an urban one, at least in numerical terms. The concentration of population via urbanization resulted in a reversal of the shares between rural and urban areas. Over the past 45 years, the proportion of people living in urban areas increased to 61.7% in 1992 as compared to 31.8% in 1946. This is consistent with the fact that most of the population increase since 1946 has been in urban areas, which grew from 7517000 in 1946 to 23740000 in 1993; by contrast, the population of rural areas remains relatively stable throughout the post-war period (Fig. 5.1). Urban growth has been concentrated in the largest cities and now over 50% of the total urban population live in cities with more than 100000 inhabitants.

Natural increase contributed 54% to urban growth, with 41% attributable to migration from rural areas; the rest is the result of the shift of administrative boundaries and the consequent reduction in status of some rural places.

The western part of the country is the most urbanized. The largest urban agglomerations are in the central and southern parts (Fig. 6.1). The presence of extensive regions of low urbanization (below 50%) in central and eastern parts indicates the importance of the traditional rural way of life there. Many suburban villages are dominated by the non-rural population, and a high incidence of commuting to work by peasant-workers has changed the rural character of those regions to only a small degree.

In the 1980s, at the national scale, the process of urbanization slowed down. At the regional scale, we can still observe a relatively strong increase in urban population in the eastern areas, however (Fig. 6.2). The process of urbanization of those areas in the 1990s will by slowed down by the unemployment and housing shortages connected with the economic recession.

Industry has become the most important urban function. The development of the city without an industrial economic base became almost impossible under communism. This created a situation in which the distribution of the workplace has largely determined the distribution of the settlement network. Urban settlements were created as an addition to industrial plants and were organizationally subordinate to their requirements. The new industrial plant was initiated and constructed first, with the attached housing for the labour force erected as a sort of patron estate

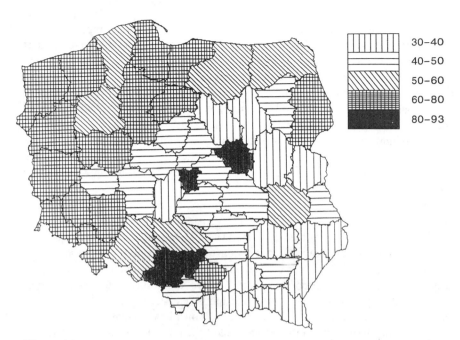

Figure 6.1 Urban population, 1992 (% of total population). After: *Rocznik statystyczny województw* 1993. Warsaw: GUS.

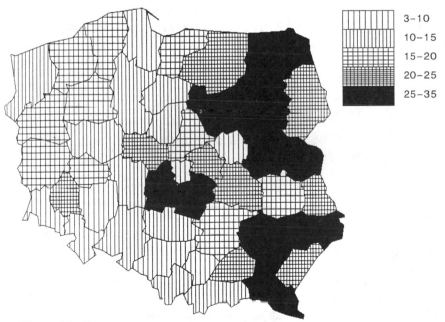

Figure 6.2 Population increase in urban areas, 1980–90 (%). After: *Rocznik statystyczny województw* 1993. Warsaw: GUS.

or company town. This concerns particularly the new industrial regions, where huge industrial plants were located in proximity to small or medium-size cities of a traditional character (for example Płock, Tarnobrzeg, Puławy or Lubin, Legnica, Konin). This type of urbanization can be treated as a precursor to urbanization proper, which occurs over a longer time and with more balanced development of other urban functions – which under communism developed with substantial delay and always in adequate quantity.

Forced industrialization stimulated huge migration from rural areas and became the leading tool of the communists for transformation of the social structure of the country. It had very evident modernization consequences and brought substantial progress as well as many problems.

The concentration on new development and neglect of the old urban infrastructure, which was not rehabilitated, became a constraint on further development. In addition, the low quality of the new infrastructure compounds the inherited problem, imposing what are now substantial constraints on economic development.

The fact that urbanization is a quite recent national phenomenon means that a large proportion of contemporary urban dwellers had no previous experience of an urban life style. The urbanization and industrialization initiated in the nineteenth century, up to the Second World War, was on a smaller scale, and in addition a high proportion of urban citizens has been killed during the war. So, contemporary Polish urban society still preserves much of its rural character, behaviour and values.

Urbanization, in terms of being a modernization process, has still to be completed. The communist period, in spite of substantial progress, introduced "lame urbanization". The most visible results are manifested inside the city. This is why particular attention has been concentrated on the intra-urban scale in the following section.

6.2 Intra-urban residential differentiation and the formation of the "socialist city"

Before the Second World War the sociospatial structure of the majority of Polish cities was similar to that of western Europe, although with many elements of pre-industrial structures. In spite of the war-time destruction, resettlement and political transformation, this structure has not disappeared, and it is still possible to trace inherited historical patterns and spatial differentiation. Implementation of communist rule had decisive consequences for the formation of the internal spatial structure of Polish cities. Ideological priorities imposed on others (social, technical or economic) led to the formation of the patterns of the "socialist city". Parallel to that, some Polish cities have developed in a more "natural" way, and most of them have become substantially different from socialist patterns elsewhere.

There is no commonly accepted definition of the "socialist city", but this is strongly connected with the notion of the "industrial city". For the ruling communist group, cities were viewed as a locus of political support from the working class, and after that as a locus of industrial production. Although old, particularly large towns were not so easy to transform and adapt to the new ideological system, the new industrial towns served as a model of future socialist cities.

The most significant features of the type of socialist city developed in Poland under communist rules, which differentiated them from the western European capitalist cities, are as follows (Węclawowicz 1992):

- Domination of employment by the industrial production sector and a low percentage of the middle class (townspeople) meant that inhabitants of towns consisted in the main of the working class (proletariat). The egalitarian principle and class homogeneity of socialist ideology resulted in relatively low levels of economic differentiation.
- The central allocation of inhabitants to particular dwellings often forced citizens to live in undesirable social surroundings, reducing the chances of creating local communities. The organization of the social life of urban dwellers was around the place of work.
- The city was absolutely dependent on central government for its finances and was "organizationally divided". The centralized authoritarian system had split off different decisions concerning the city, which came from different government departments and, at the local scale, from the authorities of particular cities. The mayor represented the interests of the state against citizens, rather than the interests of citizens against authority. Even the elected city councils represented no local interests but rather the central government and its policies. The municipal offices became units subordinated to the state administration.
- Uniformity of architecture and urban landscape created a higher proportion of waste land and led to deterioration of the old quarters of cities (except cultural heritage parts of the old towns). The builders were pressed to construct first of all only blocks of apartments, and delayed the construction of shops, restaurants, schools and post offices. As a result, in the largest cities huge homogeneous estates emerged, usually with no adequate service facilities, and frequently inhabited by more than 100000 people.
- Ignorance of the environmental problems caused by industry and urban development.
- The attempt at permanent redistribution or elimination from city space of visible presence of non-communist symbols.
- The attempt to control, by administrative means, the inflow of the people to the city.

Polish cities have conformed to these generalizations to varying degrees, while maintaining to some degree a national and European character.

The "new" industrial towns, or older medium-size towns industrialized under communism, have been characterized by the implantation into the traditional structure of new housing estates. The initial isolation of such an estate from the old part of town created a dual structure. These new housing estates represented the socialist town, the rest represented a traditional pattern; however, both parts were functionally interdependent. For example, in the beginning, new housing estates were usually isolated from the services, which meant that their residents depended on the services located in the older part of the city, which were no longer adequate for the increased population.

The two basic parts differed in many ways. The older part was usually inhabited by earlier urbanized population with an older urban tradition, of balanced and usually older demographic structure with a substantial share of service sector employment, handicraft industries and the pre-war intelligentsia. The social activity and social life was concentrated around the local community. The new part was inhabited by younger immigrants, usually of rural origin, without urban experience, employed in industrial jobs, usually as a working-class group. Most of the social activities were organized around places of work (usually industrial plants). Housing in the old part was owned by a communal administration (usually nationalized former private property), or remained private, with deteriorated or underdeveloped technical infrastructure. Housing in the new part consisted of monotonous blocks, with communal infrastructure and standard equipment, owned by a co-operative or by an industrial complex. This dual character, even if limited in some cases by the expansion of new construction, has never been eliminated and is still visible in most Polish cities because of the abandonment of the modernization of the old structure.

The new industrial towns were located in areas of new mining industry, such as coal, copper or sulphur. Some already existing towns changed character through huge industrial investment, usually in chemicals or mining. The expansion of large urban and industrial agglomerations also created new towns as dormitory satellites of a larger centre, for example in the Warsaw region. Nowe Tychy, or Jastrzębie Zdrój in the Upper Silesia coalfield, or Legnica and Głogów in the Lower Silesia copper region, could serve as extreme examples of the industrial type of the socialist city. The same concerns Nowa Huta; however, this industrial town was incorporated administratively into Cracow, and its homogeneous working-class character was partly diluted by preservation of the national and cultural elite of Cracow. The classic dual structure developed in medium-size or smaller cities (before industrialization), such as Puławy, Płock, Bełchatów, Łęczna and Tarnobrzeg. Some small towns of rural character or medium-size cities were subject to relatively small-scale transformation.

Poland has a traditionally well developed urban network, particularly in the west, so historical roots contributed to maintaining the European character of the majority of Polish cities. However, this distinctiveness has been partly preserved as the traditional, pre-capitalist or underdeveloped capitalist pattern. One of the most important factors in the preservation of the distinct form of the socialist city in Poland was the presence of many national symbols of historical value, particularly Catholic churches. Those sacred spaces have been preserved in spite of some deliberate attempts by urban planners and designers to reduce their importance. Less frequently preserved are symbols of the German and Jewish population. The similarity to western European cities has also been preserved by the dominance of Modernist ideas throughout Europe. However, in the case of Poland and other central European countries, their own forms of Modernism also served to distinguish this region from western Europe.

After the Second World War, the idea of Modernism was quickly adopted by political leaders. It became a tool used by the communist leaders to make decisions in the name of society regarding the forms and plans of the cities and the living conditions of the population. In short, after the Second World War physical planning totally conformed with the command distributive system of administration of the whole national economy, and its general system of decision-making (Kowalewski 1990). Modernism also became the theoretical background for the over-functionalization of urban spaces, particularly in the creation of enormous monofunctional housing estates, and the disappearance of ground rent and of the existing ownership structure in the space of the city.

The egalitarian tendencies of social democratic ideology and the idea of the welfare state have reduced differentiation within capitalist cities in western Europe. In spite of strong egalitarian tendencies, differentiation does exist in the sociospatial structure of the Polish city, and since the 1970s started to gradually increase, accelerating in the 1980s and 1990s. This phenomenon has been demonstrated by studies of the sociospatial differentiation of towns and cities in Poland carried out using factor analysis (Węcławowicz 1979, 1988).

The most differentiating dimension of the sociospatial structure is in terms of "socioprofessional position". The identification of this dimension conforms to the hypothesis according to which division of urban societies into social categories and professional groups is accompanied by the tendency towards spatial separation of these groups. This separation was manifested in a higher percentage of a given social or occupational group in a strictly defined area, against a lower percentage of other groups in that area. In areas with a larger percentage of higher social and occupational groups, greater availability of services and frequently a better natural environment, according to the preferences of inhabitants of a given city, are characteristic features.

The second dimension of sociospatial structure has been referred to in short as the "housing situation of households", and can be treated as forming the essential part of a more general dimension, which can be called "family status" or "life-cycle of inhabitants". This second dimension demonstrates that within the Polish city there is a tendency towards spatial separation of population according to age, family size and housing conditions. There is high degree of correspondence of certain types of apartments and housing conditions with a higher percentage of certain types of households and population groups.

Other dimensions identified in particular towns were not so general, for example, higher proportions of specific demographic groups with apartments of definite age, or of certain housing conditions with a definite of household size, as well as of dominant ownership forms of flats with definite sizes of households.

The "migration" dimension indicated the existence of concentrations of specific demographic or professional groups in particular areas of the city. In the towns undergoing industrialization the new housing estates became areas of concentration of population of rural origin or, more generally, of immigrant population. Thus, initially new inhabitants were separated from the local population. The immigrant population was also concentrated in the suburban zones of large towns.

The migration dimension was the element of sociospatial differentiation that had been evolving most quickly. Rapid development, particularly of large and industrial towns, resulted in spatial mixing of the population of rural origin with earlier inhabitants, who had usually already been more urbanized.

Generalizing, one can state that the fundamental sociospatial structures in Polish towns have been identified and their differentiation can be described with the help of the following dimensions: socioprofessional position, family and housing status, and migration status. This structure of principal dimensions remains stable up to the 1990s, only the scale of internal differentiation has increased.

In the 1970s no essential change in the structure of fundamental dimensions of sociospatial differentiation took place. In individual towns these fundamental sociospatial structures also preserved their places and positions. Radical changes have usually been related to the introduction of new housing developments in the form of new estates. Such estates, located in the vicinity of areas characterized by higher socioprofessional status in 1970, preserved their nature in that respect at the end of the decade. New estates, located less advantageously or in areas of low socioprofessional status, acquired similar character, although their position was often somewhat higher.

In the family and housing dimensions, new estates have become the areas of concentration of relatively young population with children, that is, of population with normal family structures. Such a selective concentration undoubtedly contributed to deeper spatial differentiation. Besides that, the areas of old housing construction have become partly areas of outflow of population of the economically most active age, and areas with higher shares of the elderly population.

Generally, the 1970s were dominated by a stabilization of sociospatial structures, both in terms of socioprofessional position and of family and housing status. However, an increase of spatial segregation of certain demographic and social groups occurred for the first time on a noticeable scale.

The sociospatial patterns of the Polish towns involved elements of all the standard geographical models, that is, the concentric, sectoral and policentric. Some towns had a mosaic or nodal–linear pattern. In no case did one typical model pattern appear, so that most often sociospatial structures were mixed. In the most general terms it would be sufficient to describe them with the help of geometric analogies taken from the classic models of towns. In a more detailed description such terms as a mosaic, linear or nodal pattern can be identified. These generalizations refer to the physical form, whereas their social content is often completely different.

The general regularity of distribution of urban society, in its breakdown into socioprofessional categories, consists of concentrations of the higher categories within the central parts of towns. This general regularity, however, is limited by several constraints resulting from the island-like locations of physically deteriorated buildings, as well as socially degraded areas. On a more detailed scale one can also find in these central areas (i.e. among the areas generally inhabited by upper social categories) many representatives of the lower social categories – the elderly as well as socially and economically "weak" persons. Spatial micro-units emerge, inhabited by those in lower socioprofessional positions.

A question therefore arises as to what the decisive factors are for the simultaneous appearance of these two groups in the downtown areas, and for their spatial segregation. It seems that the main reason is apartment quality. Downtown areas have been relatively quickly reconstructed, and their further development caused strong differentiation of apartment quality. Inadequate development of mass and individual transport, poor service network and monotonous architecture of new housing estates contributed to a higher evaluation of the older but reconstructed and modernized apartments located in downtown areas. Such apartments have been to a large extent acquired by people in the higher socioprofessional categories. When lower social groups had been the first to occupy these areas, higher and economically stronger groups took over. Such a process would not have occurred with the same intensity in the case of flats of lower standard, although similarly located.

Similarly, the generalization that the farther one moves into the peripheries, the higher the share of the lower socioprofessional groups, is significantly disturbed by the island-like locations of estates of higher housing standard, of single-family housing areas, of areas of better transport accessibility, or of higher natural environmental value. Physical structure and quality of housing environment had a decisive influence upon the location of particular social categories and professional groups. The spatial distribution of socioprofessional position takes on a concentric pattern in the downtown areas, becomes radial or sectoral with increasing distance from the centre, and may even turn partially policentric in the peripheries. This general image is disturbed by the scattered occurrence of small spatial units having a socioprofessional composition distinctly different from that of the surrounding areas, so that an overall impression of a mosaic or patchwork sociospatial pattern of towns is created.

The above generalization applies principally to large cities. Physical structure of small towns is often of a bipolar nature. Medium-size towns develop in a more multidimensional way and display more complex physical patterns. At the macro-spatial scale of agglomerations, the policentric pattern appears.

The distribution of individual social groups, classified according to the size of family or household and to demographic features, tends to be strongly correlated with definite types of housing conditions. A characteristic example is provided by the higher shares of small households and of the elderly population in the central parts of towns, in older apartments with lower equipment standards. As distance

from the centre increases and housing estates are newer, the shares of younger, pro-
fessionally active population and of children also increase. A general proposition
can be formulated according to which the size and age structure of apartment determines to a large extent the predominant household size and structure. Given low
intra-urban mobility, caused mainly by a shortage of new housing, it is quite common for inhabitants to age together with their flats. Consequently, in different
stages of the life-cycle through which families pass, their housing conditions cannot satisfy their changing needs.

6.3 The role of housing policy and housing issues

The explanation of intra-urban social differentiation created under communism
could refer to different spheres. The first would be political, the second ideological, the third economic and the fourth living conditions. The sociospatial structure
inherited from the communist period is the final outcome of decisions undertaken
in all these spheres. Among these decisions, of fundamental significance in shaping sociospatial structure was the industrialization process and associated housing
policy aimed at distributing the housing stock among different social groups.

The requirements of industrialization, the fundamental process transforming
the social structure of towns, brought progress, but also gave rise to many contradictions. The most important was the delay in creating adequate living conditions
for the population, in comparison with the outlays on means of production.

The mass public housing construction was not satisfying increasing needs.
Housing resources became scarce goods and, as such, the object of competition
among particular social groups, and access to these resources became one of the
factors in the formation of ad hoc interest groups. Better or worse housing conditions and flat locations became partly an indicator of the political strength of particular social groups.

The second factor having direct influence on the formation of differentiated
sociospatial structure was housing allocation policy. This policy had been undergoing constant modification according to the needs of the ruling strata. When con-
sidering the influence of housing policies on the shaping of the sociospatial
structure of the cities, basic significance should be attributed to the appearance of
two contradictory tendencies. These are the tendency of egalitarian distribution of
housing conditions and the tendency towards selective housing policy granting
privileges to certain social and professional groups.

In the formation of structures of sociospatial differentiation, the following criteria of access to housing resources, in force during the whole post-war period, had
significant influence (Węcławowicz 1988). The first was the social value of the
labour force, related to the nature of the profession exercised and the actual job
performed. Current value of the labour force was often determined via the labour
market but more frequently by political decision. Flats were more easily obtained

by those people who represented professions in short supply at a given stage of development of a town. The second criterion was related to hierarchical position in the political or economic or administrative bureaucracy, together with the system of informal connections and access to information. Third was the criterion of previous housing conditions and the number of family members. Fourth was the financial situation of the family. Fifth was the length of period of residence in a given town and the waiting time for a new apartment.

6.4 The evolution of social and spatial differentiation

Since the beginning of the democratic transformation in 1989 up to the time of writing (1994), no explicit urban policies have been formulated. So the question of what to do with the "socialist city" in post-communist conditions is resolved in practice rather than in intellectual terms. We can, however, observe a process of evolution towards market-oriented patterns and the creation of a new type of city. Whether Polish cities become versions of the capitalist city is a question for the future.

Polish cities to diverse degrees are beginning to release themselves from the principal features of the "socialist city". This phenomenon is highly differentiated regionally. The most radical evolution has occurred in western Poland and in larger agglomerations. The process of transformation is far from complete; however, it is in an advanced stage in the largest cities and prosperous regions, and in the initial stage in most of the smaller cities and of recession regions.

The most important trends are as follows (Węclawowicz 1994):
- the return of the importance of land rent and the increased number of actors competing for space
- the return of self-government, the shift of absolute control over space from central to local
- the increase of social and spatial differentiation and the changing rules of spatial allocation of peoples from political to economic criteria
- the transformation of employment structure from domination of industry to domination of the service sector
- the substantial transformation of the urban landscape and architecture
- the transformation of values and symbols, mostly by replacing many mani- festations of politically symbolical space by other function and symbols.

The most direct influence on the transformation of sociospatial differentiation in the cities would appear to be via the formation of a new social structure. This is accompanied by the redevelopment of social networks (which were systematically constrained under communism), at a higher level than friends and family circles, such as real interest groups defined locally and regionally.

The newly emerging sociospatial structure now includes a middle class that is independent from the state sector. The speed of growth in size and importance of this group will depend on the process of privatization and general economic prospects. A substantial drop in the importance of the working class, particularly workers in the "productive sector", in favour of workers employed in services has occurred. The evolution of the labour market in the larger cities, as well as privatization tendencies, had started before 1989 in the development of co-operatives.

The change in labour demand has been caused by the economic recession and economic de-activation of population, but first of all by ownership transformation. Expansion of the private sector is especially important. New well paid and high-skilled jobs have emerged in businesses such as banking and different financial institutions, and managerial and professional consulting. The expansion of the private sector has also created demand for skilled jobs such as vendors, clerks, financial staff, secretaries and semi-skilled labour. In this sector, employees are much better paid and become more efficient compared with the public sector. Additionally, the "shadow economy", in terms of employment and production, must have a strong role in the transformation of urban places. This is not just a mass of street vendors and many illegal markets, but a large if inestimable share of all kinds of trade and production.

The formation in the social structure of the city of the new social groups, such as the middle class independent from the state sector, is the result of post-1989 privatization and booming development of the private sector. The increase of the self-employed and diminution of the working-class groups are two opposite social tendencies.

The increase in social and spatial polarization is one of the most frequently described phenomena of market transformation, not only in urban areas but in the whole country. All citizens could be classified as gainers or losers from the transformation.

The increase in poverty in Polish cities has been very evident, especially homeless persons, and elderly pensioners. In addition, the many people employed in administration or dependent on the state budget are highly differentiated and generally poorly paid, creating a group that regard themselves as losers. The cities, particularly the largest ones, have become very expensive to live in for an increasing number of their citizens. These people can still survive, often with a niche in the informal sector of economy. This phenomenon contributes substantially to an increase in social polarization, having its impact on spatial segregation.

The most rapid formation of a new sociospatial structure has occurred in the central parts of the cities. New elite enclaves have formed in redeveloped parts inside or next to deteriorating neighbourhoods and housing inhabited by the poor and elderly. The increasing scale of contrasts in social status and wealth in close spatial proximity creates a sort of dual city where the poor and rich live in the same areas. However, they use different spaces: luxury shops or street bazaars, private cars or public transport, different places of work and for services.

Lifting the administrative restriction on settlement in the largest cities opened them up to uncontrolled immigration, but in-migration has now fallen. The cities became administratively open but economically closed. For many citizens they have become too expensive to live in; however, there is no chance to move out, because of the housing shortage and unemployment. For new poor immigrants they have become inaccessible, or such people are marginalized to very poorly paid jobs and poor housing in emerging slum areas. Parallel to this is the inflow of wealthy population, which creates further polarization.

The rent reform in housing, however far from completion, has brought rent increases in co-operative and municipal dwellings, partially withdrawn from subsidies. Together with the declining income of many families, the problem of rent arrears has emerged. For example, in Warsaw in 1993 over 38% of co-operative tenants were not paying rents and 7.1% were indebted longer than 3 months. In municipal housing, 20.8% of occupants have financial problems and 8.4% are indebted longer than 3 months.

The most highly differentiating new factor in the prosperity of cities is unemployment. On a regional scale, the unemployment pattern is an indicator of spatial polarization. The labour market is relatively healthy in Warsaw, Poznań, Wrocław, Cracow, Gdańsk and some other large or medium-size and economically diversified cities. Other large cities, particularly those with a specialized industrial structure such as Łódź and Katowice, or monofunctional medium-size cities such as Mielec and Wałbrzych, now have substantial problems.

The new legislation encouraging self-government facilitates the formation of local connections and ties, and, more importantly, provides opportunities for newly formed social groups to press their demands and needs on the democratically elected representatives in local government. This inevitably facilitates the identification of inhabitants with the environments in which they live. However, it is worth mentioning that not all social groups have been formed into social interest groups. Some of them are unable to express their own interests (as a result of long-imposed passivity) or are unaware of their interests in the structure of the city.

The introduction of self-government in 1989 has had positive consequences for most urban areas. One of the very few negative results was the division of Warsaw into seven independent communes with inadequate co-ordination of responsibility for the whole city. The greatest attention of the new self-government structures has been turned on the local interests and struggles with the inherited poor infrastructure and everyday issues. The strategic development of the whole city has been partly neglected.

Rejection of socialist ideology will reorientate local government attention from place of work to place of residence. Under socialist conditions, the attention of urban authorities was concentrated on the production function. The factories and the state as employer were frequently the only organizers of social and cultural life and the only providers of food and services. Now the main arena of social activity has to a large extent become the local community around the place of residence. Social life has come to be organized more by the private sector and individual initiatives.

The rapid shift of control over urban space, from central to local, created many problems at first. The new self-government had not been prepared to deal with the

81

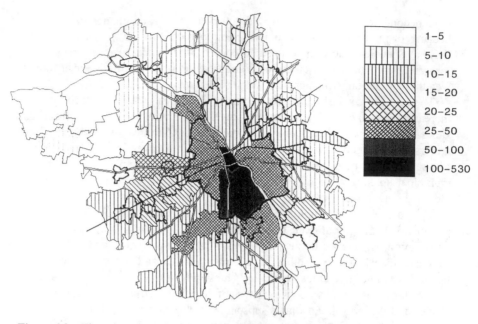

	1-5
	5-10
	10-15
	15-20
	20-25
	25-50
	50-100
	100-530

Figure 6.3   The price of construction plots in Warsaw voivodship, June 1993 ($). After: *Gazeta Wyborcza*, June 1993.

emergence of many new actors, mostly from the private sector, competing for space. The latest developments, particularly those imposed by the left-wing government elected in 1993, gradually curbed the prevailing shift of power over space from central and public to private actors.

The changes in urban landscape can best be described as changes of function and intensity of land use. The most characteristic has been the transformation from administrative and political to commercial functions, and from industrial and production to commercial or warehousing.

Parallel to transformations of function is the radical increase of intensity of land use. Many empty spaces have started to be intensively used for commercial purposes. The continuous emergence of the new investment, in the form of hotels, banks, trade and business centres, and newly designed offices, creates further intensification. Many new restaurants, shops, kiosks and bazaars or street markets have emerged.

These accelerating changes started chaotically in 1989, such as people selling from the pavement or from their own hands standing by the side of the street. Now some of these traders are located in places prepared for informal retailing, gradually moving to more permanent small shops or shopping centres. This private retail trade practically eliminated the problem of obtaining everyday products from the agenda of daily life, even in the large new housing estates where provision of goods and services was previously so poor.

The most rapid transformation has occurred in several areas with good transport connections and a tradition of private sector development. The lack of commercial facilities in the best locations resulted in strong competition for available space and also contributed to the price differentiation of the land. The structure of prices of land, as for example in the case of the Warsaw region, indicates the quickest developing areas (Fig. 6.3).

6.5 The urban system in the Polish and central European context

The lifting of many political and economic barriers in an international context created a new challenge for the Polish urban system: competition for a place in the emerging urban hierarchy of Europe. The outcome of this competition will influence the prospects of all urban places for prosperous development at the turn of the century. Also important are questions of the internal development of the economy and the political structure of the country. The drift towards political decentralization, initiated at the beginning of the transformation, has been limited by the latest post-communist government. The policentric urban system, with several large urban centres and agglomerations, is advantageous in the context of the regionalization of Poland, for it facilitates some dispersal of prosperity.

Under communism the significance of urban places as concentrations of the working class and of industrial production had the greatest priority. However, attempts to limit the growth of some of the largest cities were implemented. For example, restrictions on migration for permanent residence were effective in Warsaw, Cracow, Lódź, Poznań and other large cities.

In the 1990s, the pre-eminent position of Warsaw has been challenged by Cracow on the grounds of its cultural, scientific and spiritual significance, by Gdańsk on the basis of political power, and by Poznań by dint of its economic leadership in the transformation. Warsaw's regional location has offset the gradual decrease of its importance on the national scale. Warsaw is located in one of the underdeveloped regions of Poland, so that one of the basic conditions of Warsaw's future development is the reduction in the serious existing economic imbalance between the city and its surrounding region. As a great economic centre and capital city, Warsaw has a substantial influence on the diffusion of the modernization process in the eastern part of the country. This influence has been substantially increased by the rapid development of the private sector; however, the spatial concentration of economic activities also contributes to an increase in regional disparities.

The greater integration of Warsaw and the settlement system of Poland with that of western Europe is inevitable. Looking at the relationship between post-communist cities and western European cities, one can see the former perhaps fulfilling a distant suburban or satellite function for the western metropolis within close proximity (for example, Bratislava in Slovakia as a suburb of Vienna). A similar situation could developed with Polish cities in the case of Poznań, Szczecin and Wrocław, in relation to Berlin in Germany.

In the context of European integration and decentralization of national administration, alternatives to Warsaw could develop for close economic co-operation. For example, Gdańsk could become a partner of Copenhagen, Wrocław a partner of Prague, Cracow could establish closer ties with Vienna and Budapest. So the challenge for Warsaw, and for the regional policy of Poland in general, is the question of Warsaw becoming more attractive than other large Polish cities, or merely a "capital" for eastern Poland. The possible future economic integration of the Polish regional system, particularly with neighbouring Germany, could also create a contra-reaction to the increasing functional integration of the national system in political and cultural terms.

CHAPTER 7

The ecological consequences of industrialization and urbanization

Ecological problems are part of the wider social and economic crisis of post-communist Poland. Social awareness has emerged, associated with the increasing scale of the problems and with the growing political activity of society. Communist censorship and lack of reliable assessments suppressed information about environmental destruction. Following the Solidarity revolt of 1980, the state of the environment became one of the main issues for many political groups and ecological movements. The scale of the hazard has reached catastrophic levels in some areas, and is extremely differentiated regionally. The catastrophic state of the environment is in almost every case attributable to industrialization. An additional factor is the low level of protective infrastructure in urbanized areas and its absence in rural areas. The scale of the crisis will have many consequences and cannot be eliminated in the short term.

At the macro-spatial scale, environmental problems increase from the northeast and north of Poland, with unpolluted areas towards the southwest, with the highest pollution in Upper Silesia and the Turoszów brown coal basin on the Polish/Czech and German border. This triangle, covering $37400 \, km^2$ of Polish, Czech and German territory (referred to as "sulphur", "black" or "dirty" because of its brown coal exploitation and power-generating plants), is one of the largest sources of pollution in Europe.

The government decision in 1983 to identify 27 areas of ecological hazards was the first attempt to concentrate action (Kassenberg & Rolewicz 1985). These areas, representing 11.2% of the country areas, accommodated 35.4% of the population, that is, 13.5 million people in 1992. The ecological hazard areas were characterized by much greater urbanization: 85% of the population living in urban places in 1992 compared with 61.8% on the national scale. These areas were the source of 74.4% of dust emissions, 81.4% of gas, 56.9% of waste water and 92.6% of total industrial waste in 1992 (GUS 1992).

These delimited areas did not include all sources of pollution generated by transport and agriculture. As they excluded such highly polluted urban centres as the Warsaw agglomeration, probably for political reasons, they revealed only part of the problem that existed at the beginning of 1980s. The statistical analysis (ibid.) extended to urban areas identified 80 cities with high ecological hazard, located

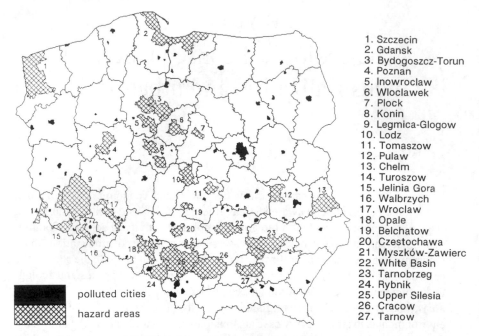

1. Szczecin
2. Gdansk
3. Bydogoszcz-Torun
4. Poznan
5. Inowroclaw
6. Wloclawek
7. Plock
8. Konin
9. Legmica-Glogow
10. Lodz
11. Tomaszow
12. Pulaw
13. Chelm
14. Turoszow
15. Jelinia Gora
16. Walbrzych
17. Wroclaw
18. Opale
19. Belchatow
20. Czestochawa
21. Myszków-Zawierc
22. White Basin
23. Tarnobrzeg
24. Rybnik
25. Upper Silesia
26. Cracow
27. Tarnow

polluted cities

hazard areas

Figure 7.1 Areas of ecological hazard and strongly polluted cities. After: *Obszary ekologicznego zagrożenia w Polsce* 1992. Warsaw: GUS.

outside the originally identified 27 areas. This made it possible to produce a more accurate picture of the ecological problem areas (Fig. 7.1).

Industrial activity in the hazard areas had an impact on the environment elsewhere, manifested, for example, in the deterioration of forest and contamination of soils on a much wider scale. On these grounds, larger agricultural areas should be excluded from food production.

On the national scale, the economic losses caused by environmental pollution are estimated at between 10% and 25.8% of GNP (Piontek 1993).

Air pollution creates one of the greatest threats, and is still at one of the highest levels in Europe. Only 21.4% of gas pollution has been reduced. In 1993 it was 10 tonnes per km^2 of gases, which contains 6 tonnes of SO_2 per km^2. The regional distribution of air pollution overlaps with the hazard areas (Fig. 7.2). At the more detailed scale of the hazard areas, the emission of SO_2 in 1990 was: 1524.4 tonnes per km^2 in Belchatów, 345 tonnes per km^2 in Turoszów, 236 tonnes per km^2 in Plock and 125 tonnes per km^2 in Upper Silesia (Rolewicz 1993), to mention just the largest.

The water pollution has left no really clean water in the river system. The rapid increase in treatment plants has ameliorated the situation; however, 328 towns still have no treatment facilities. Almost 36% of waste from the sewage system of the cities, and 25% of waste from industrial plants, comes directly into the hydrographic system without any purification. Also, lack of treatment of industrial waste

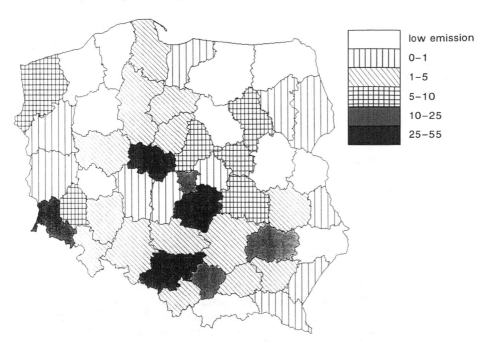

	low emission
	0–1
	1–5
	5–10
	10–25
	25–55

Figure 7.2 Emission of SO_2 in tones per km^2, 1992. After: *Rocznik statystyczny województw* 1993. Warsaw: GUS.

and municipal waste causes degradation of huge areas of the country. The degradation of soil in 1993 covered over 90000 ha. In the voivodship of Katowice Jeleniogórskie, Konińskie and Tarnobrzeskie, over 5% of the area is degraded irreversibly, unless there is huge investment in restoration.

The degradation of forest is most conspicuous in southern Poland. The coniferous forest has almost disappeared in Sudcty and in Western Carpatia. Of what still exists, 92.7% is affected in the Wrocław voivodship and 88.6% in the Katowice voivodship. Farther north and east the degradation of forest gradually diminishes; however, almost the whole of Poland is affected in some way, and even in the Bieszczady mountains (southeastern corner of Poland) the consequences of air pollution are visible.

Environmental pollution has a direct impact on the health of the population. It contributes substantially to mortality and reduced life expectancy. Particular attention should be paid to Upper Silesia, with its high concentration of pollution together with the concentration of population and economic activity. For example, detailed research indicates that nearly half of the pregnancies in the Katowice voivodship are abnormal, along with several times the national levels of throat and lung illness, cancer and genetic deformation of children. Infant mortality in Upper Silesia is one of the highest in Poland, at 17 per 1000 live births, but in the most contaminated city of Bytom it reaches 50 (Gołębiowski 1994). The cities of Chorzów and Zabrze are also very high risk areas.

The international transfer of air pollution contributes greatly to ecological degradation. In 1988, Poland "imported" 246000 tonnes of SO_2 from Czechoslovakia and 468000 tonnes from East Germany, and "exported" to those countries 126000 and 36000 tonnes respectively. Polish emissions of SO_2 have partly been "exported" to the former Soviet Union (518000 tonnes). It is worth mentioning, however, that the Polish share of gas emissions responsible for global warming was only 1.3% in 1987, as compared with 2.7% for the United Kingdom, 17.6% for the USA and 12% for the Soviet Union (Leszczycki & Domański 1995).

The continuing increase of environmental degradation under communism had been virtually halted by the beginning of 1990s. This was partly a result of the recession, but also of the introduction of the new environmental policy and creation the necessary legislative and financial framework. Among several legislative acts, the Environmental Protection Act has been introduced, and the State Inspectorate for Environmental Protection founded. Industrial plants that caused environmental pollution can now be closed down by law. The 80 polluting companies that emit 50% of gases, 44% of sewage and 23% of total waste have been required to reduce pollution drastically in 3–5 years, or they will be closed (Bossak 1993). So far, since 1990, 7 of the largest polluters have been shut down, 22 have been restructured to non-polluting production, and 20 have significantly reduced emissions (Gołębiowski 1994). The National Environmental Protection and Water Management Fund, the commercial Environmental Protection Bank, and the regional Environmental Protection Fund have also been established.

An important role could be played by foreign aid, and particularly an initiative to reduce foreign debt in exchange for environmental protection or "ecoconversion". This initiative, of buying Polish foreign debts in exchange for spending money on environmental protection, has offered a financial mechanism for creating an ecological fund and it will play a crucial role in improving the poor state of the environment. So far, foreign assistance accounts for around 5% of total expenditure for environmental purposes.

The progress in environmental protection can be attributed to a gradual increase of environmental investment. For example, this expenditure grew from 0.6% of GNP in 1988 to 1.3% in 1993. The decrease in pollution has also been the result of the recession, however, and it was greater than the fall of GNP. It is estimated that between 1988 and 1993 pollution decreased by 30% (Bossak 1994).

It is worth adding that in spite of substantial environmental problems, over a quarter of the national territory is clean and represents an asset on a European scale. This concerns particularly 19 national parks covering 244000ha of greatest ecological value. It is estimated that 19% of Polish territory of forest and traditional farming is characterized by sustainable ecological practices, and about 8.5% remains relatively unscathed by development (Gołębiowski 1994).

PART III
Post-communist transformation and its spatial components

The post-communist challenge

The transformation in Poland has occurred in various interlinked arenas. In political and ideological terms it has concerned the re-creation of democratic administrative and organizational structures for the whole of society. In psychological terms, it has concerned the evolution of people's attitudes; that is, the drift towards abandoning the "claims mentality" in favour of a more individualistic behaviour and the entrepreneurial type of self-made man. In the economic arena, substantial modernization demands reorganization of the entire economic structure, making it more efficient and competitive in terms of the requirements of the capitalist world economy. In technical and organizational terms the process of introducing a new infrastructure has been initiated: for example the organization of a proper banking systems and an efficient telephone network.

During the first years of transformation the political scene in Poland was dominated by the sharp economic recession. The dramatic drop in production, increasing unemployment and decreasing national income have been the pivotal points for political discourse. The response of society has been to question the consensus reached at the "round table" conference. The compromise between the Solidarity government and labour organized in many trade unions did not anticipate the relatively high social cost of rapid economic transformation.

Solidarity came to power in 1989 on slogans of abandoning the centrally planned socialist economy and of returning to market forces. The government drift to the right was prevented by the power of the electorate, strikes and growing strength of the post-communist opposition. However, a combination of a weakening state, an emphasis on law, and an economic doctrine that saw market forces as the solution for all inherited problems of the centrally planned economy, has failed. The Solidarity government's aims were to reduce inflation and to establish market forces as dominant in the country's economy. The continued economic recession in the period of rapid transformation has reduced the belief that this strategy would improve the standard of living. The general decline in votes cast and support for the Solidarity-based government has meant that no Solidarity government has been returned with a majority of votes cast.

There has thus been a crisis of legitimacy, and a steady decline in the belief that politicians can solve Poland's economic ills. The widespread strikes in 1992 were partly an indication of some of the social costs of transformation and partly the reflection of a climate of opinion dominated by perception of corruption and of increasing unjustified inequalities. In particular, there has been an attempt to constrain the privatization process. This has been a major political theme since mid-1990.

The government's attempt to reduce expenditure is confronted by the strength of various lobbies. To convert the collective social provision of the communist period to the social attitude of individualism, self-reliance and family responsibility seems impossible in the short term. The successive Solidarity governments have interpreted the role of the state as maintaining the market-oriented transformation.

The unsatisfactory process of transformation raises the question of the way ahead. It is obvious that there is no way back to socialism, yet there is no full acceptance of the present underdeveloped capitalism. As a third way, the social market economy is frequently under discussion. However, the latter solution and all notions of a third way are strongly criticized in government circles.

The transformation occurred in the absence of guiding experience of any similar examples. There was no single country that had been transformed from socialism to capitalism. There are no theories of this kind of transformation of economic and social systems.

In terms of popular perception, the transformation seems to have been based on a transition from a poor society into a society of poor and rich; or from an egalitarian society, at least in theory, to an inegalitarian society with very evident divisions based on wealth. The question arises: what will be the proportions of these groups? A similar question concerns the spatial scale: which regions will profit from the transformation and which will lose?

Sometimes the pattern of a Third World country is under discussion; that is, we could have a very narrow wealthy elite and large social groups in poverty. This way seems impossible to accept, because society rejected the same pattern of a narrow privileged elite of communist rulers and a large working class. The alternative of a more advanced capitalist country, with large relatively wealthy social groups and small groups of poor and elite, needs certain specific conditions. First of all there is a need for an inflow of large quantities of capital and investment goods, together with modern technology, organization, and know-how. Secondly, political and social stabilization is crucial.

One of the most important challenges seems to be a struggle for a new model of the state, or the role of the state in the economic, political and sociocultural life of the country. It is obvious that the only possibility rejected is the communist state model, which is totalitarian in character. All other models or directions of developments should be considered, because they are all possible; however, some tendencies become clearer than others.

The crucial factor seems to be the evolution of the mentality of Polish society followed by the evolution of its opinions. However, this evolution, manipulated by politicians and influenced by all kinds of political and economic events under democratic conditions, provides some basis for understanding the transformation.

The split between progress in macroeconomic terms and the evaluation of experts, on the one hand, and the individual citizen's perspective on the other, has its parallel in the split between value systems and attitudes in relation to the economy. The evolving economic situation of particular social categories has a significant influence on the evolution and transformation of social stratification. This is followed by transformation in value systems and attitudes.

According to Marody (1994), the first transformation in people's attitude concerns the attitude of the winners. The evolution of this attitude is based on the increasing share of people who believe that the top level of politics has an impact on individual life but that conditions are not created by particular leaders, that is, people who accept individual responsibility at the micro-level of everyday life. The winners also believe that personal responsibility for individual material conditions is crucial, whereas the losers support more frequently the view that someone loses in order that someone else can win.

The changing attitudes of people to the transformation have been of crucial importance. The collapse of left-wing ideology seemed to be final, just after the beginning of the transformation. The new economic reforms rapidly liquidated many elements of state collectivism, together with some social security systems. The aim was a sort of social engineering, to change the attitude of people towards more individualism. This appeared to be partly successful. A majority of the population reacted to the new situation with enthusiasm, or managed to adapt. The rest of society was waiting, and through the democratic process gradually changed the external conditions in order to maintain former privileges and benefits. Those people became the electorate of many populist prophets such as Tymiński and Lepper, and later on the consolidating left-wing parties of opposition. It so happens that this consolidation has been organized by post-communist parties.

The right-wing orientation and, for some sociologists (Boski 1993, Reykowski 1994), left-wing orientation, provide two main axes along which Polish society is differentiated. One dimension is the opposition between the liberal state (in the economic sense) and the protective state. The second dimension is the opposition between the secular European state and the religious national state. So, one dimension of differentiation is connected with economic freedom and the second with social values. Similarly, another sociologist (Jasiewicz 1993) identified two dimensions: liberalism option versus populism; and European versus xenophobia.

CHAPTER 8
The social consequence
of transformation

8.1 The transformation in social structure

The social structure of Poland after the Second World War was created by the new division of labour imposed by the communist system and by the transformation of what was inherited from the capitalist past. In the socialist society the absolute control of the economy by the state and Communist Party apparatus reduced the significance of ownership of the means of production as a criterion of class division (Słomczyński 1994). After the elimination of large landowners and the bourgeoisie, only a relatively weak working class, intelligentsia and peasantry remained. This general division of Polish society just after the Second World War gradually become too simplistic. Under the process of industrialization and urbanization the working class grew in number and significance. In spite of the unification tendencies, under communism social stratification had been evolving and gradually increased in complexity.

The lack of theoretical explanation of the collapse of the communist system and its impact on social structure, except some preliminary proposals elaborated by Staniszkis (1994), is probably a consequence of the very short time perspective. In practice, the social structure of Polish society started changing dramatically after 1989; however, some trends were visible before 1989. In general, the "socialist society" is supposed to be transformed into the "capitalist society". The large-scale process of class recomposition has started involving the changing structure of ownership, the distribution of income and wealth, consumption, cultural behaviour, political significance and prestige. However, the formation of a new social structure is a long-term process.

The different segments of social structure have clarified their consciousness and started to articulate their interests more strongly than under communism. Now, the very existence of some classes is threatened, whereas the expansion of others is even supported by the state. It becomes obvious that the main pre-existing social groups – workers in large state industrial plants and peasants – have little chance of surviving in the emerging market system, and their influence on the political evolution of the country and on the distribution of earnings has been eroded. These social groups provide the political base for modification of the process of transformation, through trade unions or political parties, but primarily electoral behaviour.

Even if the political parties do not fully represent the interests of these groups, the split between the political elite and society divided into interest groups is gradually diminishing.

The main supporter of the transformation became the state, particularly when it was run by the Solidarity governments. Based on their ideological vision, the leaders of the anti-communist movement became the leaders of the transformation. They immediately adopted the strategy of the system just destroyed: the principal objective was the creation of supporting classes or social groups. For example, the new middle class has been promoted automatically, almost in an administrative way. It also seems that the government run since the 1993 parliamentary election by post-communist parties maintains this strategy in their own elites' interests. The resistance to this policy gradually increased. It appears that the persistence of "socialist" attitudes is stronger than expected. In addition, the old social classes started to struggle for survival; this concerns primarily the peasantry and the labourers employed in large state-owned companies.

The emerging new social structure will be based on elements of the social structure formed under communism and some elements that survived from the pre-war structures. Słomczyński (1994) identifies the following classes in the late stage of socialism: managers, first-line supervisors, experts and professionals, office workers, state factory workers, petty bourgeoisie, farmers, and private enterprise workers. In the period of transformation, the new categories emerging are a capitalist class and the unemployed. According to Wesolowski (1994), the last transformation indicates the resumption of the Weberian class scheme with the return of the importance of economic resources, power and knowledge as an elements determining position in the class structure. So in central European countries the following social classes exist: working class, petit bourgeois, intelligentsia and specialists without property, and the privileged classes. In the Polish situation we should also add the peasants.

In the situation of abandoning communist system rules and introducing new rules the following process will possibly be observed (according to Wesolowski 1994):
- the restitution of a privileged class based on the criteria of property and education
- the return of private property will change the role of intelligence
- the increased role of a middle class
- the restructuring and diminution of the economic and political importance of the working class
- the beginning of deep restructuring and decreasing importance of the peasant class.

The social structure could be interpreted in different ways, depending on the theoretical assumptions. The period of transformation required less strict definition of wider groups but more narrow identification of empirical attitudes. It seems that the concept of occupational categories, less abstract than social classes, will be a useful tool for description of the transformation in social structure. The notion

of social structure is, however, not precisely defined; it comprises the class structure, professional or occupational structure, organizational structure, professional
position, educational status, prestige, income, family origin, and so on. The difference between social groups has been increasing during transformation. As data
from Table 8.1 indicate, the distribution of income, material wealth and cultural
attributes between social and occupational groups has been changing. The greatest
progress has been made by managers and state administrators, their monthly
income per family member increasing to three times the average level. Relative
improvement can also be noted in the case of the intelligentsia, engineers, private
businessman, and administration in general. A relative decline characterized all
manual social categories, particularly unskilled workers and peasants. These
categories were below national average in 1987, but in 1993 their situation had
deteriorated further (Table 8.1).

Table 8.1 The evolution of income, material and cultural position of households.
According to: Domański 1994, p. 55.

Socio-occupational categories	1978[1]	1993[1]	1987[2]	1993[2]	1987[3]	1993[3]
Managers and higher state administration officials	145	317	43.8	76.9	259	298
Non-technical intelligentsia	145	226	56.7	74.4	251	907
Engineers	123	134	47.4	76.0	304	542
Technicians	104	101	37.9	65.0	191	294
Middle-grade clerks	112	129	43.9	68.8	241	325
Lower-grade clerks	103	105	39.9	63.7	146	182
Businessman	146	144	52.4	77.0	173	271
Employed in sales and service	98	91	34.6	62.8	105	247
Foreman	100	85	28.6	50.8	344	243
Skilled workers	95	79	28.3	55.5	83	84
Unskilled workers	91	68	21.9	45.6	47	65
Manual workers in service	80	63	25.6	45.8	67	62
Employed in farming	77	58	21.0	50.1	48	75
Farm owners	88	57	22.1	40.1	48	68

1. Monthly family income per person, in relation to national average.
2. Material positions as a percentage of possession of seven goods in household.
3. Number of books in a household.

The highest position on wealth, measured by technical household equipment
(refrigerator, washing machine, colour television, computer, video, telephone)
goes to private entrepreneurs and the intelligentsia, including managers of the
highest level. At the bottom of this scale are unskilled workers and peasants

(Domański 1994). In the cultural dimension, measured by the number of books in households, the distinction is similar; however, the position of owners is much below that of the intelligentsia.

The mechanism of distribution of income according to sector of the economy, which had been created under communism, has been eliminated. However, despite the strength of the existing differentiation and the re-establishment of the former connection with property holdings, the activity of trade unions and the political pressure on the left-wing government has ameliorated the increase in income inequality. The new phenomenon is the increase in the role of education, particularly in the private sector. For example, employees with higher education in 1993 in the private sector had 31% higher salaries than the national average, whereas in 1987 they were only 7% higher (Domański 1994).

The important conclusion from sociological research is that, as a result of abandoning the communist system, the means of interest articulation by different social groups have been unblocked. This was reflected in the fact that in 1990 74% of people indicated that freedom of speech increased compared with 1984, and 70% of respondents mentioned the increase of "reliable information" (Wnuk-Lipiński 1993). At the same time, a substantial decrease has been observed (according to 58% of respondents) in the sense of personal security in employment and financial terms.

The transformations in the social structure also have important political consequences. Assuming that transformation in general is accepted by all the political elite, it seems that, as time has elapsed, the question of who will lead the transformation has become more important – the post-communist or post-Solidarity group. Assuming further that some will profit much more from change than will others, the winners will determine the share of different segments of the social structure that could enter the elite class or the emerging upper middle class. The transformation is deeply involved in the struggle over division of national property.

With weak democratic institutions and weak organization of civil society, the expansion of the economic elite creates political tension. This is particularly true of the merger of the political elite and the economic elite, in a society still characterized by a highly egalitarian attitude. If political articulation of its interests is not very strong, this could create a non-institutionalized counter-reaction or apathy.

The transformation in Poland involves not only the process of abandoning communism, but also attempting to abandon underdevelopment dating from pre-communist times. It is an attempt at modernization (Mokrzycki 1994). The transformation is not only against the short-term interest of the groups formed under communism, but is also against the interests of social classes formed in pre-war times – the peasantry and the intelligentsia – which were effectively paralyzed by the communist system.

It seems that the process of the formation of three large social groups is under way: the elite, the middle class and the poverty class. The elite group will be constructed from the former communist elite or nomenclatura members, part of the former anti-communist opposition, and the intelligentsia. In very rare cases members of the former working class or peasants will be recruited to this elite.

The middle-class group will be formed from former communist upper- and lower-grade nomenclatura, part of the anti-communist opposition leaders, and from the intelligentsia. The upgrading of the majority of the working class will be strongly limited because of the delay in the Mass Privatization Programme, and by their low skill levels, maintenance of passive attitudes and a sense of claim or dependence on the state.

The poverty group is emerging from all social categories losing from the transformation. Above all, it concerns the unemployed, some of the unskilled workers, the majority of the rural population (particularly former peasant workers), and owners of small farms, and even part of the lower-level intelligentsia. A large segment of the unskilled working class will also be on the loser side. This also concerns the majority of elderly people.

We shall now pay particular attention to the description of the three very broad groups that will determine the future transformation: the elites and middle class, the working class, and the peasants.

8.1.1 THE ELITES AND MIDDLE CLASS

In the formation of the new elites and middle class, the issues of origin of capital and the incorporation process are of fundamental significance. We can identify the following types of capital functioning in Poland. The first is of nomenclatura or crypto-nomenclatura origin. The second, partly overlapping with the first, is illegal capital that can now been legalized thanks to the liberalized transformation conditions. The third is capital released from past savings. The fourth is small-scale foreign capital of Polish former emigrants, or of other foreign nationalities from Western countries now investing in Poland. The fifth is foreign capital on a large scale.

Capital originating from nomenclatura or crypto-nomenclatura is in the strongest position, and the only serious source of competition is major Western capital if it reaches Poland. It is not absolutely certain whether the nomenclature capital works in favour of inflow of foreign capital, because it could create potential competition for already dominated markets.

To the accumulation of capital by people connected with the former communist system – the nomenclatura – has been added the accumulation of wealth by some former Solidarity opposition members and their strong supporters. The emergence of this group, which utilized its political influence and connections in the authority structure, has been particularly frustrating and negatively evaluated by "ordinary" people. The concept of the old and the new nomenclatura has emerged in public opinion, and has diluted the perception of responsibility of communism for the past, and creating public disillusionment with the former Solidarity elite. These two groups have been referred to as the post-communist upper class (Mokrzycki 1994).

97

Today the economic elite of Poland consists of representatives of the nomenclatura, economically active groups of the former political opposition, and legalized capital of illegal origin. According to some surveys, only 6% of members of the former communist nomenclatura have retained their position in the political structure and still belong to the political class (Gołębiowski 1994). However, since the parliamentary elections of 1993 and the success of the SLD, the gradual return of further members of the former communist elite has been observed. The increasing share of the former nomenclatura is in the economic elite of the private sector and in enterprise management in the state sector.

The re-establishment of the former nomenclatura has been observed particularly during 1994, and this issue became one of the reasons for the political crisis in February 1995. The left-wing government of Waldemar Pawlak, the leader of the peasant party PSL, has been accused of disproportionate appointment of PSL members to the key economic positions in regional and state administration, even causing some conflict and tensions with its government coalition ally of the post-communist SLD party.

The new capitalist class was under formation from the very beginning. All pre-war connections, cultural, property circumstances and personal connections, were destroyed. The former private initiative from the communist period has been divided. The majority collapsed because they lost their monopolistic position in delivering products and services unavailable under the communist central economy; few have the chance to become members of the economic elite or upper middle class.

The Polish capitalist class is formed from the following components. The first is nomenclatura members, benefiting from the transformation of political and administrative power, and monopoly of information, into wealth and property. The second category is the "self-made men": different types of people but generally with higher education, gaining from the rapid formation of companies based on their own energy. The third category concerns a group of contemporary "experts", as owners of consulting companies recruiting many highly specialized professionals. This group of administrative professionals has also acquired semi-capitalistic functions. The nomination of such people by state administration into positions of influence creates the possibility of acquiring high income, information and power that can be used for future prosperous business activity. The fourth is based on the creation of a company through individual technical innovation. This category of inventors includes former scientists and staff in polytechnics, universities and research institutes of the Polish Academy of Sciences. The fifth category consists of the owners of the small companies that existed under communism and were successful in expanding to a much larger size in the new economic conditions. It is worth adding that only a part of the new capitalists acting on a huge scale are "visible"; in reality an important group is operating in the shadow economy.

The varying origins of the capitalist class will work against its quick integration and creation of a monolithic type. The higher strata of proprietors and managers are a sort of economic elite. Part of this group, of nomenclatura origin, has also managed to return to political significance.

The new middle class is emerging from the collapse of different groups of the former communist system. So the basic issue will be the process of incorporation into this group. The intelligentsia has become the main recruitment group for the middle class. The European integration scenario will lead to a crisis in the traditional role of the intelligentsia and its transformation into a modern middle class. The continuing deterioration in the prospects for the intelligentsia encourages them to move into the private sector. Groups of the intelligentsia are similar to the "knowledge class" in Western terms (Mokrzycki 1994). The crisis of the intelligentsia is a result of the disappearance of different occupations, and most of all of the collapse of science and public higher education. The alternative to the "brain drain" abroad for the intelligentsia has become the private sector, as a profitable activity or source of additional work. For the majority, however, there will be no alternative to the poorly or moderately paid public sector.

Part of the middle class is recruited as a result of the re-privatization and privatization process. In particular, privatization is one way to convert part of the working class into the middle class, for example. It is a government strategy to co-opt some segment of the working class as supporters of the transformation, by the distribution of small-scale economic opportunities, but in a situation where major opportunities have already been appropriated by the nomenclatura.

Part of the middle class will be the technical intelligentsia and profit-oriented managers employed in the state sector enterprises, which maintain their high share of the national economy, or in enterprises of mixed ownership structures. The liberal attitude is that elimination of communist orthodoxy and constraints will ensure that market forces and pro-democratic tendencies automatically regenerate the middle class. The new middle class will be gradually differentiated by origin, education and cultural background. This internal differentiation will influence its political attitudes and behaviour for a long time. For example, support of liberal reform is weaker among the private business owners than among the intelligentsia. A high share of this supposed middle class maintains a socialist consciousness. The group of owners has no common ideological or political identity. Only some small political parties organized by intellectuals are trying or claiming to represent its interests.

The formation of a middle class has not been rapid, in spite of the dramatic increase of the private sector. The origin of this class under formation is crucial. It consists of different layers, and some estimations indicate that 48% are from the former nomenclatura. Some of the members were virtually forced to work on their own account because of the economic situation. Some joined the independent sector with great enthusiasm, and some are part of the shadow economy. The emerging middle class thus consists of different layers. The top layer of big businessmen, entrepreneurs and successful owners of private companies has been estimated at 15000 to 20000 (Gołębiowski 1994).

8.1.2 THE WORKING CLASS

The working class had been struggling with communism for what could be called "socialism with a human face". Its disappointment and energy for action had been converted by the Solidarity intellectual elite into a force for the liquidation of communism. Instead of restructured socialism, liberal capitalism has now been imposed. Increasing discontent with its implementation during the first few years, and particularly the policy of shock therapy, created frustration. The crucial factor was the lack of a clear alternative to the increase in the gap between poor and rich, lowering purchasing power, unemployment and other costs of transformation. The reaction became obvious: the rejection of Solidarity leaders and parties, and the success of the ex-communist Social Democratic Alliance.

The political options of the working class have undergone constant evolution since 1989. From massive support for Solidarity in 1989–90, a gradual decline has been observed. In 1991 the political preferences of the working class were divided between several parties that gained around 10% support.

The majority of manual workers support rather right-wing options. The left-wing parties and rural-based party get about one in five of its votes. The liberal option gets similar support. In the period 1992–4 a fundamental shift was visible. In 1992 the support for the left wing increased, together with strong anti-liberal attitudes. As a result, in the 1993 parliamentary election, manual workers supported the left-wing alliance (19.6%, plus 14.2% for the PSL and 7.2% for the Union of Labour). This indicated that a majority of the working class rejected the existing 1993 strategy of reform. In total, left-wing parties received twice the vote in 1993 than in 1991, the largest increase being gained by the post-communist Social Democratic Alliance (SLD).

Working-class attitudes to the economic realities of transformation have been undergoing substantial changes. First of all, the majority of the working class seems to reject modernization of the economy, which undermines the protective role of the state. The transformation has changed the prevailing attitude very little: that human beings have a natural right to basic goods and services such as housing, education and health care without regard to the input of work or to social position (Gardawski & Żukowski 1994).

The dream of a normal economy was understood to be stabilization, so the result of transformation – the uncertainty of a capitalist market – was something of a shock. The negative attitude to transformation is also the result of the many false myths about and idealization of the market economy, which were revealed for what they are under the implementation of market principles into reality. In spite of the accepted and obvious positive results, it also brings recession, unemployment and, for the majority, a decline in their standard of living. The majority of the working class expected, at the beginning, a "social market economy" with a soft transitional period. But in reality they faced a very liberal form of capitalism without state protection. The greatest concern for the working class became instability, which they had not known previously.

The three basic types of economic awareness of the working class are at present: traditional, moderate reformist and liberal (Gardawski & Żukowski 1994). The traditional type, represented by 12% of survey respondents, supports the view that government should be the manager of all companies, but under workers' control. The basic view is egalitarian, strongly supportive of equal incomes. The moderate reformist option (represented by 54.4%) supports self-government of companies and competition, preferring Polish capital and stimulation of worker ownership (akcjonariat pracowniczy). The liberal option, represented by only 3% of the working class, agreed with the necessity of unemployment and accepted foreign capital purchasing state companies.

In spite of that, the majority of workers do not wish to return to real socialism; however, they do wish to maintain a protective state that will guarantee work for all citizens. It seems that the ideal for the working-class would be the social free market economy with a strong and protective state, and with an interventionist policy in big industry.

During the years of the transformation, substantial changes of view have occurred also in relation to the widely supported idea of the role of efficiency. In 1991 around 83% of workers supported the idea that companies should be independent and that unlimited competition between them should be accepted, but in 1993 only 72.4% supported this view. The most striking change concerned the idea that ineffective and unnecessary employment should be reduced. The support for this idea dropped from 71.5% in 1991 to 37.8% in 1993. Also, bankruptcy of unprofitable companies is supported by a smaller share of workers, dropping from 72% to 56.8% in 1993. As a result, the need for unemployment ceased to be accepted at all.

The most important change in the workers' attitudes is the collapse of the idea of a meritocracy and the rule of efficiency. They suspect that the working class is the first to pay the price of efficiency improvements in an organization. Frequently, the work improvements are rejected if there is a threat of redundancy – their primary aim is to conserve jobs. Increasing hostility to restructuring, which reduces the number of jobs, will be a basic constraint on the transformation.

The attitude of the working class to Polish capital has some contradictions. On the one hand, workers prefer Polish capital as an antidote to foreign capital. On the other hand, workers believe that in Poland wealth cannot be honestly acquired, so Poles cannot be true capitalists, but only speculators. The speculator, by definition, is not trustworthy as an employer.

The working class has been split into two important segments. Those with an enterprising spirit and higher skills have moved into the private sector for higher salaries. The rest (the majority) remain employed by state-owned companies, and are strongly affected by the recession and the restructuring of the economy. This section is now the greatest opponent of fast economic transformation and it also expresses anti-market attitudes.

The resistance against transformation is connected not only with the lowering of income, which is just one element of social degradation (Mokrzycki 1994). The working class of large industrial plants struggle not only for higher wages but for survival.

The differentiation and segmentation of the working class into interest groups does not prevent it from articulating its interests. They are showing up now in electoral behaviour, not only in a verbal way as under communism. In the working-class perspective, the chance provided by the prospering private sector for a shift to the middle class is only available to a small group. For example, privatization has been treated as a way to convert part of the working class into the middle class. However, the vast majority of the working class has positioned itself rather at the edge of the poverty class, or of those really afraid to slide down there.

8.1.3 THE PEASANTRY

The peasantry is the class with the strongest sense of identity. In political terms it is the strongest opponent of the transformation to liberal capitalism and a market economy. This class consists of different layers. The strongest opponents and main economic losers are former agricultural workers on state farms, which are now in liquidation or have already collapsed. The second layer is holders of small farms, particularly those who were working additionally in industry. The economic recession and transformation resulted in many industrial redundancies in this category, so that these workers became unemployed but had a small farm to maintain a relatively low standard of living. Under the new economic conditions, the large layer of owners of medium- and large-sized farms has been pressed to increase its efficiency, and some of them, unable to do this, are losers.

The peasants' behaviour can be divided into three strategies. The first group, representing 20–30% of peasants, has a more positive attitude to the market transformation. They treat their own activity in farming as a base for modernization. Over 55% of peasants have no real plans for the future, and their strategy is to ride out the crises and produce only for their own consumption. The third group, representing 8–10%, are withdrawing from agriculture.

8.2 The evolution of public opinion

Evaluation of the transformation could be accomplished by different "objective" statistical measures, or by indications of public opinion. I believe that the actual state of social consciousness is just as important as sophisticated statistical instruments. This could be partially revealed by questionnaire studies conducted over several years in Poland. This section has been based on surveys conducted by the Public Opinion Research Centre (CBOS) from 1991 to the first month of 1995. The aim is to identify the basic characteristics of the self-evaluation of society over the transformation, which seems to be crucial for any prediction of future development.

This type of survey is often treated as not reliable; the behaviour and opinion of society was frequently not predictable by politicians and commentators on the social and political life of Poland. Despite all the methodological and interpretive reservations about this kind of investigation, their results may reflect quite accurately the state of society.

Trying to answer the question of who gains and who loses in the transformation, we describe and interpret different surveys, providing sometimes direct, but more often indirect, answers. It must be borne in mind that the interpretation of questionnaire studies prepared to fulfil other objectives should be treated with caution. Assuming that the gainers will be satisfied by the transformation and the losers will not, the interpretations will be based on various general and more specific questions.

The state of consciousness inherited from the communist period still has some influence on the level on satisfaction. Describing this state, the important point seems to be two sets of stereotypes and myths.

The first set of myths concerns the relationship of society with the authorities. A very common belief is that authority is all powerful and that human beings have no influence on their life chances, resulting in the alienation of the majority of the population. This alienation is expressed as passive behaviour during elections.

The authorities, even if elected in a fully democratic way, are still treated as an enemy of the citizen. This attitude has long historical roots, dating from the nineteenth-century partition of Poland and, later, the imposed communist government. Under communism the opposition had one constant objective: to struggle with the government and with the existing system. This mind-set remains, and may now have even deepened in the new conditions extended. The mass media have contributed substantially to maintaining this attitude, usually presenting reality in the most depressing manner and overstating the worst elements, thus exacerbating the frustration and pessimism in the popular consciousness. Society is still under the strain of negative feelings towards the system emerging after the rejection of communism.

Responsibility for the many problems in everyday life and for the prosperity of citizens is also attributed to the authorities. The attitude of making claims on the state developed under communism has not vanished. Usually, those who have criticized the state most severely have succeeded in obtaining better salaries, subsidies and other privileges. The state was treated as being responsible for the distribution of wealth. So, access to power and authority was the main source of wealth, and one's own work and skill were of secondary importance.

The second set of myths is connected with egalitarian attitudes. Slogans such as "everybody has the same stomach" have become more and more popular. Rejection of differences in wealth arising from the input of one's own work dissuades those with greater initiative from making the effort. It is a common belief that enrichment by one's own work and enterprise is wrong and is against social justice. The prosperous man still arouses suspicion and hostile attitudes.

103

8.2.1 THE SOCIAL MOOD

In response to the most general question – "Has the general situation in Poland developed in a good or bad direction?" – the number of pessimists usually exceeds the number of optimists. Comparing the situation in November 1991, when this question was posed for the first time, to the latest answers, we see slight differences. Only 23% of respondents in 1991 and 28% in June 1994 evaluated the situation as good, and 58% and 53%, respectively, as bad. This general proportion radically changed only in May and June 1992, when the share of optimists fell to its lowest level of 11% and 10%, whereas the share of pessimists increased to 74% and 71%. This was during the collapse of the Olszewski government and the political crisis. The situation was reversed in December 1993, when the pessimist evaluation dropped to its lowest level of 30%, whereas the share who evaluated the situation of Poland positively (43%) for the first time overtook the pessimists; this was just after the parliamentary election won by left-wing parties, and the expected radical changes (Fig. 8.1).

This rise of optimism associated with an election has become the typical reaction of Polish society after each change of government. The sociologists interpret this as an expectation of a better life, which will be delivered from the top, not as a result of individual initiative. Since December 1993 social optimism dropped again, to March 1994, and since then has gradually increased but at a relatively low level. This slow increase in social optimism could be attributed to positive economic trends, such as the increase of production and the stabil-

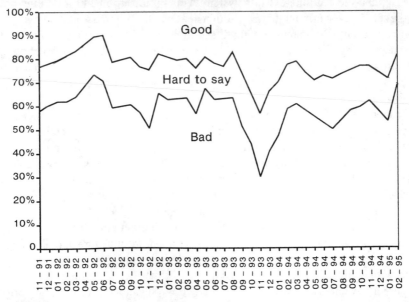

Figure 8.1 The social mood: has the general situation in Poland developed positively or negatively?

ization of unemployment, which people have begun to believe will continue.

The direct questionnaire studies of gainers and losers from the transformation distinguished between the perceptions of particular social groups and of general opinion. According to general opinion, the gainers are the owners of private companies, those employed in state administration, those employed in private firms, and former opposition activists from the 1980s. The highest price of free market transformation has been paid by unqualified workers, peasants, and manual workers with qualifications. Self-evaluation compares closely with general evaluation: the workers and farmers are conscious of having lost out most.

According to general opinion, the introduction of the free market is merely an opportunity for rich people; disparities between rich and ordinary citizens will increase in the future. Opinion is very clear. Only 5% believe that all people will have more wealth, whereas 88% believe that ordinary people will be poorer and poorer; that is, a tiny group will be more and more wealthy. The majority consider themselves to be part of the group that will be poorer in future.

The questionnaire studies (September, October, November 1992) indicate that 61% of respondents were living on the edge or below the social minimum accepted standard. Even if the respondents exaggerated and did not reveal their real income, the figure is very high. The estimation released by the Institute of Work for the same period evaluated the figure of those living below or at the edge of the social minimum standard as 40% of families.

The financial shortage caused different reactions: active or passive. The most common behaviour was passive, such as limiting spending and borrowing. Of 83% of families estimating their income as too low, only 15% wished to undertake additional work for the improvement of their financial situation (CBOS 1992a). This indicates the predominance of egalitarian and claiming attitudes in society.

The maintenance of an egalitarian attitude is also reflected in the questionnaire studies about "the rich in society" (CEBOS 1993a). First of all, in December 1992 more than 67% of respondents noticed the increase of rich people as compared with 1982. The majority (57%) of respondents evaluated this phenomenon positively whereas 23% evaluated it negatively. Now (1994), more frequently, society does not accept wealth differentiation; however, the groups representing "sensitiveness to wealth" remain minorities. Those that accept the extent of existing income inequalities represent 17% and those that do not account for only 9%. "Sensitiveness to wealth" depends more on the level of material wealth of respondents than on their personal attitudes to wealth differentiation in general. The notion of wealth is associated in public opinion with business and the emergence of a new middle class.

The evaluation of the origin of wealth is divided nearly equally between positive and negative characteristics. A slight majority of respondents attached intelligence, diligence, laboriousness, persistence, courage, venture, work and organizational talent to the origin of wealth, whereas 41% associate wealth with theft, smartness, swindles, scheming, smuggling, the use of political and administrative influence and gaps in the law.

The growing impoverishment of society could be reflected in the fact that 48% of respondents do not know anyone who can be considered as rich, whereas only 24% know one or two families like that and 27% know several rich people and families. Differences between the lowest and the highest salaries are negatively evaluated by 84% of respondents.

As a measure of social acceptance, a question about esteem and respect of wealthy people was asked. There were 30% positive answers and 45% negative. Only two groups have a opinion different from the predominant negative social attitude to wealth: the youngest group and wealthy respondents. For example, the level of acceptance of wealth is different according to the age of respondent and is twice as great in the youngest group than in the oldest.

One of the journals summarized the emerging new dimension of differentiation in Polish society as between those who are in Europe and those in the Third World. This is similar to the pre-war division between Poland "A" and "B" (west and east). The boundaries became visible in social and economic terms, in voting behaviour, and also at the regional scale; however, the regional dimension is still not as clear. The surveys indicated that the division between those satisfied and unsatisfied with the latest changes seems to be more stable throughout time.

Confrontation between gainers and losers is evident. Those satisfied, who gained from transformation, are in a minority. The losers comprise large groups of people, including those who were trying to maintain their jobs in collapsing factories or farms.

The "Polish phenomenon" is a split between economic status and satisfaction level. The average salaries in mining industries are very high, much higher than those of white-collar workers. However, the miners organized a strike. The September 1992 strikes were organized by the richest groups of workers, employed in factories without threat of staff cuts or economic problems. The Minister Jacek Kuroń interpreted this as a threat to their privileged positions in times of transformation of the whole economic system.

The workers employed in the largest socialist industries are now the most conservative group opposing free market transformation. They support the view that the state should organize production, guaranteeing employment, good economic conditions and good salaries. This view is supported by the most radical trade unions and by some political parties.

The unemployment rate in the groups with higher education is a third of the average for the whole country and a quarter of the population with vocational education. Surprisingly, the population with only primary education has adapted more quickly. One explanation is the so-called "pit rule", which suggests that those with vocational and secondary education (the core of the working class) and reasonable economic status remain in "the pit"; however, the well educated and wealthy people have enough knowledge and courage to abandon the old system and manage to adapt to transformation. The people with primary education and few job skills, who are the first to lose jobs, learn to behave very quickly without struggling against the trend. This explanation is partly confirmed by the fact that the greatest support for the transformation is in the youngest groups and elderly people.

The survey studies asked the question: "How in comparison with the situation five years ago do particular socioprofessional categories prosper today?" (CBOS 1994a). The following social categories are seen as better off: owners of private companies by 82% of respondents, priests by 73%, former opposition activists by 55%; directors and managers of state enterprises by 53%, and Solidarity activists by 48%. However, 87% of respondents believe that unskilled workers are now in a worse situation, and 70% believe that it is the case for peasants, 45% for teachers, and 53% for skilled workers.

In general, the transformations are seen as good for the economic, political and social elites. The elites are now perceived as the people connected with private business, that is, owners of companies and employers in the private sector: people controlling decisions and their associates. The outsiders are the rest of society.

8.2.2 THE PERCEPTION OF SOCIAL DIFFERENTIATION

The most frequent criterion of social differentiation is wealth (for 72% of respondents), whereas only 15% of respondents perceived class differentiation. Very low significance in differentiation has been attributed to education (only 7%) and profession or type of work (only 5%).

The wealth criterion was perceived by 40% as a rich/poor divide; 32% of respondents did not adopt a dichotomous view. This sort of perception has sometimes been interpreted as evidence of Polish capitalism evolving in the direction of Latin America, that is, consisting of a tiny financial elite, with the rest of society at the edge of poverty. Attitudes unconcerned about a divide could be interpreted as perception of the evolution towards a modern diversified society with a significant position for the middle class, in the western European model (CBOS 1995).

The survey studies from the end of 1994 (CBOS 1995), concerning the perception of personal position in society, indicate that only 1.5% of respondents locate themselves in the highest level of the hierarchy, with 19.4% at the very bottom. In total, 14% feel that they are above average, whereas 52% feel below average. Comparing this result with similar studies from 1987, a decrease in respondents locating themselves in the middle of the hierarchy and a marked increase of those locating themselves at the bottom has been observed. This indicates an increase in the gap between aspirations and the existing living conditions of the population. The system transformation has made a substantial contribution to this increase.

The survey of perceptions of the social structure indicates the formation of a new vision (CBOS 1995). Polish society is commonly perceived (for 44% of respondents) as a society with great social differentiation; with a narrow elite, small middle groups and a broad majority at the bottom. A quarter of respondents perceived social structure in the form of a classic pyramid with a broad base tapering slowly to the top, and 8% in a similar way but with a narrower group at the bottom.

In total, over three quarters of the respondents perceived social structure in a way that placed the majority at the bottom. The most surprising finding is, however, the lack of differentiation in opinion according to the income level, or other sociodemographic characteristics of respondent. It indicates that this perception is shared by all social categories (CBOS 1995).

In general, one can conclude that following the transformation the social structure is more frequently perceived as exclusive, and the share of those who perceive it as egalitarian has radically decreased.

8.2.3 THE PERCEPTION OF CONFLICTS

The perception of the most important conflicts in Poland has substantially changed. The conflict inside the authority structure is perceived by respondents as increasing; from 16% in 1990, to 33% in 1992 and to 46% in 1994. The former basic conflict under communism, between society and authority, which was the source of the transformation in 1998, has again come to be perceived as important. It has increased from the lowest position of 4% of respondents in 1990, to 23% in 1992, and 20% in 1994 (CBOS 1992b, 1994a).

A new phenomenon of perceived conflicts in Poland is the belief that the most important conflict is between rich and poor. This opinion is held by an increasing proportion of respondents: 4% in 1990, to 9% in 1992 and to 21% in 1994.

The most important conflict, according to public opinion surveys, is political. The high percentage (46%) who treat conflict inside authority as most important indicates the continuation of confusion and frustration and general rejection of state policy and politicians. The latest parliamentary elections have not changed the situation. The perception of existing conflict inside the political elite became even stronger in 1994.

The surveys from the end of 1994 show how strong particular conflicts are. For 67% of respondents, the conflicts between rulers and ruled is "strong" or "very strong". A high proportion (62% of respondents) perceived strong and very strong conflicts between those at the top and at the bottom of the social hierarchy. The conflict between rich and poor as strong is perceived by 16% and as very strong by 39% of respondents. Also, a very strong or strong conflict is perceived between managers and workers by 48% of respondents; however, 47% of respondents evaluate conflict between the working class and middle class as not so strong, and for only 24% it is strong.

In general, the intensity of the particular conflicts has increased during the past few years. The greatest increase in intensity of conflict occurred between rich and poor, and between managers and workers.

8.2.4 THE EVALUATION OF TRANSFORMATION

The vision of the transformation is not optimistic. The gainers are the social categories perceived as the new elite. The losers are the workers, peasants and employees in the state sector or public administration. The position of individuals in society is shaped to an increasing extent by level of wealth, and this is a source of increasing conflict.

Most people are in favour of the substance of the transformation. To the direct question: "Was it worth changing the political system in Poland five years ago?", 60% of respondents reacted positively, 29% negatively, and 11% didn't know.

In spite of the worsening of living conditions, the majority accept the change of political system; however, they estimate that life under communism was better. The scale of support is strongly correlated with the level of income. Generally, the higher the income the higher percentage are supporters of the changes, reaching 78% for the income categories of 22 259 000 zl per household member. Similarly, the higher the educational level or professional status, the higher the acceptance of the changes. For example, 82% of people with higher education positively evaluate the changes, and only 47% of those with primary education. It is also characteristic that if we divide the respondents into political orientation categories of "left", "centrist" and "right", 82% of those representing the rightist attitude react positively to changes in the political system, 63% of centrist supporters and 50% of these with left-wing political attitudes.

The losers in the changes, the poorly educated people without entrepreneurial attitudes and the economically non-active, feel that they are marginalized. According to CBOS, this belief is so popular that it is surprising to find a high level of support for the transformation.

8.2.5 RELIGION IN PUBLIC PERCEPTION

Being a Catholic became the most important criterion of Polish identity over the past two centuries, particularly during the nineteenth-century partition of Poland and during the Second World War. This type of combined national and religious identity was strengthened by the post-war struggle of communism with religion and the unsuccessful attempt to gain control over the Catholic Church. The Catholic faith created the distinction between "we = Catholic = Poles" and "they = communists". The level of religious commitment declined, however, and in the 1960s and 1970s only three-quarters of Poles described themselves as Catholic. The declining tendency was reversed in the mid-1970s, and the process of returning to Catholicism become evident, particularly among the intelligentsia (Grabowska 1994). This process was strengthened by the appointment of a Polish bishop from Cracow, Karol Wojtyla, to the Papacy.

The collapse of communism in Poland created a new situation for the Church as an institution in relation to the democratic state and the new transformation processes. The unquestionable support of the Church for the democratic transformation gave it a crucial role at the beginning. For many Poles the Church became the power that ruled over the country, and its position in politics and public life became questioned by deep believers.

The rise of interest in religion and the attitude of Poles to the different issues connected with religion can be described by questionnaire studies. "Religiosity" has been measured in different ways and the methodology has been changing through time. In the first research conducted by CBOS in 1984, the basic question was posed: "What is your attitude to religion and religious practice?" In response, 70% of the population declared its faith as regularly practising, 20% declared its faith as not practising, 8% declared themselves atheists, and 2% practising religiously in spite of being atheist (CBOS 1994b).

Between March 1986 and February 1992 CEBOS conducted comparative research that provides reliable material for estimating religiosity and its evolution. The general conclusion is an increase in religiosity between 1986 and 1989. Between 1990 and 1992 there was a period of fluctuation in the practising of religion. The highest period of practising was in 1990–91.

Differentiation at the regional scale, measured by the percentage of pupils attending religion classes in primary school, is very visible, particularly between the rural east and the centre as compared with the more secular west and urban areas (Fig. 8.2).

In 1992 over 95% of Polish society considered itself as Catholic and 2% identified with other religions. In spite of the fact that 97% of Poles declared their faith, only 77% had communion once a year, 83% wished to send their children to religious classes in school, 31% had contact with its parish church (excluding masses), and 37% has contact with a Catholic priest. The religious rules and principles, however, have been treated less rigorously. Over 48% were against a ban on divorce, whereas only 43% treated this as good; 56% were against abortion prohibition and believed that abortion should be legal, whereas only 29% support prohibition; 69% was again prohibition of contraceptives and 54% accepted premarital sex (CBOS 1994c). These figures suggest that the religiosity of Poles is very selective.

The perception of the activity and role of the Church in the social life of the country has evolved very radically. In 1992 more than 82% of respondents rejected the involvement of the Church in political life, and 68% were against shows of religiosity by employees of the state administration. This indicates the separation in people's consciousness of the spheres of religious life and public life. The activity of the Catholic Church reached nearly 87% acceptance in the late 1980s. This reflects the positive opinion in the first years of transformation; the later decline was probably the result of the change in opinion about the Church under the new system. Since 1989, however, approval has dropped substantially, to its lowest level of 46% in November 1992, and stabilized afterwards at 54%. However, 34% of Catholics in April 1994 had a poor opinion of Church activity. A large majority of respondents are against the political role of the Church, and support the idea of separation of religious from public life (CBOS 1994b).

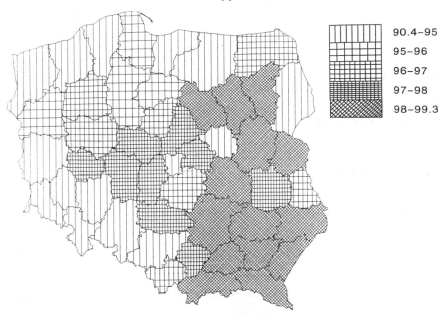

	90.4–95
	95–96
	96–97
	97–98
	98–99.3

Figure 8.2 Pupils attending religion classes at schools as a percentage of total pupils in 1998. Source: *Rocznik statystyczny* 1991, p. 53.

The conflict over the concordat between Poland and the Vatican has been rather ignored. According to a poll, over one-third treat this problem as having no impact on the average citizen, and nearly 50% have no opinion.

The Catholicism of Poles is based in general on religious practices, but also, in the light of public opinion polls, seems to be to a large extent based on historical and customary social behaviour and spiritual symbols. This conclusion could also be supported by a survey published in October 1994, about the institutionalization of religious values in social life. According to this survey, Polish society could be divided into two more-or-less equal "traditional" and "secular" groups. Only slightly more than half of Poles support the view that religious lessons should be introduced in public school. This proportion has not changed from November 1992 to July 1994, in spite of the fact that the permanent presence of religious teachers and priests in schools has become normal. Also, the changes in views about abortion are not significant (CBOS 1994c).

The general idea of the place of religious values in the state is split into two options: traditional, characterized by the acceptance of the role of the Church, and secular, which separates Church involvement and religious values from the state. The conclusion of this analysis is that the traditional and the secular are nearly equal. The largest proportion of society (29%) represents a moderate secular option, and a slightly smaller group (25%) represent a moderate traditional option. However, relatively high proportions represents an extreme traditional option (17%), and an extreme secular option (17%).

The past few years of gradual decline of religiosity, secularization of Catholic tradition and ceremonies, and the very selective attitude of Poles to the Ten Commandments, indicate together that the notion of Poles as a Catholic nation in the heart of Europe is partly a myth. Also improbable is the prediction, based on the "demonstrative" increase in religiosity of the late 1980s, that Poland has became the source of a revival of Christianity in Europe. If the imposed communist system, together with urbanization and industrialization, created the first phase of secularization of Polish society, the last years of transformation to democracy could be treated as a second phase of secularization. The evangelization endeavours of the Church are partly reduced by this secularization.

CHAPTER 9

The new political structure

Electoral behaviour is a "new" element of regional differentiation. It is new in the sense that, for the first time since the Second World War, we have been able to reveal the politically differentiated structure of Poland's space. This has deep roots in the economic and social history of particular regions. The geography of electoral results since 1989 provides a reliable source of information and becomes an additional tool for the interpretation and description of regional differentiation. The explanation of voting behaviour is usually based on a whole range of social, economic, demographic, and psychological phenomena. It also includes an analysis of perceptions, attitudes, emotions and value systems.

An important component in understanding the new political structure of Polish society is the analysis of the emerging party system and the spatial differentiation of voting behaviour. This concerns both national and regional scales. The spatial distributions of the supporters of different political options have become important elements in the general social characteristics of given areas. Electoral geography has become an important element in the prediction of the future transformation towards a democracy and market-oriented economy.

9.1 The parliamentary election of 1989

The first almost democratic and unfettered parliamentary election since the Second World War was arranged for 4 June 1989. It was the result of an agreement, after the Round Table negotiation, between the ruling Communist Party (PZPR) and the democratic opposition represented mostly by Solidarity leaders.

It was agreed that 35% (of all 460 seats) of parliamentary (Sejm) members would be elected on the basis of free competition, whereas 60% would be reserved for communists and their alliance parties, that is, the United Peasant Party and Democratic Party; the rest (5%) would be reserved for Catholic organizations. The election to the newly established Upper House (Senate) would be completely free. Two groups of mandates were formed: the first for the communist coalition, and the second for the non-communist coalition and candidates of Solidarity. The electoral contract, however, did not determine that all mandates of the non-communist coalition would be allocated to Solidarity. The communists believed that at least some of those places would be gained by communist supporters (Raciborski 1991).

In this way the communists guaranteed for themselves substantial political control over the future government and political situation of the country.

During this election, no real choice was offered of any realistic economic programme or shape of the future political system. For the opposition represented by Solidarity, the crucial issues were the rejection of communism and the introduction of very general democratic and market-oriented reforms. From the very beginning, it was a sort of national referendum on the basic question of being for or against communism.

The main forces – Solidarity from the democratic opposition side and the Polish United Workers Party (PZPR) from the communist side – had no reliable knowledge of the degree of social support for their political options. The result of the election had been unanticipated by either side: for Solidarity, the extent of victory and for the communists, the extent of defeat. Of 100 seats in the Senate (upper house of Parliament), Solidarity won 99, and one was gained by an independent candidate. In the Sejm (lower house) the results were: communists (PZPR) 173, the United Peasant Party 76, the Democratic Party 27, and the Catholic organizations 23 seats. Solidarity won 161 seats. It is important to stress that only 5 candidates of the communist coalition won a majority, from 295 seats reserved for them in the Sejm.

This parliamentary election, although not genuinely democratic because it was to an extent predetermined at the Round Table negotiation, was the legal basis for a peaceful transformation, abandoning the communist system in Poland. The direct result was the formation of the first non-communist government in this part of Europe.

9.2 The presidential election of 1990

A fully democratic power structure was created as a result of the next elections: the local government election of 27 May 1990, the presidential election of 25 November (first ballot) and 9 December 1990 (second ballot). However, the most important were the parliamentary elections of 27 October 1991, the first fully free election at this level in 60 years.

The electoral success in 1989 gave the Solidarity elite considerable autonomy in determining the future development of the country. At that time there were few rivals, and other political structures were weak. The communist elite had disintegrated and the opposition political groups that had not participated in the Round Table negotiations were at that time at the margin of political life (Wasilewski 1992). The candidates from the opposition-side list, the alternative to Solidarity, had not received a single seat. The election was also a referendum in favour of Solidarity (Wiatr 1993). However, this situation did not last long; Solidarity was finally split, post-communist groups (i.e. most of the new left) were consolidated, and other political fractions emerged or re-established themselves in the political arena.

114

The results of all the next four elections were very surprising for the political elites representing particular political options, for researchers and for journalists. This could be partly explained by the speed of social transformations in Poland, but above all by lack of information about the real preferences of society. The failure to anticipate the behaviour of electorates was also explained by disorientation and by social and political anomie. Additionally, the party system, not yet mature and only partially reflecting the political differentiation of society, contributed to the unpredictability of future voting behaviour. This system had been under constant construction and reconstruction.

The dichotomy between Solidarity and communism had slowly become less important. Three major tendencies were visible in the political arena. The first concerned the split of the Solidarity movement, the second the re-establishment of post-communist forces, and the third the formation of interest-group oriented parties. The phenomenon common to all the tendencies was the abandonment or diminishing importance of values in favour of interests.

After the unquestionable victory of Solidarity in the Parliamentary election of 4 June 1989, and in the local government election of 26 May, there was a systematic decrease of Solidarity's support during the following elections. This tendency began at the end of 1990, during the first direct presidential election. The victory of Solidarity in 1989 was obvious. However, if one evaluates the Solidarity support as a percentage of the whole electorate, it turns out that nationwide it was between 33% and 38%. During the presidential election in 1990 the two Solidarity candidates together gained the support of 34.6% of the whole electorate. Additionally, in the second ballot Wałęsa was supported by 38.7% of the total electorate (Jasiewicz 1991). This can also lead to the interpretation that, in reality, Solidarity never received active support from more than 40% of the total population.

The sizeable decrease of support for Solidarity was connected with an important decrease in popularity of the first non-communist government, which was quite unable to solve all the economic problems inherited from 40 years of communist rule. An important factor in this decrease was disagreement within the Solidarity camp.

The results of the presidential election, particularly the first run (25 November 1990), were surprising at that time. There were six candidates, and five of them received more than one million votes: those of Solidarity – Lech Wałęsa, Tadeusz Mazowiecki, Roman Bartoszcze; post-communist and left-wing candidate Włlodzimierz Cimoszewicz; the leader of oldest opposition party (under the communist system) outside the Solidarity camp – Leszek Moczulski; and, unexpectedly, Stanisław Tymiński, a Polish businessman from Canada.

The winner was a representative of Solidarity, Lech Wałęsa, gaining 40% of votes in the first run (at 60.6% participation), and 74.3% of votes in the second run (at 53.4% participation). The success of "the man from nowhere", Stanisław Tymiński, who received 23.1% of votes, was a great surprise. Another Solidarity candidate, former prime minister of the first non-communist government, Tadeusz Mazowiecki, received 18.1% of votes and was eliminated from the second run.

115

Unexpectedly large support was gained by the candidate of the post-communist camp, Włodzimierz Cimoszewicz, who was supported by 9.2% of voters.

At the regional scale, Lech Wałęsa had the largest support in southern and central parts of the country, in addition to the Gdańsk voivodship (Fig. 9.1). Wałęsa had the absolute majority in 10 voivodships. These were the same voivodships that gave the highest support during the 1989 parliamentary election. Stanisław Tymiński had the largest support north of Warsaw and in most industrialized voivodships of Silesia (Fig. 9.2). Tadeusz Mazowiecki was supported in larger proportions in western voivodships, particularly in Poznań and Szczecin, and in the south only in Cracow (Fig. 9.3). Włodzimierz Cimoszewicz, the communist candidate, was supported mostly in northern and eastern voivodships. He obtained particular support in Białystok voivodship, inhabited partly by a Belorussian minority (27.2%).

In the second run of the presidential election, Lech Wałęsa competed only with Stanisław Tymiński. He gained additional support in all voivodships and as a result had more than 58% of votes. The regional pattern of support was similar to the first run (Fig. 9.4). Stanisław Tymiński obtained less support in 16 voivodships and a substantial increase of support (over 10%) in 9 voivodships. On the regional scale, the changes in Tymiński's support indicated a north–south polarization, except for the larger agglomerations.

A specific feature of this election was the social heterogeneity of each of the three main candidates' supporters in general. However, several trends were evident in the composition of supporters: Lech Wałęsa gained the greatest support from

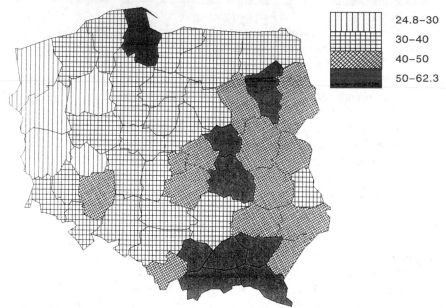

24.8–30
30–40
40–50
50–62.3

Figure 9.1 Support for Lech Wałęsa (% of votes), first ballot 25 November 1990.

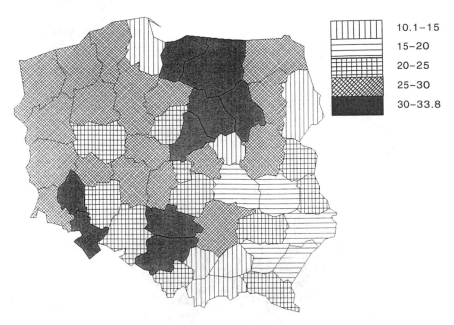

Figure 9.2 Support for Stanisław Tymiński (% of votes), first ballot 25 November 1990.

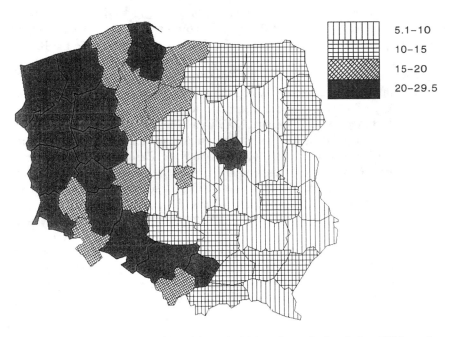

Figure 9.3 Support for Tadeusz Mazowiecki (% of votes), first ballot 25 November 1990.

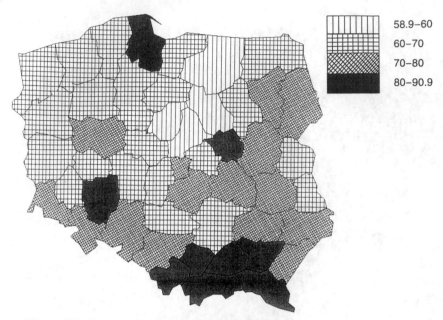

⬛ vertical lines	58.9–60
⬛ grid	60–70
⬛ cross-hatch	70–80
⬛ solid	80–90.9

Figure 9.4 Support for Lech Wałęsa (% of votes), second ballot 9 December 1990.

elderly groups and people with only basic education and with lower incomes. Stanisław Tymiński was supported predominantly by inhabitants of small urban places, people with vocational education and the youngest groups. In the 18–25 year old age group the winner was Stanisław Tymiński, not Lech Wałęsa.

Tadeusz Mazowiecki, the second Solidarity candidate, was supported mostly by inhabitants of large cities and by population with higher education. More than half of the votes for Mazowiecki come from cities larger than 100 000 people. For sociologists, the electorate of Tadeusz Mazowiecki became a new phenomenon in the political arena of Poland and was sometimes named as urban professionals (Jasiewicz 1992). Among people with university education, 35% were Mazowiecki supporters, 15% for Wałęsa and only 5% for Tymiński. This sort of social polarization occurred for the first time; before then all social categories were represented on both sides of normally dichotomous political groups. The supporters of Tadeusz Mazowiecki became the first social group where a political position was defined by social position and interests, not by value system and symbols.

The supporters of Włodzimierz Cimoszewicz were supporters of the former communist system. The supporters of Roman Bartoszcze, the fifth candidate, who received more than 1 million votes, had obvious rural origins.

9.3 The parliamentary election 1991

The parliamentary election of 27 October 1991 for the first time posed the electorate a real choice between different programmes. A characteristic feature of this election and the political situation, however, was the fact that particular parties were able only partly to express the real interests of particular groups. All political parties were trying to represent the interests of the whole nation. As a result of this attitude the political parties were not transparent and did not represent clearly distinctive features. The absence of a very stable political structure representing clearly defined economic interests of particular social groups coincided with the lack of a permanent political orientation of the majority of the electorate. In this situation, abstention from voting was very common.

A diversity of political proposals, together with tiredness, confusion and frustration on the part of the electorate, resulted in a very low participation rate (43.2%). The psychological state of society was referred to by some sociologists as political anomie. Before this parliamentary election only around 30–35% of Poles expressed a relatively stable political orientation in voting behaviour (Raciborski 1991).

With this election, the Polish electorate saw for the first time the relationship between voting behaviour, the creation of economic programmes, and the actual functioning of the elected government afterwards. Hitherto, this sort of relationship had never existed, which was one of the reasons for decreasing participation in successive elections. Low participation was not a great tragedy, merely one element of normality, particularly if we take into consideration the fact that, for the first time since the communist rule, people regained the right to stay at home at elections. In the 1980s, non-attendance at an election had a substantial political meaning: it was one of the very few ways to express one's political disapproval of the communist system. In general, people who participated in the election represented, disproportionately, the population with higher education, professionals, people of an economically active age, and inhabitants of larger towns.

The basic result of the election was the negation of both the pace and the extent of the transformations to a market economy, and also, in part, the direction of those transformations. The worsening economic situation, the high price of the reforms and the consolidation of interest groups against the transformations, together with the loss of patience by society, resulted in a constant erosion of political support for the Solidarity movement, which had in popular opinion been responsible for the last years of transformations.

The election finally demonstrated the disappearance of the political division of Polish society between "us" (Solidarity), and "them" (communists). The post-Solidarity groups gained decreasing support in successive elections. This support, in terms of percentage, was relatively stable, at around 50%, but in a situation of declining participation. This parliamentary election definitively destroyed the myth of a Solidarity society. Altogether the supporters of the Democratic Union, Liberal-Democratic Congress and Centrum Alliance attracted only 35% of the votes, in absolute numbers fewer than 4 million inhabitants, or only 14% of the electorate.

The first elections had been shaped by the issue of abandonment of the communist system. During this election, anti-communist slogans were of minor significance. The negative stereotypes of post-communist forces to a great extent ceased to exist. The election indicated the process of consolidation of anti-transformation forces based on group interests: groups with their privileges and interests rooted in the centrally planned economy. Some politicians even claimed that, if the political structure represented real group interests, it would result in a complete standstill of further reforms. Overall, that seemed to threaten radical economic transformations in combination with a parliamentary democracy.

The winner of the election was the Democratic Union (UD), which gained 12.31% of votes, supported mostly by people with higher education and particularly the intelligentsia and students. It was supported also by a self-employed group, particularly younger businessmen. Regionally, this party gained the greatest support in the western part of the country and in large urban agglomerations. UD received the largest share of the support in 10 electoral districts (Fig. 9.7).

The post-communist Democratic Left Alliance (SLD) received the second position (11.98%), and became the second largest party in the parliament. This alliance gained support from an electorate similar to the Democratic Union, except for a larger share of workers; it was mainly the intelligentsia and the inhabitants of larger towns. The difference was that SLD electorate voted for a communist candidate Włodzimierz Cimoszewicz or for Stanisław Tymiński during presidential election, whereas supporters of Democratic Union voted for Tadeusz Mazowiecki (Żukowski 1992). The largest share gained by this Alliance was in 10 electoral districts located in northern and western parts of the country and in the region of Białystok and working-class areas of Sosnowiec and Łódź (Fig. 9.5).

The third place, with 9.74% of votes, went to the Electorate Catholic Action (WAK) and particularly The Christian National Union, which received the highest share in three electoral districts but with the greatest support gained mostly in eastern parts of the country. The supporters of this political group consisted mostly of the elderly population and those with only basic education. The majority of this electorate had been supporters of Lech Wałęsa during the presidential election.

The Civic Centrum Alliance (POC), having 8.71% of votes, gained its greatest support in the southeastern part of the country, but they won only in the Warsaw region (except for the city of Warsaw) and in the Nowy Sącz voivodship. The supporters of this alliance were mostly those who had voted for Lech Wałęsa during the first-run presidential election or more generally were mostly from the urban population. They represented partly the pro-Wałęsa white-collar worker faction of the intelligentsia.

The Confederation for an Independent Poland (KPN) was supported mainly by workers and by the younger generation and by white-collar workers without university education. This party, with 7.5% of votes, gained the largest share of the electorate in one district (Lublin voivodship), but generally the greatest support

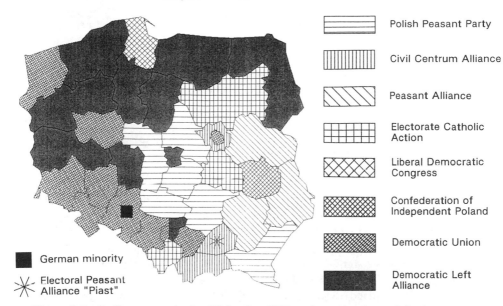

German minority

Electoral Peasant
Alliance "Piast"

Polish Peasant Party

Civil Centrum Alliance

Peasant Alliance

Electorate Catholic
Action

Liberal Democratic
Congress

Confederation of
Independent Poland

Democratic Union

Democratic Left
Alliance

Figure 9.5   Parliamentary election 27 October 1991 – winners by electoral districts.

was in the southern parts of the country in both rural and industrial areas. KPN received relatively strong support in the Szczecin voivodship.

The Liberal-Democratic Congress (KLD) was ruling during the last year before the election, and as a consequence was seen as responsible for the successes and failures of the contemporary transformations. It received only 7.49% of votes. The greatest support was gained from intelligentsia and students. Regionally, KLD succeeded only in the Gdańsk district, but relatively strong support was gained in the largest urban agglomerations.

The Polish Peasant Party (the former communist alliance party), having 8.67% of votes, was the winner in rural areas and was supported by one-third of the total peasant electorate. This party also beat the pro-Solidarity Peasant Alliance, with 5.47% of votes.

The many other political parties and coalitions obtained very little support. Over 5% of votes went to the Peasant Alliance and 5.05% to Solidarity as a trade union.

During this election an ethnic minority was visible for the first time. In one electoral district, Opole, the winner was the German minority, in front of the Democratic Union. On the national scale the German minority received 1.18% of votes. Because of political fragmentation and spatial dispersion, other minorities had no influence on the final results.

The parliament elected in October 1991 very quickly became unrepresentative of the power structure and the preferences of society. The coalitions and political structures in parliament were reconstructed, by creation of new alliances and shifting members of parliament between factions, or by the creation of new political groups. This also indicated the low level of identification of parliamentary members with their electorates. As a result, between December 1991 and June 1993 the prestige of parliament, government and political parties, as measured in public opinion polls, dropped considerably (Gebethner 1993). At that time, most political parties were losing support; only PSL maintained support, whereas SdRP gained substantial increase in support.

9.4 The parliamentary election of 1993

Only six political parties and coalitions gained parliamentary seats (four seats were reserved for the German minority). First place, with 20.41% of votes and 171 seats (37.17%) went to the Democratic Left Alliance (SLD). Second place went to the Polish Peasant Party (PSL), with 15.5% of votes and 132 seats (28.69%). The leader in the parliamentary election of 1991, the Democratic Union (UD), gained 10.59% of votes and 74 seats (16.08%). The second left-wing party, the Labour Union (UP), received 7.28% of votes and 41 seats (8.91%). The Confederation of Independent Poland (KPN) and the Non-party Bloc for Support of Reforms (BBWR) got 5.77% and 4.41% of votes, and 22 (4.78%) and 16 (3.47%) of seats respectively.

The Senate was more differentiated; however, of 100 seats, the SLD had 37, and PSL 36.

The spectacular success of the SLD was based on doubling its number of supporters as compared with the 1991 parliamentary elections, and on the amplifying effect of the new electoral law that reduced the number of parties in parliament. The Polish Peasant Party (PSL) also doubled its support, and became the second largest party in parliament. Thus, two parties of post-communist origin received an absolute majority, having together 65.86% seats in the Sejm. The Democratic Union (UD) in general maintained similar (2% smaller) support as in the 1991 election, but was pushed into opposition in spite of the fact that it received more parliamentary seats. The Labour Union achieved a strong position in the political arena, having the support of more than 1 million voters, and became the fourth largest party in parliament. The Confederation of Independent Poland, in spite of losses as compared with 1991, maintained its position in parliament. The new political formation initiated by President Lech Wałęsa, the Non-party Bloc of Support for Reforms, became the weakest political formation in parliament.

The result of this election caused confusion and frustration among transformation supporters. The first interpretation, and the most popular explanation, held that the right was beaten because it was divided, whereas the left was united. The damaging conflict in the post-Solidarity camp (started by the war at the top) and too great involvement of the Church in policy were also mentioned.

The results of the election were widely evaluated as not good for Poland and have been compared with the return of communists to political influence in Italy and France in the 1950s and 1960s. The results were treated as a protest of part of society against the erosion of its standard of living, political errors of the right, and particularly the strong internal divisions. Additionally, the results stemmed from a reduced appreciation of differences between the communist past and the present democratic conditions. Insufficient support of the democratic transformation in Poland by Western democracies has also been mentioned.

One of the expected consequences of the election results was reinforcement of the old communist nomenclature and a slowing down of the transformation. In international economic comparative perspective, in 1992 and 1993 Poland finally became the leader of the transformation, the only central European country with economic growth. The results of the election could reverse this with a damaging effect on the economy. For example, a frequently raised issue is that the results of the election would be used by the European Union as an excuse for the imposition of trade restrictions with Poland, slowing down the integration process and the reducing the chance of Poland joining NATO. The question was raised whether the anti-communist tendency would now be replaced by anti-Solidarity.

It is often said that the government of the PSL is particularly dangerous for the Polish economy, because of its unique character as a class-oriented party, serving the interests of peasants and small agricultural holdings. It inevitably leads to more restrictions on food imports, and price increases.

Many reacted to the election result with surprise, and a frequently asked question was whether Poles were able to forget so quickly how communism worked. The result must be interpreted also in terms of the shift of political opinion and in terms of the new election law. Both those had substantial influence on the final result. The new electoral law amplified the shift of public opinion to the left. The introduction of the new law was the result of the bad experience of the first fully democratic parliament of 1991, frequently paralyzed by political fragmentation (i.e. of 29 political parties). According to the new law, the opportunity to enter is open only to those parties who can cross the 5% barrier of the vote, and 8% for coalitions, and the 7% barrier for political groups that will participate in the proportional distribution of seats from national lists. This barrier does not address national minorities' lists. The electoral law, based on a proportional system, provided preferential distribution of parliamentary seats to the larger political parties.

The smallest political parties, with less than the minimum 5% support, in sum received 4 727 972 votes. These votes were lost in parliamentary representation, yet they represented 34.5% of all those participating in the election. These were primarily for the right-wing political parties. The theoretical "right-wing alliance" had 19.4% in total, that is, support nearly equal to that of the Democratic Left Alliance (SLD).

In general, the parliamentary election indicated the radical shift of political preferences of Poles to the left. In political terms, the parliament was, however, more left-oriented than society as a whole (Wiatr 1993). The supporters of SLD and UD represent partly similar social categories. Both parties were generally supported by populations with better education and living in larger settlements as compared with supporters of other parties.

123

In order to evaluate the congruence between the policy of the winning parties and the political views of their supporters from the parliamentary election of 1993, a survey was carried out by CBOS (1993b). The supporters of SLD were distinguished from others by more frequent membership of the former Communist Party, low religious activity, higher than average education, settlement in larger cities, and a critical attitude to privatization.

The supporters of PSL, as a peasant party, were more radically differentiated from other electorates. The key characteristics were the low level of education, low average income per family, and more religious behaviour.

The Democratic Union was supported by the educated population with a positive attitude to transformation. In general, its supporters were wealthier than average, expected an improvement in the economic situation and its chances in future, expressed satisfaction from functioning democracy and were convinced that the present system is better than the former. The Democratic Union supporters had liberal and less egalitarian attitudes than supporters of other parties. In the final analysis, the CBOS indicated that UD supporters were people with higher education and were satisfied with democracy in Poland.

The supporters of the Labour Union (UP) shared the general views characteristic of left-wing parties; however, attitudes to economic issues were not so consistent. For example, UP supporters wanted more active involvement of the state in the economy, yet disagreed with full employment policy. This is typically a party of town people.

The Non-party Bloc of Support for Reforms (BBWR) was supported by the most liberal electorate. As a "presidential" party, it supported the idea of allocating more power to the President. Its supporters more frequently backed privatization and closing down inefficient factories, and were satisfied with the contemporary democratic system. This political coalition, formed just before the election, eroded support for the Liberal-Democratic Congress (KLD).

In the 1993 parliamentary election, the basic division of the electorate appeared as social categories, as various surveys and general observations indicate. The post-communist SLD gained greater support from all social groups. The greatest increase of support came from workers, medium-level specialists, professional groups and the retired. The Democratic Union, although losing support in all social categories, had the greatest losses among the intelligentsia, which partly moved its support for left-wing parties primarily to the Labour Union (UP) and Democratic Left Alliance (SLD).

The Polish Peasant Party (PSL) gained increased support from all social groups, absolutely dominating the rural areas and becoming a typical class party representing the interests of peasants. The other peasant party of post-Solidarity origin, the Popular Alliance (PL), lost most of its supports in favour of PSL.

All other major political parties and coalitions from the 1991 election were losers in 1993. Even the Liberal Democratic Congress (KLD) partly lost its support from the self-employed and businessmen.

The regional pattern has not changed very much. We can observe substantial continuity, since 1989, of the spatial preference for particular political options (Fig. 9.6). The distribution of participation in elections is, for example, in general the same as participation in all elections since 1989. The better developed voivodships with a tradition of self-government and political activism were generally characterized by a greater participation rate (Fig. 9.7). The only exception is the Katowice and Opole voivodships. All central parts, the northeast and the territories along the border participated less.

The national-scale winner, the SLD, was also the winner in 26 voivodships (out of 49), located in northern and western parts of the country, plus the Warsaw and Łódź agglomerations (Fig. 9.7). The greatest support gained by the SLD (over 30%) was in Włocławek voivodship, and over 25% in the northwestern part (Fig. 9.8) – the areas where during the 1991 parliamentary election it was also the winner, although with no more than 20% support.

The Polish Peasant Party was the winner in the most rural and underdeveloped areas in the central and southeastern parts of the country. The PSL got more than 25% of the vote in all voivodships surrounding Warsaw and in the south (Fig. 9.9), generally the areas with the strongest individual and traditional agriculture.

The Democratic Union (UD) was the winner in only two voivodships: Cracow and Poznań. It had relatively more support in southern parts of the country, in Silesia and in Pomerania together with Warsaw and Łódź; however, in the rest of the country it received below 10%, or even 5%, of votes (Fig. 9.10). The Labour Union (UP), competing for the same electorate as the SLD and UD, received relatively large support in Warsaw, Łódź and Poznań, and in the industrial region of

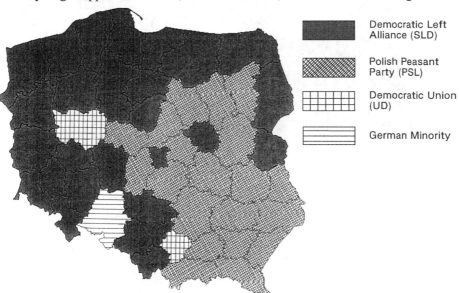

Democratic Left
Alliance (SLD)

Polish Peasant
Party (PSL)

Democratic Union
(UD)

German Minority

Figure 9.6 Parliamentary election 19 September 1993 – winners by voivodships.

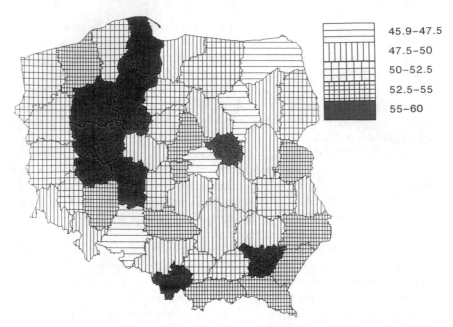

Figure 9.7 Electoral attendance (%), parliamentary election of 19 September 1993.

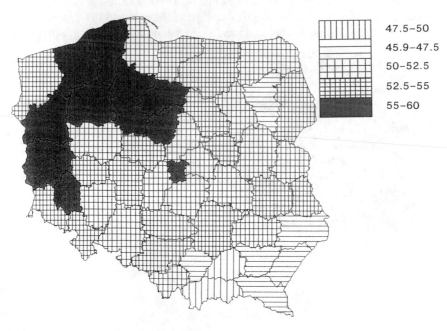

Figure 9.8 Support for Democratic Left Alliance (%), parliamentary election of 19 September 1993.

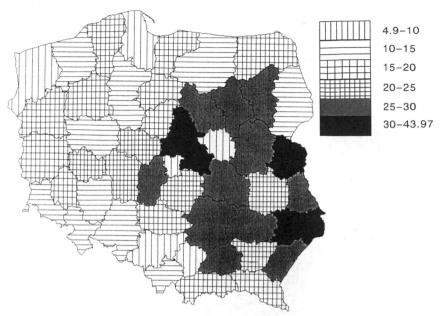

	4.9–10
	10–15
	15–20
	20–25
	25–30
	30–43.97

Figure 9.9 Support for Polish Peasant Party (%), parliamentary election of 19 September 1993.

Legnica and the very rapidly declining areas of Walbrzych (Fig. 9.11). The Confederation of Independent Poland (KPN) marked its presence in the regional structure of Poland in the southern and southeast parts of the country (Fig. 9.12), with the larger share of support, over 10% of votes, in Cracow and Bielsko–Biala voivodships. The BBWR gained relatively good support in the south – Nowy Sącz and Bielsko–Biala voivodeships (Fig. 9.13).

The rest of the political parties usually had fewer than 10% of the votes in each voivodship. Only the Electorate Catholic Committee "Homeland" (Ojczyzna) obtained more than 10% support in the northeast of Warsaw and in the four Carpathian voivodships. The Liberal-Democratic Congress (KLD) received 10.8% in Gdańsk; the Self-Defence Committee of Lepper received more than 10% of support in its homeland voivodships of Koszalin and Slupsk; in Opole voivodship, the German minority got 18.9%.

9.4.1 THE REACTION OF POLISH SOCIETY TO THE RESULTS OF THE LATEST ELECTIONS

The best sources available to describe the reaction of Polish society to the results of the 1993 election, and particularly the success of the post-communist camp, are the CBOS studies from October 1993 (CBOS 1993c). The success of the SLD has been predictable, but the scale of the victory and the scale of the catastrophe for the right-wing parties was a surprise.

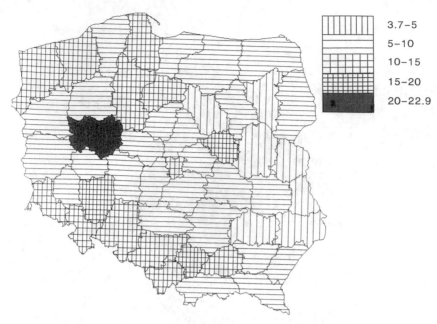

	3.7–5
	5–10
	10–15
	15–20
	20–22.9

Figure 9.10 Support for Democratic Union (%), parliamentary election of 19 September 1993.

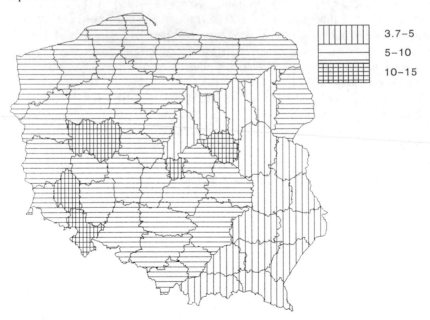

	3.7–5
	5–10
	10–15

Figure 9.11 Support for Union of Labour (%), parliamentary election of 19 September 1993.

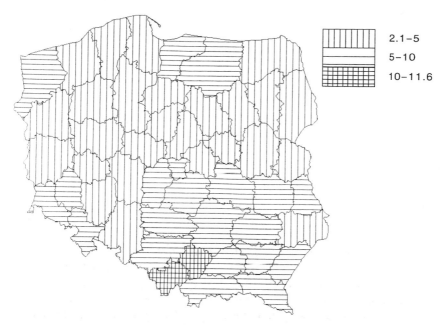

	2.1–5
	5–10
	10–11.6

Figure 9.12 Support for Confederation of Independent Poland (%), parliamentary election of 19 September 1993.

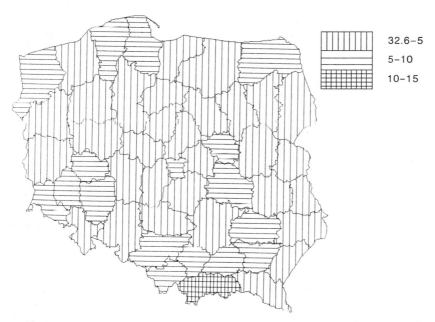

	32.6–5
	5–10
	10–15

Figure 9.13 Support for Non-party Block of Support of Reforms (%), parliamentary election of 19 September 1993.

Two types of the explanations were presented: "negative" and "positive". The negative explanations are based on the assumption that the success of the SLD was the result of protest against the economic policy imposed by the Solidarity elite. The policy had not fulfilled the great expectations of society. The positive explanations referred to the attractive political and economic programmes of the SLD, proving the skill and credibility of its representatives.

The surveys also indicate that the negative explanation was more typically shared by people with higher education, managerial and private entrepreneurs, generally by people interested in politics, and with right-wing attitudes. The positive explanation and opinion about the result of election was shared in a higher proportion by inhabitants of villages, the unemployed, the lowest income category, and those with rather left-wing attitudes. In general, the supporters of the latest years of transformation and economic reform acknowledged that society voted against those reforms.

Answering the question of why so many people voted in favour of the SLD, 36% of respondents explained that it was because "government ignored the affairs of ordinary people". In addition, 19% supported the idea that "under communist government it was better"; and 17% explained that the Solidarity camp was split, and different parties struggled between themselves. The question that suggested that support for the SLD was large because under the Communist Party regime life was better was answered positively by 25% of people with primary education, 33% of peasants, 31% of unskilled workers, and 34% of the unemployed, but by only 8% of people with higher education and by 8% of managerial staff.

The election results and the results of questionnaire surveys indicate that transformation in Poland has challenged the deeply rooted egalitarian attitudes and expectations of social justice. It also indicates that the Solidarity government did not understand ordinary people and was arrogant and did not care about dialogue with society. Left-wing political orientation is perceived as more sensitive to everyday needs.

The anti-communist slogans stopped having any significant influence on the voting behaviour of the majority of the electorate. The issue of the communist nomenclature has also been dropped. The most important problems have become, for the majority, the economic situation, unemployment, the low standard of living and other social issues that do not involve a judgement of the communists. The perspective of the SLD government, as a result of the election, created in society more expectation than fear. The SLD success would not be the starting point of radical change in recent economic policy; however, 30–35% of respondents of the polls expected slight changes that would be noticeable by society. Those respondents expected an improvement of living conditions and in the economic situation, a decrease in unemployment and in the shadow economy; however, very few expected a decrease in inflation.

In general, answering the question "Has the political situation in Poland developed in a good or bad direction?", since 1992, the only period when the share of optimism prevailed over pessimism was just after the election. But at the same time many groups felt that there would be no changes.

9.4.2 THE FORMATION OF THE NEW POLITICAL STRUCTURE AND THE LOCAL GOVERNMENT ELECTION OF 1994

The rejection of the totalitarian system was characterized by domination of symbolic values. In the next stage, a new political system was formed and a new economic order begun. First came the parliamentary election of 1989, which destroyed the existing political system. The next step was economic reforms, very effective and modern but imposed in political terms. After that, the real process of the formation of a new political structure started. Important factors were the existing cultural or political traditions, and uncontrolled individual ambitions.

As a result, the origin of the majority of political parties has an immediate "contextual" character (Grabowska & Szawiel 1993). This means that they were formed as a result of political and economic events, or through personal animosities of political leaders.

The traditional western European labels of political parties do not fit perfectly in Poland; for example, the left/centre/right divisions. In the economic dimension, indicated by the issues of privatization and the role of the state in the welfare programmes, the KLD is situated to the right, UD and PC in the centre and ZChN in the centre but further to the left. The SdRP and contemporary Democratic Left Alliance (SLD) are situated to the left. The very inconsistent political dimension is shaped by the self-evaluation of those parties and quickly evolving general opinion. So the SLD is extreme to the left and ZChN to the right; whereas the UD, KLD and PC are treated as a fluid centre. In the cultural dimension, measured by the issues of the role of the church and religion, ZChN is situated to the right, SLD and UP to the left. The KPN is in the economic dimension located to the left, whereas in cultural and political terms it is to the right.

The local government election of 19 June 1994 has partly stabilized the political structure in the spatial dimension. The electoral attendance was very low (33.8%) and was much higher in rural areas (over 40%) than in urban areas (around or below 30%). Traditionally it was higher also in the western and southern parts of the country and lowest in the eastern part, except the largest urban agglomeration (Fig. 9.14).

In political terms, it was won by the independent candidates, proposing solutions to local problems or becoming famous at a local level. Most of them were allied to single parties after the election; however, some of the elected candidates use political party support only for representing local issues, and remain relatively independent.

The success of the SLD in the 1993 parliamentary election was consolidated in 1994 and it gained many more seats on local councils. In most of the cities in the north and west the SLD enjoyed an absolute majority and in many other cities it

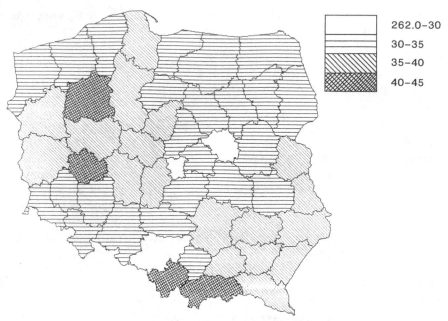

	262.0–30
	30–35
	35–40
	40–45

Figure 9.14 Electoral attendance (%), local government election of 1994.

became the strongest political coalition. Also in Warsaw it became the strongest political party in local councils; however, it is able to rule without centrist or even right-wing support.

The PSL maintains it strongest position in rural areas but had some losses in electoral support. The post-Solidarity parties, the Democratic Union (UD) and the Liberal-Democratic Congress (KLD), had united into a new party – the Freedom Union (UW) – of rather centrist character. During the local government election it had moderate success, particularly in large cities and in the cities of the south.

The right-wing parties succeeded in the east and managed to become the major-ity political formation in many eastern cities. The coalition of the Freedom Union and some right-wing parties was often organized to exclude the left-wing coalition from local government.

This election maintained the political division between rural and urban areas, and between eastern and western parts of the country. The frequent alliance of centrist and right-wing parties, particularly in urban areas, created a new political division between left-wing oriented central government and local government. The balance of power between local and central government remains, determined in favour of the left-wing coalition; however, the right-wing and centrist opposi-tion received the mandate for political action.

CHAPTER 10

The emergence of
new regional differentiation

The spatial structure of Poland has been shaped in the past by the strong ideological preferences of egalitarianism. However, the policy under communism of the even distribution of productive forces became only partly effective. After 1970 the concept of moderate polarization tended to support the development of urban agglomerations. One of the results of this, and the egalitarian spatial policy of the past, is the settlement pattern of policentric and moderate concentration. This pattern could be regarded as advantageous for future development, because in comparison with Western countries regional disparities in Poland are relatively small.

The regional structure of Poland, shaped partly by the imposed socialist industrialization policy, has brought for some regions more negative consequences. Now the economic structure of those regions is a fundamental obstacle in future modernization. The extreme example is Upper Silesia, the most important industrial region in Poland, but also a region of structural backwardness and ecological catastrophe (Kukliński 1991). The future development of this region in the traditional style of heavy industry based on high consumption of raw materials and energy, with growing environmental pollution, will lead to catastrophe. However, this fact is not fully perceived by the population of the region.

The spatial structure formed during the communist period will not disappear over night. For a long time all economic and social activity will be carried out within the spatial framework created for other economic objectives. The new economic enterprises and activities will merely modify the existing spatial structure. In spite of that, the new more "natural" tendencies will lead inevitably to the concentration of the most prosperous economic activities and to stronger polarization in standards of living.

The process of transformation is strongly differentiated regionally. An increasing polarization between rapidly advancing regions and those regions affected by unemployment and recession has been observed. Recession has had a strong influence on the decline of urbanization and has even reversed de-urbanization in some cases. This is a result of the slowing down of rural–urban migration, return migration to rural areas and a substantial decline of farmer–workers commuting to work.

The first government priority in recent years has been the rationalization of the national economy by elimination of inefficient sectors. Because of the political and social constraints, it has been only partly successful. In a situation of dramatic recession, the regional policy of the state has been limited only to social assistance in the most backward regions. The regional policy was in this way following the economic development in particular voivodships rather than shaping it. The voivodships will be strongly differentiated in future according to the regional potential for adaptation to the evolving economic situation and constraints.

The concentration of government attention on specific problem areas could be only partly effective. It is an illusion that each region will maintain in the future its economic base by modernization and restructuring. This is of particular concern to the old industrial regions of Katowice (Upper Silesia), Lódź and particularly Wałbrzych voivodship, and also areas of depopulation along the eastern border. The question that arises is whether the existing population distribution will be preserved or whether a process of substantial redistribution will be introduced.

A new phenomenon is the impact of international factors. This concerns particularly the regions along the newly opened frontiers. The greatest external stimulus for development is in the western areas with direct contacts with the European Union. The eastern regions along the former border with the Soviet Union have a chance to overcome stagnation, but so far the negative consequences of this border opening are quite marked. Other issues concern international transport and development of proper infrastructure.

The neglect of regional policy after 1989, in favour of the market mechanism, has been a part of the liberal economic strategy adopted as a base of transformation. In spite of that, policy slowly became directed towards ameliorating the costs of transformation, and regional strategy will probably be reintroduced as a part of a modern market economy. The new regional policy is under formation and is now a mixture of the old centrally oriented attitudes and the free market orientation. Before such a policy is formulated, it is necessary to identify the main actors of regional development and the areas of interest for international capital. The criteria of allocation and location of investment are different from those under a centrally planned economy, so the pattern created will be re-evaluated by the new (market economy) criteria.

The spatial behaviour of foreign investors and the private sector in Poland indicate preferences for particular areas and very slight interest in others. The most rapid developments have occurred in Warsaw and its region, Poznań and Gdańsk voivodship. The less preferable areas are the old industrial voivodships and eastern rural areas.

The transformations immediately after 1989 were accompanied by a drop in national product. The stabilization of GDP in 1993 and increase in 1994, if renewed decreases are avoided, will be the basis for new attitudes; however, the budget constraint in principle leaves little room for the government to conduct an effective regional policy.

There is no commonly accepted method for the evaluation of the consequences of the pro-market transformation in a regional perspective. The analysis of various economic, social and political indicators, however, usually provides a fairly comprehensive picture. The most general indicator is gross domestic product: regional disparities in GDP are examined later in the chapter.

Other indicators will differentiate the regions as gainers or losers from the transformation. The most important new phenomena having direct impact on regional differentiation – the process of privatization, unemployment, electoral preferences and ethnicity – will be analyzed in separate sections. The phenomena selected do not cover all components of regional differentiation; however, they are fundamental to the description of the economic, social and political space of Poland.

10.1 The ownership transformation

In Poland, private property and enterprise were never abolished and have a long tradition, but their operation under the communists was strictly limited and indirectly incorporated into central control. Throughout the whole post-war period the Polish private sector was the largest in central Europe. In the 1970s, it started gradually to increase in size, partly as a result of permission being given to Polish residents of Western countries to register partnerships. In the mid-1980s it began to expand more rapidly.

Following the collapse of the economic reforms introduced after the imposition of martial law of 1981, the desirability of the extension of the private sector was accepted by reform-oriented communist elites. For example, in 1988 the "counter-revolutionary" proposal was made (by orthodox communists) to turn state enterprises into joint-stock companies and to sell their assets to the public. However, social acceptance of the private sector was at that time much wider. The private sector was not regarded as a source of socio-economic inequality or of a non-egalitarian distribution of wealth, but as a means of escape from the inconvenience of the state system (Kotlarska-Bobińska 1994).

The expansion of the private sector was made easier because of new legal regulations. Particular importance can be attached to the new legal opportunity to register limited liability companies in accordance with the pre-war Commercial Code of 1934, the new Foreign Joint Venture Law of 1986, and the Law of Freedom of Economic Activities of 1988. It is worth emphasizing that all this legislation was introduced by the communist government. In addition, the spontaneous involvement of the nomenclatura had been accelerating, by exploiting legal gaps or through corruption and developments on the fringe of legality.

Two possible explanations were provided: one that the communist elite accepted the drift towards the free market in order to reform the economic system; the second that a main aim was only to safeguard their personal economic positions in the face of the collapsing communist system. The development of this sort of privatization was restricted by the first non-communist government, but not reversed as some opposition leaders proposed.

The model of an efficient property-owning democracy immediately became an alternative to that of inefficient communism. Privatization was treated as the basis for transformation to a market economy. It was assumed that privatization could fulfil three very important functions: the ability to respond faster to changes in economic circumstances, the rejection of political interference in economic life, and the discipline it imposed on the state budget.

The idea of privatization has been used as a principal means of improving the efficiency of the whole economy: as the only way in which the old collective irresponsibility and culture of dependence could be replaced by a new individualistic economic behaviour and entrepreneurial attitudes. The idea of privatization therefore not only had an economic rationale but also an ideological underpinning. It was treated by the new political elite as one element of the transformation to capitalism, by assisting in the formation of a supporting middle class. In the short term it was supposed to fill the gaps in the state budget, and solve the most urgent economic problems (for example, the monetary deficit).

The drive towards privatization has had great political significance, which is reflected in the fact that more than 15 proposals had been under discussion before the first privatization law was approved by the Polish Diet in 1990. The formation of legal structures, in April 1991, and constitutional guarantees for the development of the private sector during 1990 ended the chaotic phase of privatization. The newly created Ministry of Ownership Changes became the co-ordinator of the privatization process.

In 1990, there was rapid development in the private sector, but this process began to slow down in 1991. This was caused by the lack of domestic capital, the absence of major inflows of foreign capital, the reduction of public support for privatization, the over-emphasis by the public media of any faults with the privatization process, the disproportionately large participation of former nomenclatura members in the process, the conspicuous displays of wealth by private entrepreneurs in conditions of drastic reductions in the general standard of living, and the prevailing egalitarian attitudes of society. The huge expectations attached to the market transformation had no immediate impact on the standard of living of the majority of society, and the result was widespread frustration.

A substantial problem emerged to augment the recession, with the general failure of attempts to restructure state-owned enterprises. These enterprises were attempting to preserve the status quo. In addition, high taxation of salary increases (popiwek) and imposed dividends on state-owned enterprises that refused to enter the privatization process were introduced. However, the large state companies mostly adopted a passive strategy and delayed reorganization (Dąbrowski 1993). This soon resulted in the collapse of state budgets, because the expected rapid mass privatization had not contributed significantly to an increase in public spending, in spite of drastic cuts in subsidies. The expected results of rapid mass privatization had not materialized.

The first phase of pre-privatization was controlled by communist leaders with the aim of empowering the nomenclatura. The second, after the collapse of communism in 1989, was the spontaneous private development phase, up to the 1990 legislation. During the third, running from 1991 to 1995, the control of the privatization process was in the hands of the government. The privatization process of the first five years of transformation experienced two slow periods: during the Olszewski government and during the left-wing Pawlak government.

The state's own privatization agenda notwithstanding, spontaneous privatization has been very successful. The lifting of political constraints in 1989 created a social climate as favourable to entrepreneurs. As a result, the number of small and medium-size private enterprises outside agriculture grew (for example from 353 000 to 814 500 units in 1989 alone). This sort of privatization, sometimes called "founding privatization", is based on the creation of new private firms. The success of this type of privatization in the Polish economy establishes the foundation of future transformation.

In popular opinion, privatization as a whole is the key to Poland's future. The hope is that the attitudes encompassed within enterprises will develop, both as a way to overcome recession and to ensure that a new middle class will emerge as a basic support for the democratic system.

10.1.1 TYPES OF PRIVATIZATION

The process of ownership transformation has consisted of different phases and policies. Two basic components of the transformation are very evident. The first is founding privatization, a process that is organic in character and can be seen as privatization from below. This is taking place alongside the growth of existing private businesses and the sale or mass leasing of state enterprises and co-operative assets very cheaply to private owners (Gomulka & Jasinski 1994). The second concerns the large-scale privatization of state enterprises.

The direct outcomes of this transformation are the changes that have occurred in the ownership structure of the national economy, although this impact differs markedly by region. The means of implementation of this transformation caused differentiated reactions within society, and an emerging division between gainers and losers.

The new law of 13 July 1990 introduced two paths to privatization: the capital path and the liquidation of state-owned companies. Under capital privatization a state-owned company first has to be transferred to a joint-stock or limited liability company held by the State Treasury, after which the sale of shares to the public can take place. Usually the shares go to investors chosen through long negotiations or to the managers and employees of the enterprise concerned. The capital privatization path was eased by the opening of the Warsaw Stock Exchange at the beginning of April 1991.

Initially, the capital method predominated through the public sale of the stock of five companies: Exbud, Krosno, Kable, Tonsil and Próchnik. Later the shares of other companies were traded: Swarzędz, Wólczanaka, Pywiec, Wedel, Irena, Okocim and Elektrim.

137

Privatization by liquidation follows two possible paths, using either the Privatization Act or the Law on State-Owned Enterprises. The use of the privatization act involves medium-size state companies in particular. First such a company has to be restructured and dissolved and a new company set up by the former employees. Sometimes part of the assets are sold to external investors, but usually the employees have a preferential claim to the assets. Obviously, this procedure is very popular with employees (Gomulka & Jasinski 1994).

The frequent financial deterioration of state enterprises is ameliorated by privatization through liquidation using the law on state-owned enterprises of 25 September 1981, as amended in 1991. The founding body – usually a branch ministry – decides what to do and how to liquidate the company; selling directly, restructuring first and/or creating a new company that is thereafter sold or leased.

In addition to these "standard" ways, in 1992 the "Privatization Express" was introduced as a sort of liquidation privatization for medium-size state-owned companies employing fewer than 500 people. The sale is conducted by the founding ministerial body.

A specific type of privatization involves the state-owned farms. It covers over a thousand farms that existed in 1989 and employed over 440000 people. The financial bankruptcy of the majority of them forced the government to form the Agency of the State Treasury. The Agency has been trying to sell or lease these farms to private buyers, but the limited demand for land and the heavy indebtedness of the farms have rendered this process unsuccessful.

The new technique of combining privatization with restructuring was introduced in 1992 (ibid.). This policy, labelled the commercialization method of privatization, involves the introduction of a management team to govern the company to be privatized. This is only a transformation of the method of management and not of ownership. In the first stage the reform of the company is achieved, whereas in the next, true privatization is achieved through the public sale of shares to private investors chosen through negotiations, or through the sale of stock to the management or workers. However, limiting privatization to commercialization serves as a means of withdrawing from privatization completely or of slowing down the process. This method is now (1995) extensively used by the leftist government to divert the hostility of that segment of the electorate opposed to privatization and to avoid the accusation by international capital of withdrawal from the process of transformation.

The Mass Privatization Programme was introduced on 15 June 1993, when the Act on National Investment Funds was approved. According to the Ministry of Privatization there are 367 enterprises involved, with State Treasury corporations being included in this programme from the beginning of 1994. The Selection Commission that determines which enterprises are to be privatized is composed of representatives of government, parliament and trade unions. The number of companies taking part in this programme will rise in 1995 to about 470. It was expected that, following the establishment of the National Investment Funds in mid-1994, the distribution of share certificates would start at the beginning of 1995, but this has been delayed.

10.1.2 THE SCALE AND SPATIAL DIFFERENTIATION OF PRIVATIZATION

The scale of the transformation can be measured in different ways: by the level of employment, the volume of production or the number of business entities in the national economy. Additionally, one should distinguish between "nominal" and "real" privatization. Presenting statistics for formerly socialized sector co-operatives as now a constituent part of the private sector is an example of nominal privatization. Such statistical manipulation is particularly evident in the housing sector. However, nominal privatization can be treated as a first step towards real privatization.

According to data released by the Ministry of Privatization, of 8441 state-owned enterprises at the end of 1990, 2611 (i.e. 31%) had been privatized by March 1994, 1595 had been liquidated in order to be administered by the State Treasury, and 271 were communalized by regional authority (voivodships). In the 362 state enterprises, the legal process of liquidation is under way. Altogether, in 1994 over 56% of state-owned enterprises have been affected by ownership transformation. By sectors of the national economy; 1070 were in industry, 716 in construction, 295 in agriculture, 240 in trade, 149 in transport, 12 in forestry, 1 in telecommunications and 128 in the remaining sectors (*Dynamika prywatyzacji* **20**, 1994, Warsaw).

The course of privatization of state enterprises since 1990, according to the Central Statistical Office (GUS 1995), is presented in Table 10.1.

Table 10.1   State-owned enterprises under the process of ownership transformation.

	Total	1	2	3	4	5
31 Dec. 1990	130	58	72	28	44	–
31 Dec. 1991	1,258	308	950	534	416	–
31 Dec. 1992	2,478	480	1,459	797	662	723
31 Dec. 1993	3,932	636	1,956	1,091	865	1,340
30 Sept. 1994	4,585	780	2,170	1,200	970	1,635

1. Transformed into one person companies of the State Treasury. 2. Under liquidation – total 3. Under liquidation – under State Enterprises Act (Article 19) 4. Under liquidation – under State Enterprises Privatization Act (Article 37) 5. State farming enterprises taken over by the Agency for State Treasury Farmland Property. Source: *Prywatyzacja przedsiębiorstw państwowych według stanu na 30.09.1994* 1995. Warsaw: GUS.

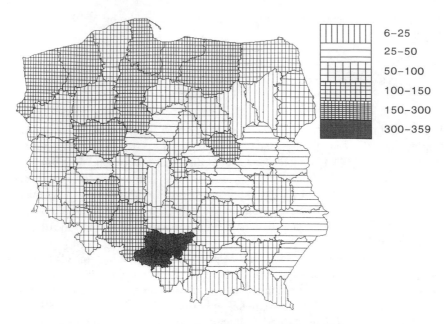

6-25
25-50
50-100
100-150
150-300
300-359

Figure 10.1 State owned enterprises under the process of ownership transformation, 30 September 1994.

The regional differentiation of the privatization process only partly reflects the economic structure of the country and the distribution of state enterprises. The largest number of state enterprises under privatization are in the most developed western part of the country, whereas the number of cases in the less developed northern voivodships reflects the privatization of the former state farms that dominated in this region (Fig. 10.1).

One of the outcomes of ownership transformation has been the growth of foreign capital in Poland. By law (since 14 June 1991), companies with foreign capital are entitled to the same treatment as Polish investors, and are guaranteed unrestricted transfer of profits abroad. According to the Central Statistical Office (GUS 1995), by the end of 1993 there were 19312 companies (mostly joint ventures) with participating foreign capital, and 587 foreign owned small-scale enterprises.

Domestic private investors and the owners of foreign capital have locational priorities that differ from those of the old central planners. Thus, foreign capital has concentrated in large agglomerations (Fig. 10.2), particularly in Warsaw, which has 34.2% of all economic units with foreign capital. Altogether, the eight most urbanized voivodships contain over 74% of all economic units with foreign capital. Concentration is also characteristic of foreign small-scale enterprises (Fig. 10.3), with 27.3% being located in the Warsaw region, 9.8% in Poznań, and over 3% in Łódź, Kraków and Gdańsk.

The status of some companies is still not fully determined. This occurs particularly where shares are split between different partnerships, which are at different

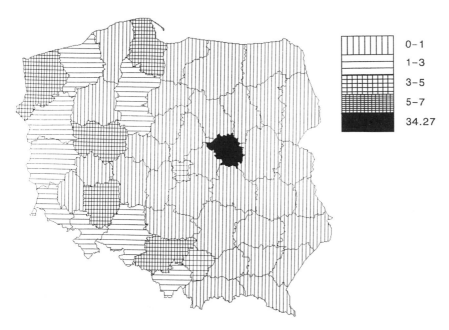

Figure 10.2 Economic units with foreign capital participation (%), 31 December 1994.

stages of ownership transformation. In banking, for example, the state sector dominates, although its direct and indirect shareholdings (around 80%) are in the hands of various institutions and companies.

The number employed in the private sector expanded from 37% in 1989 to 58% in 1993. Privatization contributed to this change, particularly the expansion of the organic private sector itself, which developed more rapidly than in other central European countries. Of enterprises formally privatized, a substantial contribution has been made by the success of the small-scale retail trade and service sectors.

10.1.3 PUBLIC OPINION

The very positive initial attitude towards privatization was eroded relatively quickly. The positive aspects of privatization, particularly the liquidation of the shortages previously endemic in everyday life, were negated by the recession and the worsening economic situation of much of the population. The declining popularity of privatization has been reflected in public opinion polls and in the sharp fall in support for parties with liberal programmes in each successive election.

Nevertheless, the attitude of society to privatization is very ambiguous: full of hope, but also full of distrust and fear. This is very apparent in the case of the re-privatization issue. During the past four years more than 50% of respondents to Public Opinion Surveys (CBOS 1994d) agreed with the idea of re-privatization, in

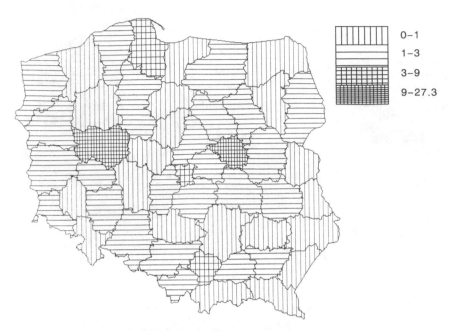

Figure 10.3 Foreign small scale enterprises (%), 31 December 1994.

	0–1
	1–3
	3–9
	9–27.3

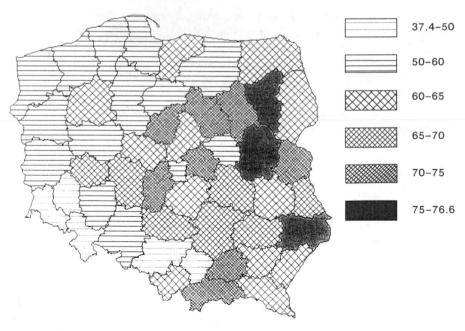

Figure 10.4 Employment in private sector as a percentage of employment in national economy, 31 December 1993.

	37.4–50
	50–60
	60–65
	65–70
	70–75
	75–76.6

spite of increasingly contradictory media coverage and increased knowledge of the financial limitations of the state budget. However, the proportion of supporters did fall from 64% in March 1991 to 56% in May 1994. Also, the share of respondents against re-privatization increased from 28% to 41% in the same period. The least politically fragile and most accepted aspect of the programme is the re-privatization of small enterprises such as stores, craftsman workshops, and pharmacies, whereas the re-privatization of larger enterprises and large landholdings has been rejected by a majority of respondents.

As yet, there is no consensus regarding re-privatization, with continuing political controversy over the issues between interest groups. The highest proportion of opponents of re-privatization is among those with only primary education, inhabitants of rural areas and small towns. The peasants are usually against the re-privatization of large farms, whereas workers object to the re-privatization of large industrial enterprises. Predictably the greatest share of support for re-privatization is found among the socioprofessional category of private sector employees.

The surveys since April 1994 indicate that in all social categories except the peasantry more respondents think that privatization is good for the Polish economy than that it is bad. The strongest support for privatization is to be found among private entrepreneurs (61%), managers and the intelligentsia (51%). The lowest level of support occurs among unskilled workers (26%), whereas 38% of peasants are against privatization compared with one quarter who support the policy. Positive evaluations of privatization increase with education; only among respondents with elementary education do a larger share (28%) of respondents claim that there are unfavourable consequences, compared with 25% who return positive evaluations. Among people with higher education, positive attitudes prevail, with 62% in favour and only 4% against. At the regional level, only in the eastern voivodships is there more opposition than support for privatization (CBOS 1994e).

In total (in April 1994), 35% of respondents believed that privatization was good for the Polish economy (in January 1991 it was 47%) whereas 21% held that it was not. However, when asked about the personal consequences of privatization, 28% perceived these to be unfavourable and only 21% saw them as favourable. The gap between the support for privatization at the general and the individual levels represents a difference between hope for the success of the national economy through this policy and the attendant personal economic insecurity associated with change (Kolarska-Bobińska 1994).

Surprisingly, although it is politically very controversial and often discussed in both Parliament and the media, the issues raised by the Mass Privatization Programme are to a large extent ignored by public opinion. In contrast to the above findings regarding privatization as a whole, surveys concerning Mass Privatization reveal that over 50% of respondents have no idea about this programme. Also, 60% of respondents claim that it could not improve prosperity (CBOS 1994f).

10.2 Unemployment

10.2.1 THE EMERGENCE OF UNEMPLOYMENT

Labour market indicators are among the quickest to react to the pace of transformation. In particular we can note: the decreased economic activity of the population, the shifts of employment between ownership sectors and branches of the national economy, and the expansion of employment in the shadow economy. However, the most spectacular new phenomenon is unemployment.

The over-employment, or latent unemployment, of the centrally planned economy had, by mid-1990, been replaced by manifest open unemployment. In the 1980s there were still regularly 400000–500000 vacant jobs, but after mid-1989 this number fell rapidly to 35000 at the beginning of 1990, whereas the unemployment level reached 55800 persons.

Registration of unemployment started at the beginning of 1990. At first the appearance of unemployment was not a result of the economic crisis but rather a result of the opportunity to register existing unemployment legally and of the availability of financial benefits for the unemployed. But, since the second half of 1990, the increase was an inevitable result of the deep recession associated with the transformation of the economy. In short, the recession reduced the demand for labour. In just a few months the situation in the labour market had been reversed. From having a shortage of labour, Poland suddenly faced increasing unemployment. However, certain commentators, such as Witkowski (1992), attribute this unemployment solely to the recession and not to the structural transformation of the national economy. The gap between job creation and job destruction has been widening all the time, in spite of the booming development of the private sector.

The collapse of the planned economy and the general desire for a more efficient economic system led, at the outset, to widespread acceptance of the unemployment associated with the radical restructuring process. However, public opinion quickly turned against the scale of unemployment implied by transition. In spite of social progress and the elimination of shortages, the growth of unemployment implied the growth of poverty. The political and social resistance generated by unemployment soon became one of the major critical reflections on the contemporary state of transformation.

10.2.2 THE SIZE AND STRUCTURE OF UNEMPLOYMENT

The rate of growth of unemployment has been remarkable. From officially being zero in January 1990 it jumped to 1140000 in December 1990 (6.1%), 2155573 (11.4%) in December 1991, and 2509342 (13.6%) in December 1992. The latest figure (December 1994) reached 2.8 million, or 16.0% of the economically active population. However, if we exclude agriculture, the rate of unemployment is over 26%.

The foregoing information is culled from employment agency data. However, the Quarterly Labour Force Survey is an alternative information source. This is undertaken according to the methodology elaborated by the International Labour Organization. It indicated that the rate of unemployment in 1993 was smaller (by 0.5–1%) than that recorded by the administration.

Unemployment is a problem not only for those without work but also for nearly 2.2 million households within which at least one member is unemployed. In consequence, over 8 million people have direct personal contact with unemployment (Witkowski 1994a).

Unemployment is a particular concern in urban areas. According to the Labour Force Survey of November 1993, unemployment in urban areas was 1751000, whereas in rural areas it was 844000, of which 304000 included individual private farms (Król 1994). The real problem in rural areas is that of hidden unemployment, particularly in individual agriculture (one-person farms). The private and individual sectors of agriculture have acted as a shelter in the face of the current economic crisis, but this has become a negative force for the future development of this backward sector of the economy.

The population of rural areas is, however, differentiated in terms of activities pursued. The population directly involved in agricultural production (i.e. living in households that own land) represented 60.1% of the population in November 1993, whereas the population without land represented only 39.9% of the total. Unemployment among the rural population connected with agriculture was only 6.2%, whereas among inhabitants of rural areas not connected with agricultural production it was 25.5%. This last figure is higher than for the urban population (16.9%).

In tandem with the national economy as a whole, the population working in individual farms has declined over the five years 1988–93. The size of the decline has been estimated at between 400000 and 500000 people (Kałaska 1994). In spite of this, the number of people who are, strictly speaking, still surplus in agriculture has been estimated at around 333000 (Witkowski 1994b). This estimate is based on statistical criteria, but if the estimation is based on the opinions of people themselves employed in agriculture it reaches 505000. This is around 16% of all rural inhabitants working in agriculture. Combining the two estimates, there were therefore about 447000 hidden unemployed workers in individual agriculture in Poland in 1993 (Witkowski 1994b). The reserve labour force in individual agriculture varies between 14% and 21% of those employed. Clearly, this situation implies future upward pressure on unemployment in the economy as a whole.

The recent substantial improvement in the macroeconomy has resulted in the stabilization of unemployment. After two years of rapid increase between 1990 and 1992, the growth of unemployment slowed between 1993 and 1994.

Those most affected by unemployment are in the 18–24 year age group, which accounted for over 31% of the total unemployed at the end of 1993. In absolute numbers this represents over a million members of the younger generation without

145

jobs. School-leavers have been particularly affected. Among those who finished their education in 1990/1, as many as 44.7% were unemployed at the end of 1991. At the end of 1993, the comparable figure was over 49%.

Differentiated by education level, those most affected by unemployment are those with only vocational and basic education (39% of the unemployed). The share of people with university education is relatively low (around 1.8%).

The unemployment rate for women is higher than average (over 51% in 1994), and in Upper Silesia (Katowice voivodship) it reaches 63%. This is partly the result of the economic situation facing whole families, but it also reflects the new legal opportunity for women to register as unemployed in regions where the proportion of economically active women was historically low. A similar situation existed in 1990 in Olsztyn voivodship, where the first group registering as unemployed were those who had never worked before: the wives of officers in the police and in the military.

The growing number of people who have been without a job for more than one year is an important issue, particularly for areas with a single economic function or that are underdeveloped. In May 1992, 24% of the unemployed had been look-ing for a job for more than one year. This will cause problems in the future, because it is recognized that the ability to re-enter employment declines with the length of time a person is unemployed. The problem had worsened by December 1992, by which time as many as 45.2% of the unemployed had been without a job for more than a year. In 1993 and 1994 the share of long-term unemployment diminished as a result of the change of the definition of unemployment, but the problem still exists. Indeed, by the end of 1993, 14% of unemployed people had been without work for over two years.

Unemployment, particularly long-term, contributes substantially to the exten-sion of the "benefit dependency syndrome", that is, those who for generations live from state support (partly families with many children and those with social prob-lems). The long-term unemployed join those people who, in spite of poor material living conditions, wish not to undertake a job but to remain on social support.

10.2.3 THE REGIONAL STRUCTURE OF UNEMPLOYMENT

From the onset of transformation, unemployment has exhibited marked spatial differences. The most seriously affected areas have been the northeastern and northern voivodships, along with the Jelenia Góra voivodship in the southwest. This general spatial pattern has remained stable, although the size of the problem has grown over time.

In 1990, unemployment exceeded 10% in only two voivodships (Olsztyn and Suwalki) but, by the end of 1991, unemployment was less than 10% in only 11 voivodships out of a total 49 (Figs 10.5, 10.6). In 1992, unemployment rates of over 20% were recorded in five northern voivodships and in Jelenia Góra in the southwest, whereas it was below 10% in only five voivodships. In 1993, all those

146

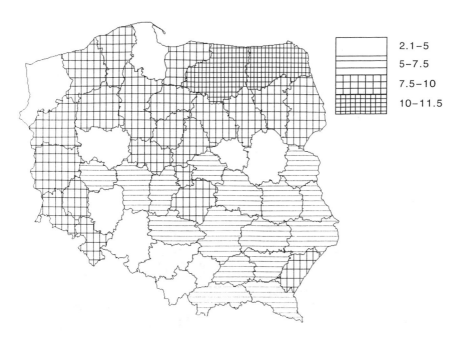

Figure 10.5 Unemployment rate in 1990 (% of economically active). Average for Poland: 6.1%.

2.1–5
5–7.5
7.5–10
10–11.5

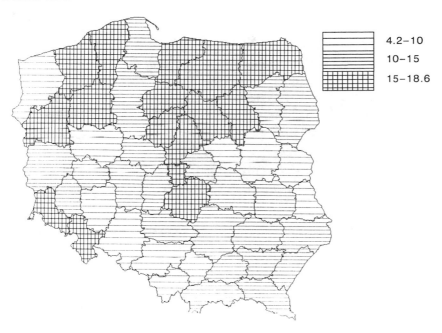

Figure 10.6 Unemployment rate in 1991 (% of economically active). Average for Poland: 11.4%.

4.2–10
10–15
15–18.6

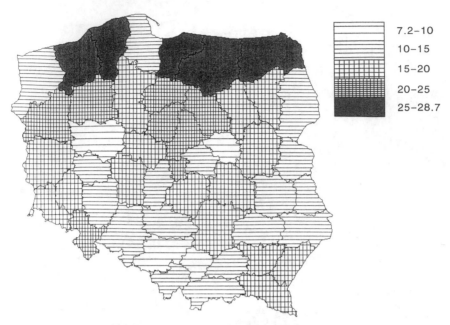

	7.2–10
	10–15
	15–20
	20–25
	25–28.7

Figure 10.7 Unemployment rate in 1993 (% of economically active). Average for Poland: 15.7%.

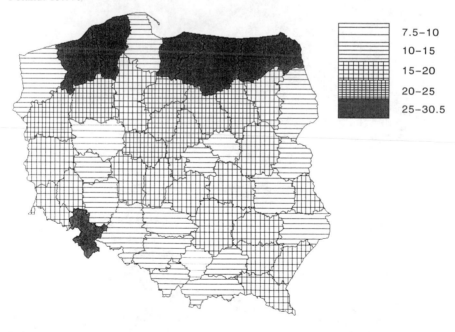

	7.5–10
	10–15
	15–20
	20–25
	25–30.5

Figure 10.8 Unemployment rate in 1994 (% of economically active). Average for Poland: 16%.

regions in which unemployment exceeded 20% a year earlier witnessed over 25% of their workforces without a job (Fig. 10.7). The reduction in the rate of increase of unemployment in 1994 has not changed the general spatial pattern (Fig. 10.8).

The persistence of this spatial regularity is the result of very low residential mobility. The national housing shortage, which affects even the more developed urban agglomerations, serves to maintain the spatial structure of unemployment. Also, the share of those unemployed for longer than 13 months (in 1994) is greater than 50% in the northern voivodships.

The labour market in Poland is therefore not national in scale; to a high degree it is segmented into many local labour markets, as a result of the housing shortage and associated low labour mobility.

In absolute terms, the spatial distribution of unemployment indicates another pattern that is even more stable (Fig. 10.9). Thus, the largest number affected by unemployment live in the Katowice voivodship (172 000), and this, together with four other voivodships (Lódź, Kielce, Bydgoszcz and Olsztyn), accounted for 20.6%, or 596 700, of the country's unemployment in 1994.

Although the spatial distribution of high unemployment rates highlights the economically weakest and most underdeveloped areas, the distribution by size indicates the areas where the restructuring of traditional industry has begun in earnest (except Olsztyn voivodship). The regional differentiation is even more visible at the scale of local labour market districts, some of which have unemployment rates in excess of 35%. At this scale the level of unemployment varied from 6.2% in Warsaw to 42.2% in Pasłęk (Elbląg voivodship) and 41.1% in Gołdap (Suwalki

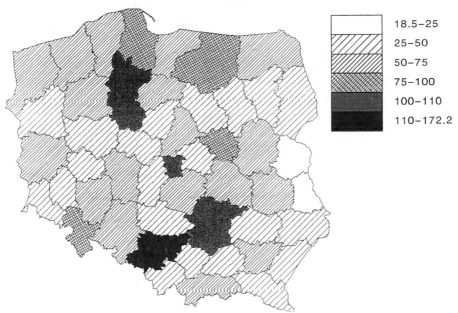

18.5–25
25–50
50–75
75–100
100–110
110–172.2

Figure 10.9   Unemployment rate in 1994 in thousands. Total for Poland: 2 838 000.

voivodship). Many communes in northern voivodships are experiencing rates of over 30%.

The lowest rates are generally in the urbanized and industrialized areas, particularly around large agglomerations were there is access to a differentiated labour market. The areas most affected by structural unemployment are concentrated in the less developed northeastern and northwestern voivodships. Generally, all of the areas in the north have unemployment rates of over 20%, except for the industrial agglomerations in that region.

The scale of the problem meant that on 24 August 1992 the Council of Ministry identified areas of severe structural unemployment, which in 1993 reached 412 communes. These areas have since been assisted by limited state intervention (Fig. 10.10). Any attempt to withdraw central government assistance, even in the face of improvements in the prevailing situation, immediately draws strong political protest from the local authority. Given the budgetary pressure that this implies, there has been only a gradual increase in the number of communes covered by specific government assistance.

There is a need to link the overall economic policy of the state with its policy in the labour market. This applies particularly to the large and medium-size industrial cities such as Lódź, Starachowice or Mielec, the economies of which are based

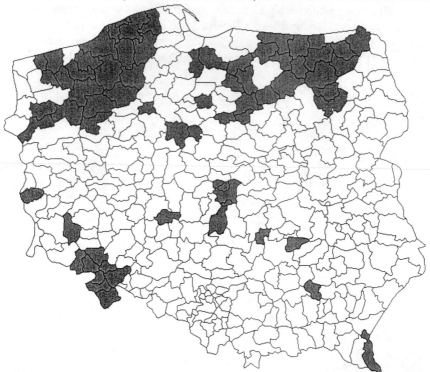

Figure 10.10 Areas of structural unemployment in 1993 by regional employment agencies.

on only one branch of industry, or even just one factory. It concerns also the northern and northwestern regions dominated by state farms, with underdeveloped individual agriculture.

10.2.4 THE PROSPECT FOR THE FUTURE

The extremely limited intervention in the labour market at the beginning of the transformation contributed to the aggravation of the unemployment problem. The allocation of full responsibility for the problem to the Ministry of Labour and Social Policy was ineffective. A more comprehensive programme for tackling unemployment as a part of macroeconomic policy should be introduced.

Also, the attitude of people to employment is slowly starting to change, from the socialist perception that jobs follow labour, to the more free-market attitude that labour should follow jobs (i.e. a recognition of the need for increased labour-force mobility). The role of the government should not be limited simply to the promotion of local initiatives, even if the main investment comes from private capital. In particular local government should attract capital inflow, whereas the state should provide a proper legal and tax environment; but first of all it should create the conditions necessary for an increase of capacity utilization within existing places of work.

To deal with the unemployment problem, Poland needs an economic policy designed to counteract its causes. Unemployment is partly a result of the structure of the economy inherited from the socialist era. The sharp recession of the early 1990s has merely increased the size of the problem.

Unemployment is an important economic and political problem that will remain for several years. There will be no large-scale investment, but rather a gradual increase of small and medium-size private entrepreneurs. During the past three years the firms that the latter control have created over 3 million jobs. The basic constraint remains the lack of spatial labour mobility from the most affected regions to those with healthier economies. This is caused by housing shortages and the low levels of education of unskilled labourers for whose services demand has fallen.

For future policy purposes, the unemployment problem should be linked with the demographic prognosis. Assuming for example that, up to the year 2010, the population of those of economically productive age will increase by 2.7 million, this increase could become the source of substantial economic progress, or it could create enormous political problems in the future. In the 1990s, in spite of a reduction in the rate of natural increase, there will be 150000 new people of productive age each year, so that between 1993 and 2000 there will be 1.2 million new job seekers. If there are no changes in the contemporary economic prospects, the level of unemployment could reach 5.2–6.6 million people by the year 2000 (Kabaj 1993). Hence, the problem will not disappear over night and the period of transition will continue to be very painful.

10.3 The rebirth of ethnic identity

"Minorities" in Poland are estimated at 1.5% of the total population (1994), compared with the pre-war situation of 35% (in 1939). Poland's population seems now to be highly homogeneous. This situation, stabilized in the early 1950s, was a result of war damage, the holocaust, shift of Polish territory towards the west, and resettlement of the population imposed by the Allies at Potsdam in 1945. After the 1950s the only changes were waves of emigration to Germany and repatriation of Poles from the Soviet Union; however, all this time there was a dearth of reliable statistical information.

The lifting of political constraints and the democratization of political and social life of the country allowed the re-establishment of ethnic identity. The lack of statistical information meant that official estimations varied sharply from those provided by ethnic minority organizations; however, the latest research and attempt at the verification (Żoledowski 1994), together with the results of parliamentary elections, indicated that official estimates are more realistic. The most accurate answer could be provided by the next National Census, if the question about national and ethnic identity is introduced.

The largest ethnic group in Poland is the German minority. The number of Polish citizens who regard themselves as ethnically German is unknown, and is still a sensitive issue. It varied from 400 000 to a much larger figure. Regionally, the German minority is concentrated in Silesia, particularly in Opole, and partly in neighbouring communes of the Katowice and Częstochowa voivodships. The concentration in the Mazurian region has diminished as a result of the constant emigration to West Germany through the whole post-war period.

The consciousness of native Silesians has for several decades been more regional than national. The Silesian culture has been formed under the influence of not only Polish and German but also Czech–Moravian cultures. The Silesian dialect has some elements of German and Czech language influence, but it is a dialect of the Polish language. On both sides of the pre-war Poland/Germany frontier, the Silesian was usually a Silesian first, a German or Pole only second (Kosiarski 1992). The end of the Second World War changed the situation. The population of Polish origin identified themselves as Silesian on former German territory, but because of the threat of deportation declared their Polish nationality. A mass "Polonization" process occurred. The reverse situation gradually developed under communist conditions. The absence of recognition of Silesian autonomy and of its culture as a part of Polish cultural tradition had been highly significant. The only way for Silesians to distinguish themselves was through a declaration of German identity. Additionally, the increasing gap between the standards of living in Poland and Germany, together with the assimilation policy, resulted in a drift towards German identity and to emigration. In 1956–81, about 586 000 people emigrated to West Germany, and in 1980–88, according to German statistics, 385 000 people arriving from Poland became German citizens. Even with this emigration to West Germany, a growing number of people still consider themselves Germans. Even if part of this national identity shift has economic roots, it has substantially changed the ethnic situation in Upper Silesia and especially in the Opole voivodship.

The political emancipation of that group developed fully immediately after the collapse of the communist system, and was consolidated during each election. During the local government election of 1990, the German candidates gained an absolute majority of seats in 26 communes in the Opole voivodship. This provided the fundaments for the formation of a national committee for the 1991 parliamentary election. At that time the German minority introduced one representative to the Senate and seven to the Sejm, and has become an established feature on the social and political landscape of Poland. During the 1993 parliamentary election, the Germans introduced four members to the Sejm and one to the Senate.

The German minority issue has great significance for the future, and is regionally specific to the most economically developed region of Poland. As one German political scientist has said, "The situation in Silesia can evolve in one of two directions . . . it can either become a time bomb or an example of the possibility of living together in conditions of mutual respect." (Kosiarski 1992). However, for a thousand years of common association, mutual economic and cultural co-operation prevailed, so after the collapse of totalitarian ideologies, this trend seems likely to prevail in future. The proper settlement of relations between the German minority and Polish majority in the Opole region is still far from overcoming historical constraints.

The next largest minority – Ukrainian – accounts for 250 000 to 400 000 people, and has not managed to introduce a single member to the parliament because of internal division and particularly because of dispersed settlement. The Ukrainian, Belorussian, and Lithuanian minorities are mostly concentrated along the eastern border. This is the result of historic relations and the impermanence of boundaries in this region for several centuries. The increase of ethnic separation is merely the twentieth-century outcome. It is worth mentioning that in 1569 the first federal state in Europe was created by common agreement between Lithuania and Poland. The eastern boundary of Poland today is in the middle of this former Commonwealth of Poland and Lithuania. The minorities along the border are, then, partly the remains of this vast multi-ethnic, cultural and religious region.

The First and particularly the Second World War caused huge migrations. The shift of the Polish border westwards and resettlement of Polish population from former eastern territories of Poland was accompanied by smaller resettlements of the Ukrainian and Belorussian population to the Soviet Union. For example, 36 000 Belorussians were moved to the Soviet Union. The size of the Belorussian minority is now estimated at 250 000 inhabitants, concentrated mostly in the eastern part of Białystok voivodship. This minority gives the region an ethnic, cultural and religious distinctiveness. Neither the Lithuanians nor the Belorussians have been the object of any deliberate ethnic policy. Their situation evolved in parallel with the evolution of the general situation in Poland (Ciechocińska & Sadowski 1989). In the case of the German and Ukrainian minorities there were many discriminatory

153

measures implemented, such as forced resettlement and dispersal of the Ukrainian population after the defeat of the Ukrainian Nationalist Army in the Bieszczady mountains, and the Polonization policy for the remaining German minorities and Silesians, Warmians and Mazurians. Now Ukrainians are dispersed partly on the "Regained Territories", and particularly in the northern part, and form the largest concentration around Bartoszyce, Pasłęk and Gorowo Ilowieckie. The relative concentration along the south eastern border has more native character.

The specific character of ethnic identity is frequently attributed to religious affiliation, but this is only partly correct. The absolute domination of the Catholic church resulted in enduring ignorance of other religious affiliations. Particularly popular is the notion of Poles as Catholic, frequently repeated under the communist regime by the opposition intellectuals, but for a majority of the population this has now lost its significance.

The presence of the Orthodox Church and the Greek Catholic Church is most visible at the regional scale, usually mixed in the same regions. The Greek Catholic church was formed in 1596 as a result of the Brześć Union, and since then has been the subject of hostile treatment by the Orthodox Church. Now the members of this church are dispersed in the western and northern territories as a consequence of resettlement after 1947, and in the southeast corner of Poland. This Union, eliminated during the partition, survived and at the end of the nineteenth century became the source of revitalization mostly of the Ukrainian identity in Poland, particularly in the inter-war period. In 1946 this Church, on former Polish territories incorporated into the Soviet Union, was liquidated by the Soviets and was integrated by force with the Orthodox Church. The same happened in Poland in 1947: the Greek Catholic Churches or so-called "Unit" Churches were incorporated into the Orthodox Church or destroyed.

In 1956, after the Polish October, the Catholic Church provided some shelter for the survival of this religion, for example by creation of a seminary in Lublin. Officially, however, the strong censorship limited any publication about this Church: all notion of "grekokatolicki" or "unicki" was banned. The contemporary name of the Byzantinian–Ukrainian Church gained full legal and status in 1989. Now it has its own regional administration and bishop, Iwan Martyniuk. The membership of this church is estimated at about 500000.

The peaceful coexistence of the Byzantine–Ukrainian Church and Catholic Church is strongly supported by both sides; however, the old national problem still persists. This was shown during the conflict in 1991 around the Cloister in Przemyśl. This Cloister had been given by the catholic bishops as the temporary location of the main church of Byzantine–Ukrainian. The protest and occupation by Catholics indicated the tension and feeling of unjustified menace from Polish. There is also, on a smaller scale, competition and tension between the Orthodox Church and Byzantine–Ukrainian Church.

The orthodox Church members in the Białystok voivodships are, in most public opinion, treated as Belorussian, but questionnaire studies of the late 1980s among orthodox church members indicated that Belorussian identity was declared by only

57.8%, Polish 28.9%, Ukrainian 2%, and 11.3% identified themselves as "local" (Żołędowski 1994).

The regionally defined ethnic minority of Kaszub origin is accounted, in the most optimistic figure, as 700000 (Pałubicki 1993), and is concentrated in Gdańsk and partly in Słupsk and Bydgoszcz voivodships. In reality only a few thousand people still use the Kaszubian dialect. This ethnic group of Slavonic origin preserved its identity under long-time Prussian and German domination and the integration policy of Polish governments. This group had a regional identity and will contribute to the distinctiveness of this region of Poland.

The smallest minority that could be defined regionally is the Lithuanians. They are concentrated in Suwałki voivodship, particularly in the communes (gmina) of Sejny, Puńsk, Szypliszki, and in the towns of Sejny and Suwałki. The total number in this region is estimated at 10000. The rest of the total of 20000 Polish citizens of Lithuanian nationality live in Warsaw or are dispersed throughout the whole country because this community was undergoing a general urbanization process. For many Lithuanians, particularly those living in the inter-war period on Polish territory and having Polish citizenship, emigration in 1945 and 1957 was the only means of escape from the KGB and other forms of Soviet oppression (Kultura 1994).

The existence of several villages with a Russian population, orthodox religious sects of the Orthodox Church such as "starowiercy" and Slovakian minorities in Spisz and Orawa (in the south of Poland), can also be noted. Around 20000 Gypsies and 8000–10000 Jews are dispersed throughout the whole of Poland.

The evaluation of the political and economic transformation in Poland by the ethnic minorities has not deviated radically from the general attitude of the citizens. The relatively low educational level and mostly rural origin of the minorities group them together as mostly peasants and people on the losing side of the transformation, at least in economic terms. The Ukrainian and Lithuanian minorities have a relatively larger share of the intelligentsia, and therefore better living standards.

The threat of serious ethnic conflict is very limited. However, real tension exists between German minorities and Poles. Other tensions have been slight, and political leaders of minorities are trying to win popularity. Nationally oriented leaders have sometimes exploited these rather superficial tensions of nationalist behaviour in marginal parts of Poland.

The public opinion survey of November 1994 (CBOS 1994g) indicated that the attitudes of Poles (classified in three categories: sympathy, indifference, aversion) to the national minorities living in Poland are very differentiated. Usually, most Poles are indifferent. Sympathy prevails in respect of Slovaks, Czechs, Lithuanians, Bielorussians; whereas there is antipathy towards Gypsies, Ukrainians, Jews, Russians and Germans.

Most Poles react positively to the idea of accepting Polish citizens of other national origins in their own family. However, 55% of respondents would not accept someone of Gypsy origin as a member of their family, and quite a high proportion are against integration with Ukrainians (45%) and Jews (43%).

The attitude towards minorities is strongly differentiated according to the education and the age of respondents. In general, the higher the level of education, the lower the level of aversion. A similar generalization is true in relation to age: younger generations represent a much lower level of aversion. For example, 66% of people aged 25–34 have nothing against Jews as a member of their family, whereas only 27% of respondents of age 65 and over accept this situation.

10.4 Regional disparities in gross domestic product

The study of regional differentiation in Poland based on gross domestic product (GDP) by administrative units (voivodships) has become possible since the Central Statistical Office and the Polish Academy of Sciences have provided information disaggregated regionally for 1976, 1986 and 1992. GDP as an indicator of regional development is too crude an instrument to measure longer-term tendencies, particularly in a time of radical transformation. Only short-term trends can be observed and there is evidence of a more constant direction of change.

The frequently supported idea of an increase of spatial polarization in Poland during the 1970s and 1980s rests on very weak evidence, in terms of the regional distribution of GDP. For example, the degree of regional differentiation between 1976 and 1986 did not change significantly at the top level of the regional hierarchy. Between 1976 and 1986 Katowice voivodship lost first place in terms of GDP to Warsaw voivodship, and generally those regions with a higher share of GDP in 1976 had a lower share in 1986. The relative stability of regional differentiation is a result of the short time period and of the basic crisis in the national economy in the declining phase of communism. The economic crises provided no scope at that time for any regional shift of investment to less developed regions (Leszczycki & Domański 1995).

After the GDP reached its highest level in 1978 (between 1971 and 1975 the average annual increase was 9.8%) it stagnated and started to decline. In the period 1976–80 there was still a 1.8% average annual increase, but for 1981–5 there was 0.8% annual decline, and for 1986–90 there was a 1% average decline each year. The slump in industrial production was even greater: for the period 1986–90 it was 3.6% on average each year (Dochód 1992).

In statistical terms, however, the regional disparities between 1976 and 1986 had slightly increased (Zienkowski 1989). The decline phase of the centrally planned economy in crisis, particularly in the 1980s, had been characterized by other researchers as an equalization tendency in regional disparities (Parysek 1986, Szul et al. 1986).

The relative stabilization of regional disparities that had formed up to the early 1970s could be supported also by the fact that gross domestic income in 1986 hardly returned to the level of 1976, after slumping around 1979–80.

The research on national income for 1992 (Zienkowski 1994) is a good starting point for the future estimation of regional differentiation caused by the introduction of the market economy. The comparison of regional differentiation in GDP in 1986 and 1992 takes two useful points in time, the first (1986) just before the beginning, and the second (1992) just after the radical transformation in 1989. The period of 1986 to 1992 should be treated as referring to a real transformation of the economic and political system. For example, the change of prices was not only the result of market forces, but was rather (since 1989) the result of the withdrawal of the state as a source of subsidy and control, and in particular of the radical macroeconomic reforms. More recently, market forces have become a more independent causal factor. Whereas disparities in 1986 could be treated as a final picture of the centrally planned economy under communism, the 1992 disparities could be treated as a starting point, when the direction of transformation had been determined, and the evolution of future disparities will depend more on market forces.

The regional structure of GDP in 1992 (Fig. 10.11) indicates first of all significant regional polarization. In spite of 40 years of egalitarian spatial policy, the Katowice region contained 11.4% of the whole national GDP, whereas 15 regions contributed below 1%. The second largest region contributing disproportionately to GDP is the Warsaw region. The share of other regions with large urban agglomerations was over 3%.

The evolution of this picture since 1986 (Fig. 10.12) shows the relative decrease of the share of Warsaw and other large industrial regions, reflecting the sharp

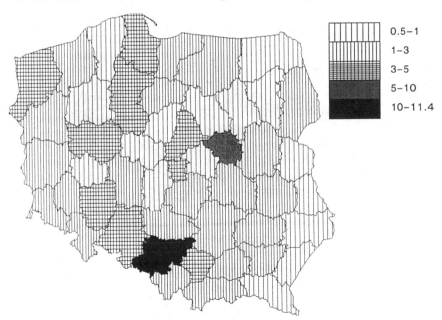

Figure 10.11 The distribution of Gross Domestic Product in 1992 (%). After: Zienkowski 1994.

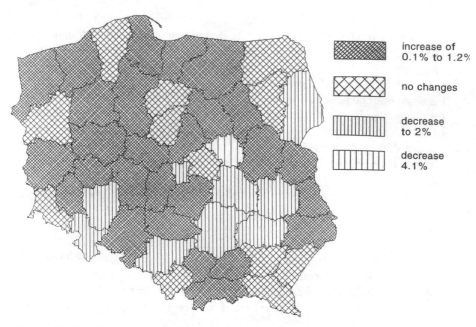

increase of
0.1% to 1.2%

no changes

decrease
to 2%

decrease
4.1%

Figure 10.12 The evolution of share of Gross Domestic Product, 1986–92 (%). After: Zienkowski 1994.

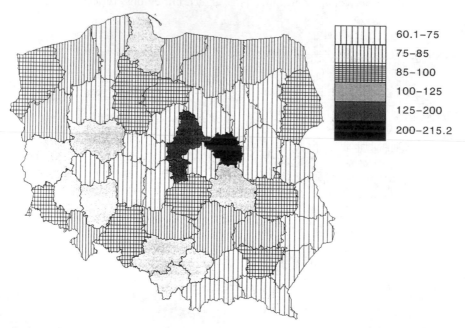

60.1–75

75–85

85–100

100–125

125–200

200–215.2

Figure 10.13 The differentiation of Gross Domestic Product in 1986 per inhabitant (%). After: Zienkowski 1994.

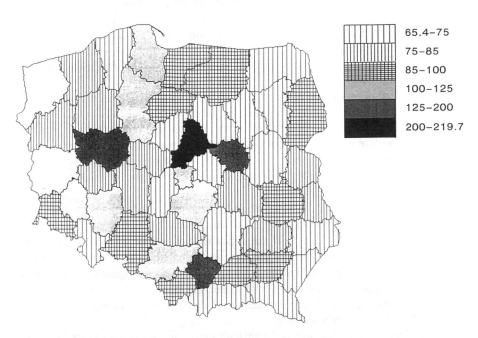

Figure 10.14 The differentiation of Gross Domestic Product in 1992 per inhabitant (%). After: Zienkowski, 1994.

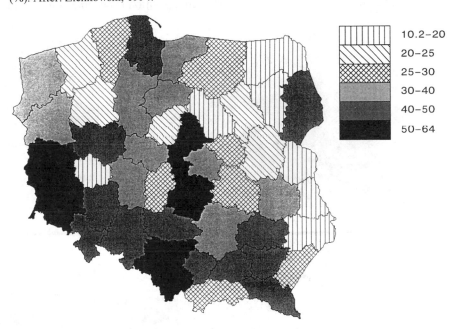

Figure 10.15 Share of industry in Gross Domestic Product, 1986, by voivodships (%).

recession of the last phase of communism and the first two years of market-oriented transformation. In the rest of the country, either the situation has not changed or the region has increased its contribution to GDP (the case with the majority of regions).

The distribution of GDP per inhabitant (Figs 10.13, 10.14) reveals the highest position of the Plock region, generated by the relatively new and modern petrochemical industry; and the Warsaw, Cracow, Poznań agglomeration as centres of the more modern economy. The industrial regions were in a secondary position. The most important change between 1986 and 1992 was the relative slump of the majority of eastern voivodships, whereas some of the western voivodships showed improvement.

The highest contribution to the national GDP is by industry. In 1986 over 50% of GDP was generated in industry in eight voivodships of southern and southwestern Poland (Fig. 10.15). The decline of importance of industry to 1992 was remarkable and only in three voivodships did industry contribute over 50% to the regional GDP (Fig. 10.16). The largest urban agglomeration also manifested the de-industrialization tendency. This relative de-industrialization of the largest industrial centres coexists with a relative increase of industries in less developed regions, for example in Siedlce, Piła, Koszalin, Leszno.

The decline in the importance of agriculture in the generation of GNP has been even more marked than in industry. In the northeast over 35% of GDP in 1986 came from agriculture (Fig. 10.17). In the west such a position is occupied only by the

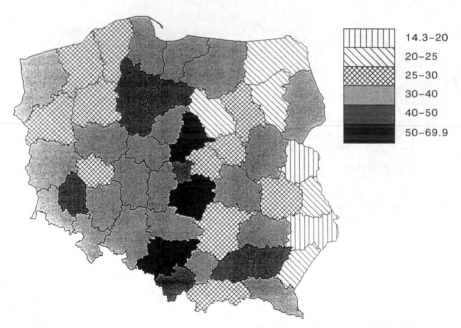

	14.3–20
	20–25
	25–30
	30–40
	40–50
	50–69.9

Figure 10.16   Share of industry in Gross Domestic Product, 1992, by voivodships (%).

160

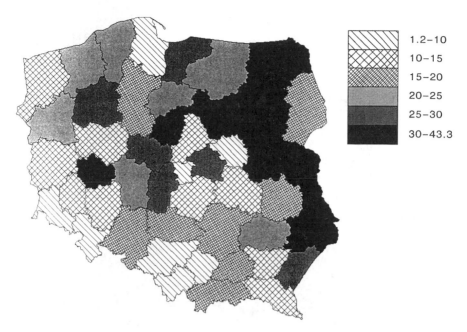

⧄	1.2–10
⊠	10–15
▤	15–20
▦	20–25
▨	25–30
■	30–43.3

Figure 10.17 Share of agriculture in Gross Domestic Product, 1986, by voivodships (%).

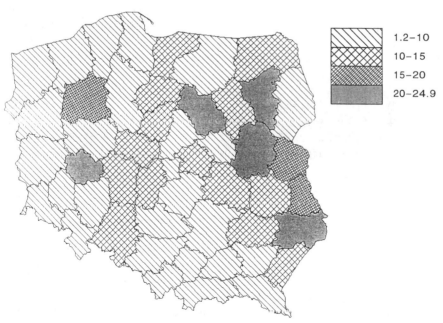

⧄	1.2–10
⊠	10–15
▤	15–20
▦	20–24.9

Figure 10.18 Share of agriculture in Gross Domestic Product, 1992, by voivodships (%).

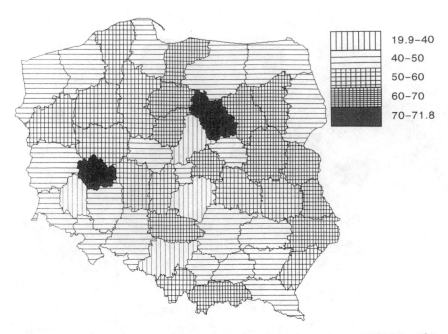

Figure 10.19 Share of Gross Domestic Product in private sector, 1992 (%). After: Zienkowski 1994.

best developed Leszczyńskie voivodships and Pila. In 1992 the overall position of agriculture had declined and there was no single region with more than a 25% share in GDP generated in agriculture (Fig. 10.18). The regional dichotomy has been maintained between the predominantly rural northeast and east and more urbanized and industrialized west.

A new phenomenon in regional change is the expansion of the private sector in the economy. The highest share of GDP generated in the private sector is particularly in the rural areas, with private farming being dominant (Fig. 10.19). In the most urbanized and industrialized voivodships or those of the west and north, the share of the private sector was still below 50% (in 1992).

10.5 The gainers and losers in regional development

The new regional structure under formation will be shaped by two basic trends: the collapse of the old industrial regions and deepening underdevelopment of already underdeveloped areas, and the formation of new prosperous regions with production adapted to the requirements of the new economic conditions, that is, the competitive domestic and international markets.

The political and economic factors that provided a privileged position for the expansion of traditional industry have lost their significance. The market economy, particularly in terms of the new international relations, has brought new conditions and tendencies into regional development. The most important are the attractiveness of particular regions for investors, the existing business environment and the state of the natural environment.

During the early 1990s the strongest industrial centres, specializing in coal mining, steel and other metal production, military equipment and shipbuilding, and the textile industry, started to decline. Their future depends on the restructuring process and on their ability to attract and absorb new capital investment. The next strongest were rural areas industrialized under communism contrary to conventional economic rationality.

The regions with economic sectors in crisis are Upper Silesia, Lódz, the Sudety region, and eastern and northern Poland. All these areas are facing problems of recession and unemployment and have little chance of recovering. This is particularly true of the eastern and northeastern voivodships.

The leaders of the transformation, that is, large cities such as Warsaw and Poznań, but also Gdańsk and Szczecin, will probably become the booming regions in the future. At the national scale, a prosperity corridor is under formation on the axes from the border with Germany (nearest Berlin) through Poznań to Warsaw.

Evaluating the regions by different aspects of pro-market transformation, the following voivodships are favoured: Poznań and Warsaw, to some extent also Cracow, Bielsko–Biala, Leszno, Kalisz, Skierniewice and the urban agglomeration of Gdańsk, Szczecin and Wroclaw. The lowest evaluation usually goes to voivodships along the eastern and northern borders, along with Jelenia Góra and Walbrzych in the southwest.

The formation of the regional structure of Poland could be interpreted in terms of change in the labour market with the unemployment problems, the development of the private sector outside agriculture, foreign investment and formation of new infrastructure and social conditions for new entrepreneurs, and by particular measures of wealth such as average monthly income or the rate of car ownership.

The fall in employment from the mid-1980s to 1993 was partly the result of demographic trends, but above all of the economic transformation and the recession. At the regional scale the decrease occurred in the whole of Poland. Relatively small decreases occurred only in already better developed areas. The dramatic deactivization of labour concerned areas also with high unemployment, particularly in the north (see §10.2).

The greatest fall in employment in absolute terms (over 200000) concerns first of all the two industrial voivodships with the largest share of the coal industry. Employment has also fallen by over 100000 in Wroclaw, Opole, Warsaw and Gdańsk (Fig. 10.20).

There have been significant changes in the employment structure. The most important shift in employment has been from construction and industry and to the service sector. As data from Table 10.1 indicate, from 1985 to 1993 there was a substantial fall in employment in the majority of sectors of the national economy. A substantial increase occurred only in trade, finance and education. In 1993 the

163

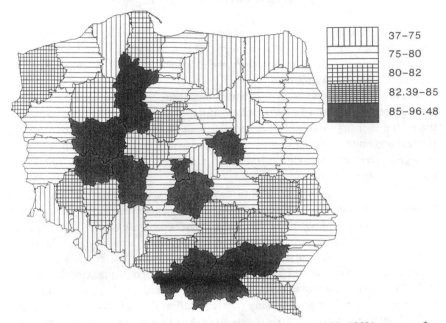

‖‖‖‖‖	37–75
▭▭▭	75–80
▦▦	80–82
▒▒	82.39–85
■■	85–96.48

Figure 10.20 Drop in employment between 1985 and 1993. 1985: 100%; average for Poland: 82.39%. After: Zienkowski 1994.

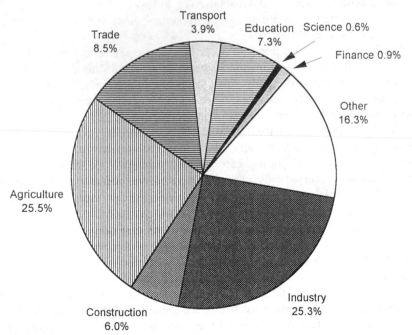

Figure 10.21 Employment by sectors of National Economy, 1993. After: *Rocznik statystyczny* 1994. Warsaw: GUS.

employment structure (Fig. 10.21) still represented the traditional pattern, with a very large share (25.5%) in agriculture.

By the more aggregated three-sector classification of the national economy (I – agriculture and forestry; II – industry and construction; III – services and other branches), the largest decreases in employment in the 1990s in sector II occurred in Lódź, Cracow, Warsaw and often in voivodships in which the old industrial regions are located. Only in Katowice voivodship was the share greater than 50% and in two (Lódź and Walbrzych) greater than 40% (Central Office of Planning 1993). The strong decline also affected economically very weak and less industrialized voivodships. The decrease in Ostrolęka, Zamość, Ciechanów and Lomża indicates a de-industrialization process that has nothing to do with transition to a post-industrial society, but for these regions rather a process of recession or even a revival of agriculture. The increase in sector III, mostly in service branches, at the beginning of 1990s has been concentrated regionally in the most urbanized areas of larger agglomerations, whereas it decreased in the central and eastern parts of the country where there was already the lowest share of service employment.

Generally, in the urbanized regions the decline of industrial employment has been balanced by the increase in service employment. In the less developed rural voivodships the sharp decline of industrial employment is accompanied by an increased share of agricultural employment and a very small increase in the services sector. This indicates that sector I (agriculture) has become the retaining sector for the labour force.

One of the results of the regional restructuring will be an inevitable shift of labour force from the traditional industrial regions to more prosperous regions. However, it will not happen in the short term because of housing shortages and a severe lack of investment capital. By the 1980s Poland generally experienced very low migration rates, which have been declining further in the 1990s. In 1993, migration was mostly concentrated on the urban agglomerations of Katowice, Warsaw and Gdańsk. The long-term stagnation of several regions will be a crucial problem of economic change in the future of Poland. The adaptation of the regional structure to the free market economy will last for a long time.

There will be two basic sources of regional development: the expansion of export sectors and the expansion of production able to compete with foreign products for the domestic market.

Evaluating the regional distribution of wealth, it is very difficult to find a reliable indicator within the existence of a vast shadow economy (usually estimated at over 30% of GDP). An indirect indicator could be the remuneration level from work and the rate of car ownership.

The regional structure of remuneration from work showed the highest monthly wages throughout the 1990s in the Katowice, Legnica, and Warsaw voivodships. Changes have weakened the domination of voivodships with traditional types of industry, whereas there was a relative improvement in the multifunctional voivodships of the largest urban agglomerations, that is, Warsaw, Gdańsk, Cracow, Poznań and Szczecin. At the bottom end of the remuneration scale, to the

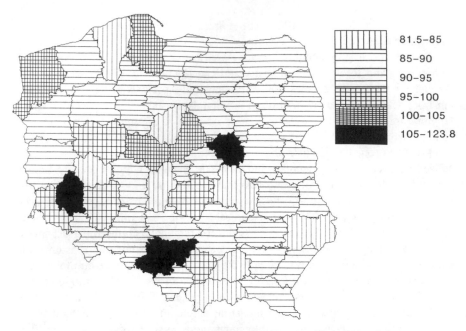

Figure 10.22 Average monthly wages, 1993. Poland: 100. After: *Rocznik Statystyczny Województw* 1994. Warsaw: GUS.

traditionally weakest rural voivodships were added other voivodships with low levels of industrialization (Fig. 10.22).

The private car ownership rate is an indicator of wealth in Poland. In 1990–93, car ownership rose from 138 to 176 per 1000 inhabitants. Inter-voivodship disparities show the highest rate in Warsaw (328) and the lowest (115) in Nowy Sącz voivodship (Fig. 10.23). So the richer regions in Poland are Warsaw in the eastern part of the country and the region between Poznań and Wrocław in the west. Above average rates of car ownership are also found in Bydgoszcz and Piła and in the industrial regions of the south.

After three years of transformation, the Central Planning Commission stated that there had been a gradual increase of regional disparities. The recession and unemployment have become the new and probably more permanent phenomena for some voivodships, whereas economic progress connected with expansion of the private sector has been concentrated regionally. So, a classification of voivodships according to economic prosperity in terms of advancement of transformation (Fig. 10.24) indicates strong spatial polarization.

The first group of voivodships, the "leaders in transformation", consist of multifunctional urbanized agglomerations such as Warsaw, Poznań, Wrocław and Cracow, along with Bielsko–Biała voivodship and the sea port agglomeration of Gdańsk and Szczecin. These voivodships are the best prepared to face the challenges of a market economy, with relatively good international connections, a diversified economic base, and a high level of labour-force skills. These areas are also characterized by the highest level of entrepreneurial attitudes of inhabitants and the quickest process of privatization.

The second group of voivodships represent "the industrial regions" and consist of the Katowice, Łódź and Wałbrzych voivodships. These areas are dominated by traditional extractive or basic processing industries, with extremely underdeveloped service functions. A major problem for these regions is the high level of degradation of the natural environment. This category of highly polluted regions is represented by the voivodships of Jelenia Góra, Konin, Legnica, Tarnobrzeg.

The third group, "underdeveloped areas", is concentrated in the northeast and east, and is characterized by low levels of urbanization and socio-economic development, domination by the agricultural sector, and low labour force skills. The privatization process and the development of the private sector is the slowest there.

The fourth group, the "north", consists of Elbląg, Koszalin, Olsztyn, Słupsk, Gdańsk and Szczecin voivodships, minus the urban agglomeration of Gdańsk and Szczecin. This part is characterized by a very deep recession and by the collapse of the dominant state-owned agricultural sector. The highest rates of unemployment in this area are spreading to the neighbouring voivodships of Gorzów and Piła.

The fifth group consists of voivodships connected with medium-size cities and agglomerations. The economic structure of this group is diversified, but there is both a shortage of infrastructural facilities and a weak service sector. For some areas, particularly for small and medium-size cities dominated by one type of industry, there are unemployment problems.

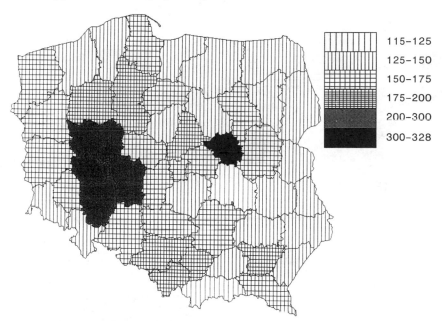

115–125
125–150
150–175
175–200
200–300
300–328

Figure 10.23 Private cars per 1000 inhabitants, 1993. After: *Rocznik statystyczny województw* 1994. Warsaw: GUS.

In 1994 the Central Office of Planning provided a similar classification of regions. In this new classification (after four years of transformation) the increase of the disparities has been noted. The regional trend in development remains similar.

It is worth adding that the second group of "the industrial regions" dominated by traditional industry, even if classified as problem areas, are still important for the Polish economy. Those seven voivodships still (in 1992) produced one-third of the gross domestic product of Poland. This group is dominated by the state sector and will remain in that position for some time. The radical transformation or restructuring is politically impossible because of the impact on the whole country. This concerns in particularly the Katowice voivodship (covering the Upper Silesian industrial region) as the most important industrial region in Poland. In spite of its high economic and political status, it is regarded by some local research-ers as an object of long-lasting discrimination. Describing the Silesian situation, Szczepański (1992) used the concept of internal colonization as an aspect of inter-dependence between core and periphery. The periphery in this case is Upper Silesia and the core is the central administration in Warsaw. This interpretation of the status of Silesia depends on recognition that a disproportionate share of wealth produced in the region goes to the disposal of the centre, that there is an asymmetry of political power, that there is an imposition of standards of national culture, and that there is a persistence of dirty branches of industry in the region. For local researchers this region is an example of so-called "long-lasting phenomena"

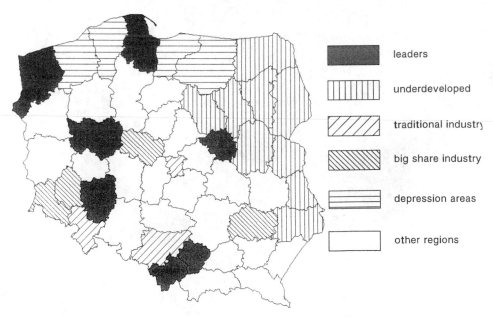

Figure 10.24 Advancement of transformation, 1990–92. After: Central Planning Commission.

because since the eighteenth century it was a peripheral region producing raw material and low value-added goods for evolving centres. Those centres were, throughout the centuries of the Austro–Hungarian empire, Prussia, Germany and Poland.

Two new regional problems have emerged: one along the western border, the second along the eastern border. On the western border, the great wealth and economic potential disparity between Germany, one of the richest countries of western Europe, and the relatively underdeveloped former Regained Territories, raises the threat of losing economic and political control to Germany. The peripheral region (in relation to other economic regions of Poland) along the western border is characterized by spontaneous economic development and seems to have a chance for more stable future development. So this region is a gainer in the latest years of transformation.

The development of the eastern border region is threatened by the political and economic instability of eastern neighbours. For 40 years the existence of a "frozen border" with the Soviet Union functioned as an eastern wall, unattractive to any economic activity and with an outflow of population. So this area has entered into the market economy with the lowest level of infrastructure, a backward agricultural structure, the lowest level of urbanization, and the demographic structure of a rural population. Human and capital resources are very limited in this region, particularly in terms of skilled labour. The spontaneous invasion of poor citizens from the former Soviet Union and the development of a mafia-like sector of the economy are exacerbating the problem of underdevelopment of the "eastern wall".

This part of the country will probably remain the backward periphery of Poland for a long time. Fundamental improvement could come only from outside. The stimulation of the economy in this region could come from the elimination of long-standing unattractive conditions and from ameliorating the prevailing economic crisis by the development of new possibilities connected with the huge transfer of goods and peoples across the eastern border. Of potential significance also is the high quality of the unpolluted environment, unusual in Europe's rural landscapes.

The future regional differentiation of Poland depends partly on the ability of particular regions to attract inflow of capital, both domestic and foreign. Each region is attractive to a different degree. In some recent research the attractiveness for investment has been measured by the level of industrialization, level of living, labour force resources and quality, the formation of a business environment, infrastructure equipment (particularly in telecommunications and transport), the activity of local self-government and the local community, geographical location, proximity for example to the economic centres or border, and natural environmental quality (Dąbrowski et al. 1995). Based on these indicators, the latest synthetic regional typology provided by the Institute of Market Economy, according to attractiveness for investment, shows regions of progress and of stagnation.

The most attractive category includes Warsaw (Fig 10 25). The high position of the Katowice region is based on the assumption that it still has great economic potential, in spite of the catastrophic state of the natural environment, and urgent

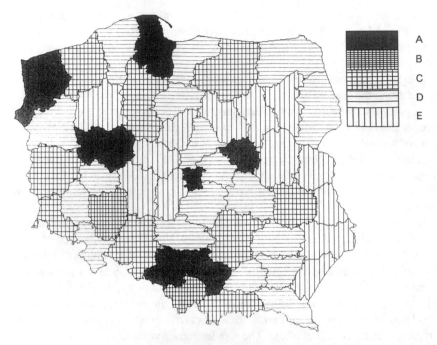

Figure 10.25 The index of investment attractiveness, 1995. After: *Rzeczpospolita* **76** (4029), 30 Marzec 1995.

restructuring problems. The high position of Gdańsk and Szczecin is based mostly on location (as gates to Poland), relative to modern industry. The position of Poznań is because traditionally it is one of the best developed and organized regions in Poland. The high position of Łódź is somewhat unexpected; in spite of severe recession in the textile industry and the general crises of the economy, the local community manages to create a relatively favourable business environment attracting much new investment. Wroclaw and Bielsko–Biala voivodships also have relatively good positions.

The worst categories are found in eastern and central Poland, which is traditionally less developed. So, if there are no basic changes in regional policy, or large-scale investment as a pull factor, this region is destined to stagnate.

The voivodships of Katowice and Cracow, classified in the category of most attractive region for investment (Dąbrowski et al. 1995), are in another classification allocated to the category of regions with the highest concentration of internal disparities and barriers – together with Jelenia Góra and Konin voivodships (Prusek & Bieda 1995). The rural and less developed eastern and central part of Poland have fewer internal disparities and barriers and could profit from apparent advantages of backwardness in future development (ibid.).

10.6 Towards a new regional policy

Regional policy had secondary economic significance during the communist period, diminishing further on the eve of the collapse. It became ineffective earlier than the whole system of central planning. Particularly important was the gradual formation of regional political lobbies, mostly based on industrial sectors accumulating as much national investment resources in their regions as possible. This policy was based above all on ideological and political objectives. The spatial plans for Poland were a sort of propaganda device of the central government, or a collection of aspirations, rather than sets of realistic objectives for balanced regional development. In reality, the economic development of some regions frequently went in directions other than those provided by plans, causing an increase of interregional disparities. Under communism, regional policy was determined by ideological objectives, so it was not necessary to have rational economic policy. The final collapse occurred in the mid-1980s as a part of the general economic crisis and the ineffective attempt at reform of the national economy.

According to the liberal economic theory adopted as the basis of transformation, market forces should regulate all the problems. The tacit assumption was that market mechanisms will replace the central planner in the allocation of resources. So, as some researchers indicate (Bagdziński & Maik 1994), there was no place in the "shock therapy" for regional policy, because macroeconomic priority prevailed. The absence of regional policy has been treated partly as a type of policy in itself. The neglect of regional policy could be partly explained also by the behaviour of the regional planners and planning staff who, as a part of the old establishment, were not as interested in the success of the transformation, whereas the pro-transformation attitude of regionally oriented professionals was not strong enough. They were passively adapting to the evolving circumstances or criticizing the trends *ex post facto*. This situation was very frustrating for the people involved in regional planning, because demand for their skills, which were not as relevant for the market economy requirements, became very limited, . Some issues of regional policy and regional planning have also been neglected by local authorities, having no will or knowledge to undertake decisive actions.

The regional structure of Poland formed under communism will be preserved to a certain extent. In spite of the restructuring process, the existing spatial pattern could have positive or negative effects for particular regions. Part of the investment process in 1990–92 consolidated the existing spatial pattern and contributed to the maintenance of the old and crisis-generating type of regional economy (Kukliński 1991, Bagdziński & Maik 1994).

The past four years of transformation dramatically exposed the weakest regions, and the hidden disproportions in economic structure. The regional structure formed for different, mostly ideological, purposes does not fit the contemporary market economy. The newly introduced elements of free market competition revealed the strong components of the regional economy. In addition, since the end of 1993, the left-wing government has been unwilling to introduce more radical

171

restructuring, in order to maintain the political support of the employees of traditional industries and of the peasants. In spite of that, the new differentiating process that began after 1989 is widening regional disparities. It highlighted the regions of economic depression and those of relative prosperity. The depressed areas particularly need immediate action, in the form of economic and social support, to prevent any social unrest and also maintain the transformation process. The attempt to formulate a new regional policy is congruent with the end of the illusion that the invisible hand of the market economy will solve all the problems.

The evaluation of regional policy (1990–93) by the Central Planning Office stresses the following points. First, regional policy has been subordinated to macroeconomic policy. The main decisions on territorial organization have been concentrated at and imposed from the central government level. Secondly, regional policy has been reduced to ameliorating the spatial concentration of unemployment. Thirdly, the areas of high unemployment have become the object of exclusive intervention from the centre in regional development. This intervention was uniform, without taking into account regional specificity. Fourthly, the central budget for direct regional policy was minimal, and other state funds ignored the state's regional policy aims. Fifthly, in the central government administration there was no structure responsible for implementing regional policy. The Central Planning Office designed only the general principles, with responsibility allocated to different branches. Only for the regions in crisis, or as a result of highly political pressure, did the inter-sector bodies try to co-ordinate regional policy. Sixthly, the regional level administration (voivodships) has lost the legal and material power to co-ordinate regional policy.

Summing up, regional policy is of minor importance in general and has been neglected until the spatial concentration of problems has accumulated to the point of political explosion. This policy is reactive rather than creating the vision for longer-term strategies. Regional policy has been ineffective because of over-centralization at the national scale and lack of financial resources. The lack of a legal basis denied this policy the capacity to co-ordinate the allocation of public resources (Pyszkowski 1995).

From the organizational point of view, an improvement would bring, some future reorganization of the state administration and a new administrative subdivision of the country. Both these developments would have a basic influence on regional policy as a tool for the socio-economic development of Poland.

The crucial legislation – the reform of territorial organization, which should be the basis for the regional formation – has unfortunately been postponed. What is expected is only the shift of different economic sectors of some fields of responsibility from the central government level to the voivodships (i.e. regional) level. This will facilitate economic activity on the part of voivodship administrations as representatives of the state in the promotion of regional economic development.

There is a need to co-ordinate and above all collect information about the real size of investment in particular regions. This investment comes from voivodship budgets, different state budget subsidies, foreign assistance, resources of different agencies and foundations of the private sector and State Treasury. So far, such information is not even collected (ibid.).

Two main programmes are under construction: the short-term programme of development for 1994–7, and the longer-term programme for the decade. As a starting point, the existing differentiation of the country has been identified and its genesis established. The next point involves the elaboration of appropriate methods of regional policy for the state. The characteristic feature of these programmes is a lack of any vision or consistent strategy. The Central Planning Office has proposed only to strengthen state administration and the role of the regional administration as agents of the centre in conducting regional policy at the national and intra-voivodship (intra-regional) scale. Except for the attempt to identify the causes of the increased disparities, it is still being considered whether it is worth undertaking any action and whether the means to influence this process exist. The aims of regional policy of the state are still under formation. The next step will be the preparation of instruments appropriate to the aims and specificity of the regions. This approach underestimates the emergence of new actors in economic development that will shape regional policy. The most important, except for private investors, is becoming local government.

The administrative organization of the country involves two tiers of territorial division. Since 1975 it has consisted of 49 voivodships and over 2300 municipalities (gminas). Up to 1990 the whole of Poland was centrally administered. Since 1990, the Local Government Act has delegated some basic responsibilities to the lower level. The authority of central government remains at the voivodship level. Democratically elected local government becomes representative of the interests of the local community rather than the state central administration.

For regional planning, physical planning, land management and environmental protection are crucially importance. The local authority has become an investor in the local infrastructure, and as owners of former communal properties obtained the power to lease or sell it.

The executive power of local government is, however, partly limited by the existence of many legislative contradictions and financial constraints. The immature legislation creates permanent conflict between the voivodships as representatives of the central government and the gminas as representatives of the local communities. Also, since 1993, there has been a gradual attempt to regain central control by the left-wing government.

The formulation of regional policy at the local government level has several additional constraints. These concern, for example, the lack of trained specialists (who would rather work in voivodship administration), access to statistical information, land registration and in some cases the lack of definitive information on landownership, and the devolution of decisions to different sectors and departments. The local physical plans, in the vast majority of cases, are rather ad hoc modifications of pre-1990 development plans. Also, the possibility of the local authority in promoting the economic development of its own commune faces constraints in the legislative field and in existing physical infrastructure provided by communes. One of the solutions was a proposal for the introduction of the county (powiats) as a second tier of local self-government. The direct control of administration at this level by an elected body would bring further decentralization and economic and political benefits on a national scale.

The withdrawal from the reform of administrative divisions by the left-wing government in 1994 could be interpreted as a final reversal of the decentralization policy adopted between 1990 and 1994, and as a limitation of local democracy.

The reorganization of public administration and the evolving role of the local, regional and central government virtually eliminated regional planning. Regional policy has been reduced to the provision of very general indications by central government and the spontaneous initiative of local government or regionally defined groups of local authorities.

The predominant regional policy of the government is the attempt to combat regional inequality in order to secure economic development of the whole country and consequent sociopolitical stability. Regional policy in the near future will be strongly conditioned by the macroeconomic priorities, the level of contemporary development, and the financial situation. There is a threat that, as during the communist period, regional policy may be conditioned strongly by political priorities. The evident drift of the government to centralization is challenged by the well established new actors: the private sector and local self-government.

Integration with the European Union would have a substantial impact on the formation of regional policy. Poland had the first indication of this transformation during the liberalization of trade with the West and the protectionist restriction imposed by the European Union on the import of Polish steel, textiles and agricultural products. So the regions specializing in those products would be the first to be affected by the transformation and reorientation of Polish trade from the East to the West.

An important stimulus for the formation of a new regional policy would come also from the association treaty with the European Union. The existence of some regional assistance programmes and gradual adaptation of the whole country to western European standards would certainly contribute to the creation of a new modern regional policy.

Contemporary developments, under the impact of the market economy and of the tendency towards integration with western Europe, will inevitably lead to the reshaping of the general spatial pattern of Poland after the year 2000. The old "traditional" inverted T-shape or triangle-like pattern of the 1950s, with its base in southern Poland (see Figs 4.1, 1.2), will shift its best developed and economically strongest southern base towards the west (Fig. 10.26). So far, the areas closer to the border with Germany have the greatest location rent for future development. Along the eastern border, some contemporary economic improvement has too little impact in compensating for the negative influence of several decades of the "eastern wall".

The belt of development between the German border and Poznań and further towards Warsaw is under formation. The secondary axes will develop towards

174

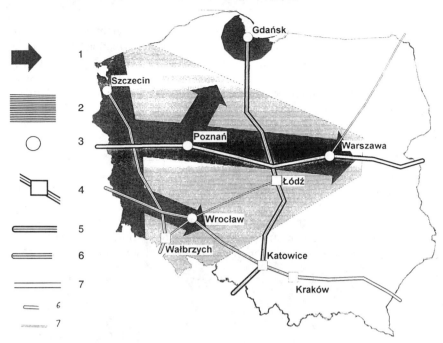

Figure 10.26 The spatial structure of Poland 2000+. 1. Main area and axes of economic prosperity. 2. Areas of potential economic development. 3. Biggest gainer of transformation and innovation centres. 4. Old industrial centres under restructuralization. 5. Projected principal motorway network. 6. Projected secondary motorway. 7. Projected additional motorway.

Bydgoszcz and Gdańsk and in Lower Silesia towards Wrocław. This area (particularly Greater Poland with Poznań) will probably become the most prosperous region in future, gaining from the proximity of Western sources of innovation and capital. The already good communications infrastructure is under rapid modernization and also the projected motorway network will improve the economic prospects for those areas. The most likely route for construction of the first motorway is the west–east line, towards Warsaw, which will attract the most support from foreign capital. This route will serve as an agent of new and modern economic development.

The north–south motorway from Katowice towards Lódź and Gdańsk, while strengthening the already existing regional pattern, is of special significance for reconstruction of Upper Silesia, Kraków and Lódź. The most rapid improvement could be expected in the Kraków agglomeration, and with successful restructuring in Lódź, but in the case of Upper Silesia restructuring will last for decades.

The "location rent" of the southwest, particularly the Sudety mountains region, is severely limited by the dramatic natural environment and the need for radical restructuring of the economy. It particularly concerns the traditional coal and textile industries of the Walbrzych region.

The northeast, which already represents the lowest economic potential, has opportunities only in ecological agriculture, tourism and recreation. However, the advantage of an unpolluted environment is not sufficient for future prosperity, without an inflow of external investment. Similarly, the eastern and southeastern parts have few opportunities, compared with other regions to attract radical inflow of capital. The situation of many towns dependent on single (now usually collapsing) industrial plants or traditional agriculture will generate an outflow of labour force.

The formation of such a regional structure in the future is also supported by the contemporary regional differentiation of peoples' attitudes towards transformation. The most innovative and active behaviour is seen in the largest urban agglomerations, in contrast to the predominantly rural areas. At the regional scale, at the level of local communities, the most active and prosperous areas are in Greater Poland. The more traditional and conservative attitudes of the population outside the urban areas are in eastern and central Poland, and the southeastern parts.

CHAPTER 11

The security and modernization challenges

Consideration of the geopolitical position of Poland in Europe over the past two centuries has been dominated by very negative attitudes. Usually Poland's geographical location was regarded as unfavourable in geopolitical terms (between the two powers of Germany and Russia), and this has been a basis for alien domination. The first sign of a more positive attitude has emerged from the unpredictable process of political transformation since 1989. The location of Poland in European space is discussed again, and often optimistically, but it is not clear yet whether it now could be regarded as a favourable element for future development.

Political transformation in Europe since 1989 seems to have created a new geopolitical situation. The following events shaped the new situation: the end of the Warsaw Pact Treaty (July 1991), of COMECON (December 1991), and the collapse of the Soviet Union. The impact of these complex events on geopolitical evolution has been overstated. The tremendous expectations of radical liberation from external dependency, particularly on Russia, has been fulfilled by the withdrawal of the Russian military presence from Polish territory. However, the expected rapid integration with western Europe has been constrained. The rejection from the Western side has given rise to many frustrating issues in internal and foreign policy.

In spite of the fact that Polish aspirations are not fully satisfied, the scale of the transformation is enormous. In just four years, starting from the status of a Soviet satellite, Poland re-established full political independence, obtained associate status with the European Union and reoriented its economic relations to Western countries. The indeterminate position of Poland in the political and military arenas of Europe has attracted superpowers, and other strong nations, to play the "Polish card" for their own interests.

The basic geopolitical dilemma remains unchanged: does Poland now become a protective zone for western Europe or a bridge between West and East? It is very clear that this dilemma will be resolved by developments in Europe, over which Poland has very limited influence and to which it will have to adapt in order to maintain its own identity. However, the will of Polish citizens is clearly determined and is congruent with foreign policy; the main objective of Poland is economic and cultural integration with the European Atlantic and Mediterranean regions.

The collapse of the communist system, and of the Yalta order in Europe, opened up new and old conflicts frozen for 50 years by the East–West global confrontation. The most important – the ethnic conflict – does not concern Poland directly.

The security challenge for Poland has its roots in an old geopolitical situation. After the dissolution of the Warsaw Pact and the collapse of the Soviet Union, Poland was for several years in a very comfortable position. However, the geostrategic vacuum has not lasted for long. It seems to have ended with Boris Yeltsin's veto of the integration of Poland and other central European countries with NATO, and with the silent recognition of this veto by the West. The illusion of security has ended.

Two-thirds of Poles, surveyed in June 1993, believe that Polish sovereignty is threatened and that this threat comes from Russia. The attempt to institutionalize security is because of the distrust of the West. More than half of respondents in 1994 "would not count on the help of the West in case of a direct threat to Polish sovereignty" (CBOS 1994h). Additionally, 50% of those polled believed it possible that NATO countries could make an agreement with Russia "behind Poland's back". This results from the belief that the most important goal of NATO is to have good relations with Russia.

The perception of the threat to Polish sovereignty, however, has fallen from the high level of 38% of respondents in November 1993 (after the success of the Zhirinowsky nationalist party in the Russian election and Russian veto of Polish and central European membership in NATO) to 21% in June 1994, probably as a result of the introduction of the Partnership for Peace and the Prague Summit (the meeting of President Clinton with central European presidents).

Of key significance for the future security of Poland is the situation in the former Soviet Union. Foreign policy has been reoriented towards Western counties since 1989 – towards the rapid integration with NATO and the European Union. The parallel political strategy has been based on conducting a balanced Eastern policy, between support of the newly independent states separating Poland from Russia and of Russia itself.

Relatively new phenomena have emerged to threaten Poland's security. Polish territory has become attractive for the transit of narcotics, the laundering of illegal capital, internationally organized crime operations and uncontrolled migration.

11.1 The menace from the East

The security challenge comes mostly from the east. Economic chaos and political destabilization could create waves of refugees to Poland. The same can be said of the possibility of another ecological catastrophe on the scale of Chernobyl.

The basic menace comes from Russia. The screen of independent states separating Poland from Russia has a very weak and temporary significance. The independence of Byelorussia and Ukraine is not fully established. The latest developments in Russia, particularly the re-establishment of the superpower policy of the former Soviet Union, raises three geopolitical issues that could have a substantial impact on Poland's security.

The first issue concerns internal developments in Russia: maintaining the territorial integrity of Russia itself and the confrontation between pro-democratic and nationalistic options. The development of conflict in the former Soviet Union, caused by the deep economic and political crisis, could create a civil war, ethnic conflicts, border confrontations or the re-establishement of some ideological orthodoxy. It could lead directly to the resurrection of Russian nationalism and attempted domination over central Europe. All this could result in huge migration waves and economic and political pressure.

It is assumed that the formation of a democratic Russia, whether territorially integrated or not, is in the interests of Poland. For Poles, however, it is very evident that Russia is moving in an authoritarian direction, and that the great significance of the military sector in the economy will result in a return to traditional imperial policy. This development will create a direct menace to the independence of our eastern neighbours and, in the next step, to Poland itself. A foreign policy oriented only towards the West is to expose Poland's security to the greater economic and political menace from the East.

The acquisition of security support from the West has not so far brought real success. The direct rejection of central Europe's integration with NATO was accompanied by the statement that the West does not intend to guarantee the security of this region, in spite of vague verbal promises made by Western politicians now and in the past. It seems that, in conditions of confrontation between East and West, Poland will have more chance of integration with NATO as a front-line state than in conditions of relaxation of Russian–American relations.

The second issue is the gradual economic and political subordination of the former Soviet republics to Russia. It is assumed that the existence of fully independent and democratic Ukraine, Byelorussia, Lithuania, Latvia and Estonia are the best guarantees for Poland and all other central European countries released from the menace of Russian domination. A substantial part of Polish eastern policy is devoted to support for the independence of these states, with the highest priority devoted to maintaining good relations with the Russian Federation (or Commonwealth of Independent States). It was a Polish initiative to sign a series of bilateral agreements, which guarantee good relations and confirm existing international borders. In spite of that, the "Polish card" (as a Polish menace) is played in the internal relations of those countries, particularly in former Polish territories. This "Polish card" concerns the rebirth of Polish national identity within some Lithuanian, Byelorussian and Ukrainian citizens, together with the rebirth of Catholicism.

The presidential election in Byelorussia in July 1994 determined the subordination of this country to Russia. Alexander Lukaszenko was elected as president, with a very populist programme that stresses the re-establishment of strong relations with Russia. The same policies were declared by the other main candidate for the presidency, Viacheslav Kielbich. This election finally destroyed any illusion about the stabilization of the screen of independent states separating Poland from Russia. Both main Byelorussia candidates were competing in the subordination of their nation to Russia.

The presidential election of July 1994 in Ukraine showed a substantial division between the pro-independent candidate Leonid Kravchuk and the pro-Russian candidate Leonid Kuchma (who could hardly speak the Ukrainian language). The strongest support for the pro-independent candidate was in the western part of Ukraine, with strong support for the pro-Russian candidate in the eastern part, reflecting the ethnic division of Ukraine, which could lead to a division of this country. This division could not occur as peacefully as in Czechoslovakia. The probability of civil war in neighbouring countries creates a direct threat for Poland. Also, the existence of a highly nationalistic tendency in western Ukraine could be a source of potential danger.

The reintegration of the Soviet Union as a federation of the three eastern Slavonic republics of Russia, Byelorussia and Ukraine is very probable. Solzenicyn would include Kazakhstan, as it is dominated by a Russian population. So the revival of the eastern dominating superpower in political terms creates a fundamental security challenge for Poland in the near future. Poland is not powerful enough to support Ukrainian and Byelorussian independence effectively.

The third issue is the attempt to re-establish Russian influence over central Europe. Russia is trying to re-establish its European influence, not only as a partner in the European security system but also as one of the guaranteeing powers. The first sign of that policy was the reaction to the idea of Poland and other central European countries associating with NATO, the pressure to attain special treatment in the Partnership for Peace, and the increasing role in the Yugoslavian conflict. Russia has already become the guaranteeing power of the new states of the former Soviet Union, except for the Baltic states. It is obvious that Russian participation in pan-European organizations has the basic aim of diluting their effective functions in order for it to attain a privileged position in European affairs. The weaker the international and collective obligation, the stronger will be the position of Russia itself.

In military terms Russia has a strategic "stick" in the Kaliningrad region. This region has a common border with Poland (200 km long) and with Lithuania, but is connected with Russia only by way of the Baltic sea. This region is a part of the former East Prussia, which since the Second World War has belonged to the Soviet Union as a part of the Russian Republic. Its strategic and particularly its geopolitical position have crucial significance for the whole of central Europe and for the Baltic states.

The withdrawal of Soviet troops from central Europe causes an additional concentration of military power in this region. It is estimated according to various sources that there are 100000–200000 (the lowest figure) and 300000–500000 (the highest figure) Russian soldiers in this region. These are the best front-line military units withdrawn from Germany and other central European countries. After the withdrawal of several Baltic Fleet bases from the independent Baltic republics, only Kronstatd (near St Petersburg) and Baltijsk (near Kaliningrad) remain as Russian bases.

Additionally, this region now has the greatest concentration of military equipment in Europe. The military might of this region is greater than the armies of Poland and the other Visegrad countries.

Since 1994, Russia has been trying to impose on Lithuania an agreement for free passage for military forces to the Kaliningrad region. This could directly threaten Lithuanian sovereignty. The direct blackmail of withdrawal of petrol and gas supplies to Lithuania indicates the direction of Russian policy.

Two future scenarios are possible for this region: to become an economic zone of free trade, as a sort of European Hong Kong, or a military base in the Baltic basin that threatens the whole central European and Baltic region. This dilemma will be resolved in the future. So far, the Kaliningrad region represents only a threat.

The possibility of the integration of Poland with NATO could contradict the interests of other eastern neighbours. One can expect strong opposition to having a new "iron curtain" along its borders. However, it could be treated also as an opportunity for those countries. Undoubtedly, it is in the interests of all to develop various economic, cultural and personal relationships as much as possible.

11.2 The menace from the West

The menace from the West has a different character. Two elements of this menace should be stressed: the development of isolationist attitudes in Western countries, and the acceptance of the allocation of Poland to the Russian zone of influence as the price of a world-scale strategy for peace.

Isolationist attitudes may well occur in conditions of the development of nationalism and persistence of economic recession. In historical terms, democratic Europe is accused of committing three mistakes. The first was the concession to Hitler in the case of Czechoslovakia, and the lack of effective support for the Polish army at the beginning of the Second World War. The second was the concession to Stalin and withdrawal from half of Europe. The third will be the re-establishment of the former zone of influence, pushing Poland together with the rest of central Europe towards Russian domination. The military crises in Russia (in 1993) and the veto of central European integration with NATO brought to public consciousness the possibility of the formation of a second Yalta.

A democratic Russia cannot reliably co-exist with the rebirth of an imperialist policy, drifting towards reconstruction of the former Soviet Union. An illusion in the West, and particularly among some Russo-centric Western politicians, is based on the assumption that co-operation with Russia guarantees security in the cheapest possible way by selling central European interests to Russian influence. It only strengthens Russian potential and encourages them to extend their domination policy in a westward direction. The alternative – a democratic and strong Russia without an imperialist tendency – is simply impossible. This distrust in Poland of Russia is a result of a thousand years of history. The non-totalitarian tendencies in

Russian history were evident only in very short periods; otherwise there has been an authoritarian style of government and an expansionist policy.

In the case of Germany, the historical distrust from the Polish side is much less pronounced. The "drift towards the east" and fascism have not been the main characteristics of Germany history. However, they have been very significant during the past two centuries. So the challenge and hope for European security is the creation of a democratic and relatively demilitarized Russia. This is possible only on the whole European scale of democratic development in a Europe in which the strength or weakness of nations is not the determining factor in international relations. The more global solution will be the integration of Russia with NATO, but this seems to be very unrealistic without a threat of world-scale conflict between, for example, North and South.

The threat of political instability in the former Soviet Union could result in western Europe using Poland as a protective zone. Central Europe will again pay for the security of western Europe. The marginalization of central Europe creates a dangerous situation for Poland. The fear is that there could be an agreement between the NATO countries and Russia about security in central Europe without Poland's participation.

It is obvious that the Partnership for Peace was launched as a substitute for full membership in NATO to protect the pact from direct involvement in security guarantees for central Europe. More important for NATO countries are relations with Russia, a nuclear superpower. So Poland is likely to remain a protective zone for Western countries rather than a bridge (in the case of democratic development in former Soviet Union) or even a "front-line state" for the Western alliance (in the case of the more imperialistic developments in Russia). The Russian veto against the integration of central Europe with NATO indicates the persistence of the old geopolitical structure. The zone of influence of the superpowers, in spite of some dilution of interest, is still present and in principle has not changed much on the macro scale. The only major change has been the inclusion of eastern Germany under the Western umbrella. The fate of Poland, the Czech Republic, Slovakia and Hungary is still not determined.

The development of Eastern pressure, with the increasing delays in military integration with the NATO security structure, together with selective and constrained economic integration with the European Union, contribute to a great extent to the creation of conditions for the re-establishment of the Yalta order. The Partnership for Peace and Poland's participation in the Consultation Forum of the Western European Union, together with its participation in the Co-operation Council of Europe and the Conference on Security and Co-operation in Europe, are very important. However, they do not fully secure Polish geostrategic interests. Only the development of a pan-European security system, which is not very probable in the near future, or full integration with NATO, can secure the existence of democracy and economic prosperity in the future.

Integration with NATO would gain for Poland not only security from Russian domination but also from German domination, because the rest of the European

Union would act as a counterbalance to any German threat. It would also reduce the threat of a Russia–Germany alliance, which in Poland's history has always had a very damaging impact. Integration with NATO would be the key factor for the inflow of foreign capital and would offer a potential for economic development in the whole region. For foreign capital, military security will be an issue of paramount importance.

For now, it is in the interests of the West to leave Poland in a protective zone. The situation of Finland, which in 1995 became a new member of the European Union, is different, because in this case the Union has obtained a long common boundary with Russia. There is no reason to be afraid of extending this boundary between Poland and former Soviet Union countries, except that Poland is located on the main geostrategic axes in Europe, whereas the geographical location of Finland is peripheral.

11.3 The internal menace

Internal political and economic development will have a substantial, if not decisive, impact on the stabilization of Poland's external security. Rapid economic development, together with the substantial modernization of social and economic life and with political stabilization, would substantially ease integration into Western structures. Poland must be modernized in order to adapt to Western legal, technical and economic standards.

The internal processes that could disturb the political, economic and military integration are the slowing down of market-oriented reforms, the persistence of all types of conservative stereotypes in Polish society, the emergence and organization of interest groups against European integration, and political instability.

For example, the success of post-communist parties has become an important factor in the rebirth of Western distrust, which impedes integration. The return of the nomenclature to power after three years of democratic transformation has its place in the central and eastern European context and has not been as strong in Poland as in Hungary. The former communist nomenclature never lost power in Byelorussia, Ukraine and Russia, nor in Romania, nor even Slovakia. In Poland, during the 1993 parliamentary elections voters supported in about the same proportions post-communist parties and the divided right-wing parties. There is no return to communism in Poland, but the virus of ideas represented by the "*Homo sovieticus*" mentality, as members of the enfranchised nomenclature, and former hard-line Communist Party members, could spread. There is a threat of stagnation of the reforms, but not of a return to a centrally planned economy. So far, Poland has been a leader in central and eastern Europe in terms of economic and democratic transformation towards a market economy, and the new left-wing government also works in favour of integration with the European Union and NATO.

The economic situation has severely limited military spending, greatly reducing the military might of the Polish forces. Additionally, there are not enough resources for re-allocation of military forces from the west, where they are over-concentrated, to the east, where they are below the level necessary for national security.

In the near future the expected cost of integration with NATO, and the adaptation of the Polish military industry to Western standards, will be difficult to meet without external assistance.

11.4 Towards European integration – the modernization challenge

Integration with the European Union is for Poland the main historical chance for secure, prosperous development and modernization. Geographical location, cultural and historical links, together with the dominant pro-European attitude of Polish society, leave no alternative.

If we attempt to place Poland in general stages of development, or classification of societies, as traditional, partly traditional, partly industrialized, modern (i.e. industrial) and post-industrial society, the most appropriate would be partly traditional and partly industrialized society. This stage of development is a result of the socialist type of industrialization and urbanization, which, as an important modernization process, has been to a great extent superficial. This indicates that the urbanization and industrialization conducted under communist conditions should now be corrected and adapted to the requirements of the world market economy, and modernized to a degree suitable for integration with the post-industrial society of western Europe. The existing development gap is the reason why many of the modernization impulses coming from western Europe are still encountering impediments. The only solution seems to be the elimination of relative isolation from the world market economy by the integration that will serve also as an aid to modernization.

This economic and political integration would seem to fulfil the following aims, which will be helpful to Polish society:
- political security from the eastern threat
- "final" association of Poland with European civilization
- stable economic growth, which will raise the standard of living to European levels
- inflow of foreign capital, which will reduce the backwardness of the infrastructure
- the unlimited inflow of cultural innovation and access to new technology as a base of modernization.

Since 1989 Poland has been very determined to join the European Union. The question is whether in future the majority of people will be really persuaded of this, if the full cost of integration is evident. This concerns first of all the social cost of economic transformation and modernization of the country. There is the possibility of increasing anti-Western sentiment as soon as the cost of integration and subordination to Western economics challenges interest groups. The best examples are the peasants and the existence of many social groups that wish to have stronger relations with the East than with the West. The economic nationalism that in Poland has had a protective character and is the result of bad historical experience could be strengthened. Additionally, there is the old communist propaganda concerning capitalist exploitation, despite its subsequent dismissal. Also, the isolationist tendency in Western countries could cause a contra-reaction in Polish society.

The interests of the European Union are not always in accordance with those of Poland. This interest has a long- and short-term character. In the longer perspective the European Union will be in economic competition with Japan and the USA, and central Europe together with Poland will be a natural ally. In the shorter term, however, the recession in the European Union revealed significant constraints on integration, which will not disappear even with the end of the recession. The European Union is perceived partly as a very elite club, protecting only short-term self-interest and having in addition very powerful political and commercial instruments to implement it.

Members of the European Union are trying effectively to defend themselves from increased imports of such things as steel, textiles and agricultural products. Poland is accused of dumping by selling at artificially low prices, and trade barriers are frequently introduced by the European Union. An increasingly protectionist economic policy makes Polish public opinion suspicious of the European Union's attitude to central European democracy.

Inside the European Union a contradiction of political and economic interests exists between the northern countries, which will support integration, and the southern countries such as Greece, Portugal and Spain, and even France, which are less enthusiastic. The extension of the European Union to the Visegrad countries will finally move the political, economic and cultural balance to the north. Integration is strongly supported by Germany, in order to secure its eastern border and open up a field for economic expansion, and the UK, which treats integration as means of political dilution of the Union.

Although the Visegrad countries expect full integration with the European Union before the year 2000, the most pessimistic prediction is 20 years. The most important constraint on full integration has an economic character, as the Baldwin report indicates:

- Central European countries are relatively poor, at 30% of the per capita income level of the European Union.
- The agricultural sector in central Europe is too large.
- The cost of integration for European Union budgets has been estimated at 63 000 000 000 ECU, so against it will be two interest groups inside the EU: the poor regions and the peasants.
- Assuming 6% annual economic growth in the Visegrad countries, and 2% in the European Union, the Visegrad countries can reach 75% of the European

Union income in 20 years' time. If the increase in the Visegrad countries is only 4% a year, it will take 30 years.

Poland is a latecomer to the well established division of production in the world-wide market, and to European integration. It is a widely shared opinion that in this situation Poland should adapt itself to the interests of the European Union. Additionally, it has become clear, through time, that the "return to Europe" will be to a great extent a return to the "periphery" of prosperity in relation to the economic standard of living and the political and cultural development of the core of western Europe.

The integration will also bring negative consequences, of which the following are most frequently mentioned:

- the subordination and loss of independence to Western capital
- the unpredictable social cost of economic adjustment before the benefits begin to function
- integration under contemporary conditions suggest that Poland would remain largely a raw material supplier, to which the labour-intensive and polluting industry will be moved from the core areas
- the expected outflow of the best educated labour to the West will reduce the chances for rapid modernization of the country.

The idea of European integration is the most challenging requirement for Poland. This concerns, for example, basic change in the social structure. The reduction of the status of the peasant class, under the impact of economic reality (the competition from cheap Western food, low-level Polish technology and inefficient methods of Polish production), is the obvious example. It must be remembered that the socialist model of industrialization and urbanization was also a kind of modernization that led to a reduction of the peasant class. This social class nevertheless survived under communism; however, its predominantly conservative consciousness is now an unfavourable element in contemporary modernization. The situation of the working class under new market economy conditions is different, but the existence of some segments of this class is threatened. Although the impact of the latest stage in the transformation is not perfect, it would appear that modernization works against the interests of most segments of the working class. It seem that the intelligentsia, particularly its younger elements, are more modernization-oriented than its old bureaucratic members. The expansion of the middle class is partly an opportunity for support of modernization. Transformation has already created a self-employment category and the tremendous demand for the new jobs required in a market economy.

The only real chance for the modernization of Poland is based on the already initiated transformation of the evolution of the social consciousness. Of fundamental importance is the substantial increase in the very dynamic and innovative social groups with highly entrepreneurial attitudes and a positive perception of modernization. The contribution of these active people, at the national and regional scale, is the best guarantee of the success of modernization, modernization in the interests of not only the whole society, in abstract, but also of individuals in real terms. The increasing share of those who perceive modernization as in their personal interest is gradually increasing. However, resistance to modernization is based on the threat to personal standards of living, to the cultural values system, or just the resistance to evolution driven by external conditions.

The most important area of economic problems that will have direct political and social impacts is in agriculture. The modernization of agriculture under pressure of the contemporary and future co-existence with the European Union raises several issues. The confrontation of the highly traditional agricultural sector of the Polish economy with free inflow of Western produce reduced demand for home food production, and the sudden introduction of loans under commercial conditions (real values) deprived agriculture of its protectionist umbrella. For nearly four decades under communism there was no competition for Polish agricultural products, and the domestic and Eastern market absorbed all production. This lack of competition contributed greatly to the backwardness of the whole sector. Agriculture now has only one option: to modernize to the requirements of the international market, otherwise it will cease production or stagnate.

Modernization must involve all production, even those lines that traditionally were regarded as being of high quality. For example, best quality Polish ham and bacon have ceased to be attractive, in spite of their "natural" flavour. Also, in spite of great progress in the packaging and food-processing industries, there is a still huge gap in the quality and organization of delivery systems.

Organizational and informational issues concern first of all the skills of negotiation and the competitive capitalist game, exploiting legal gaps, banking facilities and so on. An important factor in international competition is asymmetrical access to information. For example, any plans for quotas from the Polish side are well known long before they are implemented, whereas Western-imposed restriction came as a surprise for Polish exporters. Sudden elimination of Polish competition from particular segments of agricultural markets in Europe is a sort of deliberate protectionist policy for the EU's own agricultural production. It has a direct impact, lowering production in Poland by changes in customs restrictions and by political pressures on Poland to withdraw any protection of its own market.

Polish agriculture needs substantial improvement, but the restriction by the European Union only partly explains the problems of Polish export of agricultural products. The strong protectionism of the European Union reduces the possibility of modernization.

Agriculture apart, the most challenging issues for the future integration and modernization of the country are in education. Under communism, in spite of its ineffectiveness, the social security system, along with the educational and cultural infrastructure, created the base for modernization. However, the reward from investment in education has had very limited material consequences for individuals.

The decline in the importance of education characteristic of the last phase of communism has been only partly reduced. During the first years of transformation, as far as most people were concerned, there was no connection between investment and reward. The last year of economic growth has not reduced, so far, the diminution of the standard of higher education and scientific research. The issues of educational challenges – the unequal chances in educational system and the low quality of comprehensive education – are still not solved. The idea that a high level of education for society is a precondition for modernization, and that the contemporary situation must be changed, still has verbal rather than practical support.

The market and democratic transformation, despite very obvious positive impacts, has also contributed to the reduced educational potential. For example, the elimination of political constraints and the access to the Western scientific market has resulted in a "brain drain". The outflow of highly qualified scientists and highly skilled labour could become barriers to the future modernization of Poland. With a need for dramatic modernization of the whole country, and especially of the economy, reduced research potential is a bad indicator. The brain drain from science and research has its counterpart in the expansion of the private sector, which offers better financial conditions for researchers but is still too small to encourage research itself.

In spite of that, Poland still has huge intellectual potential, which could be hired for relatively cheap prices. The shrinking of the scientific and technological innovation sector, and the drain from science and higher education, has begun substantially to diminish the capacity to reproduce highest quality specialists, reducing in this way the future development capacity of the country (Jałowiecki et al. 1994).

The integration of Poland into the world market economy brought the basic impact of modernization, but this creates only the necessary precondition for further modernization. Poland, having partly the status of a latecomer country, must accept with modernization the parallel of dependent development, whereas the alternative of autonomous development (Szczepański 1992) seems to be less realistic. Modernization, as a process following the Western pattern, will place Poland on the periphery of the world economic core of the European Union. However, this position represents substantial progress. It is expected that the gap in the standard of living between countries in the European Union and peripheral Poland will narrow, but this is not certain in the longer term. The economic transformation and modernization of Poland is conditioned by the demands of western Europe. Full accommodation to the requirements of the European Union creates a dependent asymmetrical relationship, which, although still advantageous for Poland, does not necessarily guarantee the short-term Polish interest.

Modernization conditioned by increased asymmetrical dependency on the European Union is sometimes perceived as dependency on Germany, which detracts from the enthusiasm for the process. The experience of the Second World War and partition of Poland are still present in the popular consciousness. There is no real choice for Poland: a dependency relationship with East or West is inevitable. The cultural and economic tendencies, and most importantly the will of the people, link Poland to the West. However, once established, the peripheral position will last for a long time. The question of how far the future way of life will be from that of western Europe is the main object of the contemporary and future modernization struggle for Poland.

188

References

Bagdziński, S. L. & W. Maik 1994. Determinants of regional and spatial policy in the period of system transformation. In *Changes in the regional economy in the period of system transformation*, R. Domański & E. Judge (eds), 55–69. Warsaw: PWN.

Bolesta-Kukułka, K. 1992. *Gra o władzę a gospodarka polska 1944–1991*. Warsaw: PWE.

Bossak, J. 1993. *Poland, international economic report 1992/93*. Warsaw School of Economics.

Bossak, J. 1994. *Poland, international economic report 1993/94*. Warsaw School of Economics.

Boski, P. 1993. O dwóch wymiarach lewicy – prawicy na scenie politycznej i w wartościach politycznych polskich wyborców. In *Wartości i postawy społeczne a przemiany systemowe*, J. Reykowski (ed.), 49–103. Warsaw: Wydawnictwo Instytutu Psychologii.

CBOS 1992a. *Warunki życia i sposoby radzenia sobie w sytuacji kłopotów finansowych. Komunikat z badań – Grudzień '92*. Warsaw: Centrum Badania Opinii Społecznej.

CBOS 1992b. *Konflikty i podziały w polskim społeczeństwie. Komunikat z badań – Październik '92*. Warsaw: Centrum Badania Opinii Społecznej.

CBOS 1993a. *Bogaci w społeczeństwie. Komunikat z badań – Luty '93*. Warsaw: Centrum Badania Opinii Społecznej.

CBOS 1993b. *Wyborcy zwycięskich partii. Komunikat z badań – Grudzien '93*. Warsaw: Centrum Badania Opinii Społecznej.

CBOS 1993c. *Sukces wyborczy SLD: Przyczyny, oczekiwania, konsekwencje. Komunikat z badań – Październik '93*. Warsaw: Centrum Badania Opinii Społecznej.

CBOS 1994a. *Konflikty "stare" czy "nowe". Komunikat z badań – Maj '94*. Warsaw: Centrum Badania Opinii Społecznej.

CBOS 1994b. *Religijność Polaków: 1984–1994. Komunikat z badań – Czerwiec '94*. Warsaw: Centrum Badania Opinii Społecznej.

CBOS 1994c. *Obecność i instytucjonalizacja wartości religijnych w życiu społecznym. Komunikat z badań – Październik '94*. Warsaw: Centrum Badania Opinii Społecznej.

CBOS 1994d. *Reprywatyzacja i odszkodowania za mienie zabużańskie i pożydowskie. Komunikat z badań – Czerwiec '94*. Warsaw: Centrum Badania Opinii Społecznej.

CBOS 1994e. *Społeczeństwo o prywatyzacji po pierwszym półroczy rządów lewicy. Komunikat z badań – Maj '94*. Warsaw: Centrum Badania Opinii Społecznej.

CBOS 1994f. *Program powszechnej prywatyzacji w opiniach społeczeństwa. Komunikat z badań – Maj '94*. Warsaw: Centrum Badania Opinii Społecznej.

CBOS 1994g. *Stosunek Polaków do przedstawicieli mniejszości narodowych mieszkajacych w Polsce. Komunikat z badań – Listopad '94*. Warsaw: Centrum Badania Opinii Społecznej.

CBOS 1994h. *Między Niemcami a Rosja-Ocena międzynarodowego bezpieczeństwa Polski. Komunikat z badań – Wrzesień '94*. Warsaw: Centrum Badania Opinii Społecznej.

CBOS 1995. *Obraz struktury społecznej. Komunikat z badań – Marzec '95*. Warsaw: Centrum Badania Opinii Społecznej.

Central Office of Planning (COP) 1993. *Polska 1989–1993, Reforma gospodarcza (przekształcenia strukturalne)*. Warsaw: Centralny Urząd Planowania.

References

Ciechocińska, M. & Sadowski 1989. Białoruska mniejszość. *Studia Socjologiczne* **2**(113), 215–42.

Dahrendorf, R. 1990. *Reflections on the revolution in Europe*. London: Chatto & Windus.

Dąbrowski, J. M. 1993. *Privatization of Polish State-owned enterprises, progress, barriers, initial effects*. Warsaw–Gdańsk: Wydawnictwo sponsorowane przez fundację im. Konrada Adenauera.

Dąbrowski, J. M., Z. Dworak, K. Gawlikowska-Hueckel, B. Wyżnikiewicz 1995. Ciągle atrakcyjni nadal ryzykowni. *Rzeczpospolita* **76**(4029), 30 Marzec.

Dochód 1992. *Dochód Narodowy 1991*. Warsaw: GUS.

Domańskia, H. 1994. Nowe mechanizmy stratyfikacyjne? *Studia Socjologiczne* **1**(132), 53–76.

Dziewoński, K. 1988. Changing goals of spatial policies and planning in Poland. *Geographia Polonica* **56**, 9–15.

Dziewoński, K. & B. Malisz 1978. *Przekształcenia przestrzenno – gospodarczej struktury kraju* [Studia KPZK 63]. Warsaw: PWN.

Dynamika Prywatyzacji 1994. *Dynamika Prywatyzacji Nr 20. Departament Delegatur i Analiz Prywatyzacji*. Warsaw: Ministerstwo Przekształceń Własnościowych.

Gałczyńska, B. 1993a. Poziom wykształcenia ludności zatrudnionej w rolnictwie indywidualnym (w ujęciu przestrzennym). In *Rolnictwo i gospodarka żywnościowa w ujęciu przestrzennym 1980–1990–2000*. Projekt badawczy Nr 50281 9101. Unpublished paper, Instytut Geografii i PZ PAN, Warsaw.

Gałczynska, B. 1993b. Zmiany poziomu wykształcenia ludności zatrudnionej w rolnictwie indywidualnym 1978–1988 (ujęcie przestrzenne). In *Rolnictwo i gospodarka żywnościowa w ujęciu przestrzennym 1980–1990–2000*. Projekt badawczy Nr 50281 9101. Unpublished paper, Instytut Geografii i PZ PAN, Warsaw.

Gardawski, J. & T.Żukowski 1994. *Robotnicy 1993. Wybory ekonomiczne i polityczne*. Warsaw: Minsterstwo Pracy i Polityki Socjalnej, Fungacja im. Friedricha Eberta Przedstawicielstwo w Polsce.

Gebethner, S. (ed.) 1993. *Polska scena polityczna a wybory*. Warsaw: Wydawnictwo Fundacji Inicjatyw Społecznych "Polska w Europie".

Gołębiowski, J. W. (ed.) 1993. *Transforming the Polish economy*. Warsaw: WarsawSchool of Economics, Faculty of Foreign Trade.

Gołębiowski, J., (ed.) 1994. *Transforming the Polish economy II*. Warsaw: Warsaw School of Economics; Warsaw: World Economy Research Institute; San Francisco: International Centre for Economic Growth.

Gomułka, S. & P. Jasiński 1994. *Privatization in Poland 1989–1993: policies, methods and results*. Warsaw: Opera Minora 6, Polish Academy of Sciences, Instytut of Economics.

Governmental Population Commission 1993. *Annual report*. Unpublished paper, Warsaw.

Grabowska, M. 1994. The Church in times of change. In *The transformation of Europe, social conditions and consequences*, M. Alestalo et al. (eds), 253–66. Warsaw: IFiS.

Grabowska, M. & T. Szawiel 1993. *Anatomia elit politycznych. Partie polityczne w postkomunistycznej Polsce 1991–93*. Warsaw: Instytut Socjologii Uniwersytetu Warszawskiego, Warsaw.

GUS 1992. *Obszary ekologicznego zagrożenia w Polsce w latach 1982 i 1990*. Warsaw: GUS.

GUS 1995. *Prywatyzacja przedsiębiorstw państwowych według stanu na 30.09.1994*. Warsaw: GUS.

Holzer, J. Z. 1991. Poland/La Pologne. In *European population*, vol. 1: *country analysis*, J. L. Ralla & A. Blum (eds). Published for the European Population Conference, Paris, October 21–25 1991. Montrouge: John Libbey.

Jałowiecki, B., J. Hryniewicz, A. Mync 1994. *The brain drain from science and universities in Poland, 1992–1993*. Warsaw: European Institute for Regional and Local Development,

References

University of Warsaw.

Jasiewicz, K. 1991. Polski wyborca-dziesięć lat po sierpniu. *Politicus Biuletyn Instytutu Studiów Politycznych* PAN **1** (28–32).

Jasiewicz, K. 1992. Polish elections of 1990 beyond The "Pospolite Ruszenie". In *Escape from Socjalism,* W. D. Connor & P. Ptoszajski (eds), 181–98. Warsaw: IFiS.

Jasiewicz, K. 1993. From protest and repression to the free elections. In *Societal conflict and systemic change: the case of Poland 1980–1992,* W. W. Adamski (ed.), 117–140. Warsaw: IFiS.

Józniak, J. & J. Paradysz 1993. Demograficzny wyraz aborcji. *Studia demograficzne* **111**(1), 31–42.

Kabaj, M. 1993. Jaki program przeciwdziałania bezrobociu? In *Bezrobocie – wyzwanie dla polskiej gospodarki,* E. Frytczak, Z. Strzelecki, J. Witkowski (eds), 466–479. Warsaw: GUS.

Kałaska, M. 1994. Pracujący w rolnictwie indywidualnym. In *Sytuacja na miejskim rynku pracy ze szczególnym uwzględnieniem ludności związanej z rolnictwem indywidualnym,* 95–138. Raport z badania modułowego przeprowadzonego w listopadzie 1993 r. w ramach Badania Aktywności Ekonomicznej Ludności, Warsaw: GUS.

Kamiński, B. 1991. *The collapse of state socialism: the case of Poland.* Princeton, New Jersey: Princeton University Press.

Kassenberg, A. & Cz. Rolewicz 1985. *Przestrzenna diagnoza ochrony środowiska w Polsce* [Studia KPZK PAN 89]. Warsaw: PWN.

Korcelli, P., A. Gawryszewski, A. Potrykowska 1992. *Przestrzenne zmiany ludnościowe w Polsce* [Studia KPZK 98]. Warsaw: PWN.

Kosiarski, J. 1992. The German minority in Poland. *The Polish Quarterly of International Affairs* **1**(1–2), 47–68.

Kotlarska-Bobińska, L. 1994. *Aspirations, values and interests: Poland 1989–1994.* Warsaw: IFiS.

Kowalewski, A. T. 1990. *Ekonomiczne aspekty planów urbanistycznych w Polsce.* Wrocław: Ossolineum.

Krasuski, J. 1991. East-Central Europe – its past and future. *Polish Western Affairs* **32**(1).

Król, E. 1994. Bezrobocie i bezrobotni na wsi. In *Sytuacja na miejskim rynku pracy ze szczególnym uwzględnieniem ludności związanej z rolnictwem indywidualnym.* Raport z badania modułowego przeprowadzonego w listopadzie 1993 r. w ramach Badania Aktywności Ekonomicznej Ludności. Warsaw: GUS.

Kukliński, A. 1991. Restrukturyzacja polskich regionów jako problem współpracy europejskiej. *Studia Regionalne i Lokalne* **34**, 319–29.

Kultura 1994. Wywiady "Kultury". Rozmowa z prof. WiesLawem Lesiukiem z Państwowego Śląskiego Instytutu Naukowego w Opolu. *Kultura* **1–2**(556–557), 91–96.

Kupiszewski, M. 1993. Poland as a source of migration and travel. In *Atlas of Eastern and Southeastern Europe.* Vienna: Österreichische Ost und Südosteuropa Institut.

Kurcz, Z. & W. Podkański 1991. Emigracja z Polski po 1980r. In *Nowa emigracja i wyjazdy zarobkowe za granice,* W. Misiak (cd), 31–92. Warsaw: PWN.

Lange, O. 1966. *Ekonomia Polityczna.* Warsaw: PWE.

Leszczycki, S. & R. Domański 1995. *Geografia Polski, Społeczno-Ekonomiczna.* Warsaw: PWN.

Lijewski, T. 1993. *Zmiany przestrzennego zagospodarowania Polski w latach 1945–1989.* [Studia KPZK, tom 101]. Warsaw: PWN.

Malisz, B. 1986. Three visions of the Polish space. In *Regional studies in Poland: experience and prospects,* A. Kukliński (ed), 75–102. Warsaw: PWN.

Marody, M. 1994. Uwagi do opracowania: "Zmiany systemowe a mentalność polskiego społeczeństwa". In *Komitet Prognoz "Polska XXI wiek" przy Prezydium PAN,* 44–58. Warsaw: PWN.

References

Misztal, S. & W. Kaczorowski 1983. *Regionalne zróżnicowanie procesu uprzemysłowienia Polski 1945–1975* [Studia KPZK, tom 76]. Warsaw: PWN.

Mokrzycki, E. 1994. Nowa klasa średnia. *Studia Socjologiczne* 1(132), 37–52.

Morawski, W. 1980. Strategia narzuconej industrializacji a społeczeństwo. *Studia Socjologiczne* 4(79), 113–28.

Morawski, W. 1994. Three dilemmas of citizenship building. *Polish Sociological Review* 1(105), 23–34.

Musil, I. 1984. *Urbanizacja w krajach socjalistycznych.* Warsaw: Książka i Wiedza.

OECD 1992. *Industry in Poland: structural adjustment issues and policy options.* Paris: OECD.

Okólski, M. 1989. Demographic anomalies in Poland. In *Poland: the economy in the 1980s*, R. Clark (ed), 88–109. Harlow, England: Longman.

Pałubicki, W. 1993. Etniczna mniejszość Kaszubów w procesie przemian. In *Antynomie transformacji w Polsce, Chrześcijaństwo – Mniejszości – Liberalizm*, Z. Stachowicz & A. Wójtowicz (eds), 243–8. Warsaw: Polskie Towarzystwo Religioznawcze.

Parysek, J. J. 1986. Zmiany struktury społeczno-gospodarczej Polski w latach 1975–1982. *Czasopismo Geograficzne* 57(4), 525–50.

Piontek, F. 1993. Metody i efekty badania strat ekologicznych w Polsce. *Ekonomia iŚrodowisko* 1(3), 115–30.

Prusek, A. & M. Bieda 1995. Województwo tarnowskie w strukturze regionalnej kraju 1992–1993. *Gospodarka Narodowa* **58–9**(2–3), 19–22.

Pyszkowski, A. 1995. Zasady polityki regionalnej państwa. *Gospodarka Narodowa* **58–9**(2–3), 1–22.

Raciborski, J. 1991. Zachowania wyborcze Polaków w warunkach zmiany systemu politycznego. In *Wybory i narodziny demokracji w krajach Europy Środkowej i Wschodniej*, J. Raciborski (ed.), 112–24. Warsaw: Uniwersytet Warszawski-Instytut Socjologii.

Reykowski, J. 1994. *Zmiany systemowe a mentalność polskiego społeczeństwa.* Warsaw: Komitet Prognoz "Polska w XXI wieku", Przy Prezydium PAN.

Rolewicz, C. 1993. Zmiany wstanie środowiska przyrodniczego na obszarach ekologicznie zagrożonych w latach 1982–1988–1990. *Biuletyn KPZK PAN*, Zeszyt 165, Warsaw.

Roszkowski, W. 1994. *Historia polski 1914–1993.* Warsaw: PWN.

Staniszkis, J. 1994. *W poszukiwaniu paradygmatu transformacji.* Warsaw: Instytut Studiów Politycznych Polskiej Akademii Nauk.

Słomczyński, K. 1994. Class and status in Eastern European perspectives. In *The transformation of Europe – social conditions and consequences,* M. Alestelo, E. Allardt, A. Rychard, W. Wesołowski (eds), 167–90. Warsaws: IFiS.

Stola, W. & R. Szczęsny 1994. Struktura przestrzenna rolnictwa i leśnictwa. In *Geografia gospodarcza Polski*, I. Fierla (ed), 137–212. Warsaw: PWE.

Szczepański, M. 1992. *Pokusy nowoczesności Polskie dylematy rozwojowe.* Katowice: AMP.

Szczęsny, R. 1992. Produktywność ziemi w rolnictwie indywidualnym w Polsce. Przestrzenne zróżnicowanie i przemiany w latach 1938–1988. *Zeszyty Instytutu Geografii i Przestrzennego Zagospodarowania PAN* 7.

Szul, R., A. Mync, M. Lasecki, M. Grochowski 1986. Sytuacja społeczno-gospodarcza Polski w okresie kryzysu i reformy-ujęcie regionalne. *Przeglad Geograficzny* 4(58), 627 –660.

Wasilewski, J. 1992. The contract-based diet and elite formation in Poland. *The Polish Sociological Bulletin* 2, 41–57.

Węcławowicz, G. 1979. The structure of socio-economic space of Warsaw in 1931 and 1970: a study in factorial ecology. In *The socialist city, spatial structure and urban policy,* R. A. French & I. F. E. Hamilton (eds), 387–424. Chichester: John Wiley.

Węcławowicz, G. 1988. *Struktury społeczno – przestrzenne w miastach Polski.* Wrocław: Ossolineum.

References

Węcławowicz, G. 1992. The socio-spatial structure of the socialist cities in East-Central Europe: the case of Poland, Czechoslovakia and Hungary. In *Urban and rural geography*, F. Lando (ed.), 129–40. Venice: Cafoscarina.

Węcławowicz, G. 1994. Warsaw and its region in the process of social and economic transformation. Paper presented at the international seminar on Capital cities of central Europe: adjustment and strategy in the new Europe, Giovanni Agnelli Foundation, Turin.

Wesołowski, W. 1994. Procesy klasotwórcze w teoretycznej perspektywie. *Studia Socjologiczne* 1(132), 19–35.

Wiatr, J. J. 1993. *Wybory parlamentarne 19 września 1993: przyczyny i następstwa*. Warsaw: Agencja Scholar.

Wilkin, J. 1989. Private agriculture and socialism: the Polish experience. In *Poland: the economy in the 1980s*, R. Clark (ed), 61–71. Harlow, England: Longman.

Witkowski, J. 1992. Rynek pracy w Polsce 1990–1992. In *Gospodarka polska w latach 1990–1992: Doświadczenia i wnioski*, L. Zienkowski (ed). Warsaw: GUS.

Witkowski, J. 1994a. *Podstawowe cechy bezrobocia w Polsce w okresie transformacji* Warsaw: GUS, Departament Pracy i Dochodów Ludności.

Witkowski, J. 1994b. Próba oszacowania zbędnej siły roboczej (Bezrobocia ukrytego) w gospodarstwach rolnych. In *Sytuacja na miejskim rynku pracy ze szczególnym uwzględnieniem ludności związanej z rolnictwem indywidualnym*, 39–70. Raport z badania modułowego przeprowadzonego w listopadzie 1993 r. w ramach Badania Aktywności Ekonomicznej Ludności. Warsaw: GUS.

Wnuk-Lipiński, E. 1993. Economic deprivation and social transformation. In *Societal conflict and systematic change: the case of Poland 1980–1992*, W. Adamski (ed.), 71–92. Warsaw: IFiS.

Zatoński, W. & J. Tyczyński (eds) 1994. *Cancer in Poland in 1991*. Warsaw: Department of Cancer Control and Epidemiology National Cancer Registry, Centrum Onkologii.

Zienkowski, L. 1989. *Dochód narodowy Polski według województw w 1986r*. Warsaw: Zakład Badań Statystyczno–Ekonomicznych Głównego Urzędu Statystycznego i Polskiej Akademii Nauk.

Zienkowski, L. 1994. *Produkt krajowy brutto i dochody ludności według województw w 1992 roku, Cześć I: metodologia i wyniki badania*. Warsaw: Zakład Badań Statystyczno-Ekonomicznych Głównego Urzędu Statystycznego i Polskiej Akademii Nauk.

Żołędowski, C. 1994. Kwestia mniejszości naradowych w Polsce. In *Kwestie społeczne i krytyczne sytuacje życiowe u progu lat dziewięćdziesiątych*, J. Danecki & B. Rysz-Kowalczyk (eds), 322–50. Warsaw: Uniwersytet Warszawski Instytut Polityki Społecznej.

Żukowski, T. 1992. Wybory parlmentarne '91. *Studia Polityczne* 1, 35–59.

Index